P9-CPZ-518

Planning for MK Nurture

Compendium of the
International Conference on Missionary Kids
Quito, Ecuador, January 4-8, 1987
Volume II

Edited by
Pam Echerd and Alice Arathoon

William Carey Library

PASADENA, CALIFORNIA

Copyright 1989
International Conference on Missionary Kids
All Rights Reserved

No part of this publication may be reproduced, stored in a retrieval
system, or transmitted in any form or by any means — electronic,
mechanical, photocopy, recording, or any other — except for brief
quotations embodied in critical articles or printed reviews, without
the prior permission of the publisher.

Published by WILLIAM CAREY LIBRARY
a Division of WCIU Press
P.O. Box 40129
Pasadena, California 91114

Cover art by Jonathan Gregerson
Cover design by Paul Merrill

ISBN 0-87808-226-3
Library of Congress # 89-083397

PRINTED IN THE UNITED STATES OF AMERICA

To our children,

Daniel, Jonathan, Andoe, and Peter

and to all those working to help MKs and TCKs
like ours be all they can be for God

87951

Contents

Part III   Addressing Cultural Issues in MK Schools

Part IV   Mission Board Involvement in MK Care

Part V   Issues for MK School Administrators

Part VI   Issues for MK Teachers

Preface

We hope you noticed on the title page that this is Volume II of the Compendium of the International Conference on Missionary Kids held in Quito, Ecuador in 1987. Volume I is called *Understanding and Nurturing the Missionary Family* and is also available from William Carey Library. It is intended as an overview for anyone interested in missionary families. In this second volume we have included presentations that would be of more interest to professionals working with missionary children—teachers, counselors, school principals, house parents, mission board administrators.

We would encourage you to obtain Volume I of this set and also the Compendium of the International Conference on Missionary Kids held in Manila in 1984. That book has forty-seven chapters divided into parts on Family, Cross-Cultural Experience, Education, International Education, and The Care Network. It is available from Missionary Internship, Box 457, Farmington, MI 48024, for $10.95 in the U.S. and $13.95 overseas; both prices include postage and handling. While the range of topics covered at the two ICMKs is similar, we have included very little repetition of content. Instead, we have referred you to articles in the Manila Compendium.

Besides the thanks in the first volume, special thanks go to the people at Trinity Church who read next-to-final copy of this manuscript and to Pam's husband, Steve, who dedicated a week to reading final copy and helping Pam with last-minute corrections.

Part I

THE STATE OF MK EDUCATION AND MINISTRY – PLENARY ADDRESSES

1

The State of MK Education

Paul Nelson
Superintendent of Children's Education, Wycliffe Bible Translators

I am pleased to be able to report that the state of MK education throughout the world is just great. Over ninety percent of the students who graduate from our MK schools go on to higher education. Standardized test scores continue to go up, and students are consistently one or two academic levels above their peers back in their country of citizenship. Most graduates and parents are enthusiastically positive about the academic challenge and the high quality of instruction students receive in our schools. Most of the issues over which school administrators, teachers and communities agonize in other parts of the world are insignificant in schools for MKs. What more could anyone ask?

Objectivity. There are dozens of books and articles, some even written by our seminar speakers, which assert a particular bias either defending or attacking some element in MK schools. Both attacks and defenses serve some useful purpose in affirming what we would like to believe about the way children are being cared for in the missions community.

As I highlighted some of the glowing facts about MK schools, you may have begun to swell a little with what might be considered the Christian equivalent of justifiable pride. Others may have been feeling a little "righteous indignation" over my failure to mention the hurts and damaged self-esteem that some students have suffered because of the unrealistic pressures and demands these achievements require. Others might share the indignation, asserting that schools have more than an academic mission and should be held accountable for their ineffectiveness at creating students who are culture-free or who lack the ability to reenter their parents' home country with minimal trauma. It is these kinds of feelings, and others you have experienced throughout this week, that cloud our objectivity.

The truth is, MK schools are not utopian educational institutions nor are they culturally insensitive hothouses. Boarding is not the best experience any child could have nor is it the enemy of the family. Integrity demands that we start from the premise that MK schools exist to carry out a much higher purpose than academic excellence. There is a price to be paid to take the Good News to places where it has never been heard and we have all made substantial accommodations in our ideal educational model to carry out that higher purpose.

Those of us involved in MK education occasionally respond to criticism as though schools for MKs exist because we have discovered that educating children outside their country of citizenship is inherently superior. Critics are frequently guilty of ignoring the fact that there are constraints within each cross-cultural setting which may explain why things are being done as they are.

In our desire for objectivity, it might be considered the height of presumption for me to make generalizations about the state of MK education all over the world. If I have not been to your school recently, my observations are, at the very least, suspect because there are things about each context which are unique.

You have a point. The environment within which you work and the clientele you serve, to a great extent, determine your policies and programs. However, this claim of uniqueness, this assertion that you are the only one who knows your school well enough to suggest changes, occasionally translates itself into self-assumed autonomy which some missionary families and administrators characterize as bordering on autocracy.

At a time when educational systems in industrialized nations all over the world are undergoing some significant reforms, many of our 125 mission-sponsored schools are feeling good about being able to "hold the line." Suggestions for change in curriculum, admission policies, fee structures, student/faculty relationships, organizational structure, boarding homes, and the decision-making process itself are frequently interpreted as criticism and met with defensiveness and formidable resistance.

Educational reform in Japan, Europe, the United States, and other nations is taking place primarily because external pressure is being applied, not because a particular need was perceived. In spite of our desire for continuity and stability, change is inevitable. Students change, teachers change, political climates change, mission strategies change, school boards change, currency values change, mission and field administrators change, and they all exert their own kind of pressure on the school to change as well. Perhaps we can avoid the trauma of change under pressure by anticipating and initiating appropriate modifications which will keep us on the cutting edge in education, supportive of new mission strategies, and sensitive to the increased pressures these changes are causing for the families we serve.

One of the most positive things to come out of ICMK Manila was a perception by many school administrators that they have much more in common with colleagues in other parts of the world than they have differences. The lessons learned in one context, with all its uniqueness, really can be applied to a school continents away.

Those involved in the British O-level program at Faith Academy in Manila can profit from looking at the O-level program at Rift Valley Academy in Kenya. The successful way Pan American Christian Academy has integrated Brazilian national faculty and students into their program can be valuable to Hillcrest School in Nigeria as they work through a similar challenge. The implications of a declining enrollment of students from the sponsoring mission could be profitably discussed by Ivory Coast Academy and Sentani International School in Indonesia. The Christian Academy of Guatemala might have some helpful suggestions for Ukarumpa High School in Papua New Guinea about the establishment of a school-to-school partnership that works. The folks from the American Cooperative School in Suriname may have some questions to ask the folks from Aiyura International School about how a mission sponsored school can assume responsibility for a community school and meet the expectations of both groups. Finding effective ways to serve a changing constituency is a challenge for both Bingham Academy in Ethiopia and Woodstock in India.

The list could go on, but the point to be made is found in our willingness to de-emphasize the uniqueness and autonomy of our programs and seek out opportunities to learn from one another. That is why most of us are here, and yet it is very difficult to place ourselves in the role of the learner. We educators are accustomed to being in control of the learning environment and we do not shift roles easily. It is not easy to say, "I need your help," but when we do, things can happen. Common solutions to common problems can be found. Commitments can be made to work cooperatively to develop or strengthen a common program.

The Job Alike/Interest Alike workshops today are designed to help you initiate these kinds of relationships and establish some working plans for cooperative efforts. Networks need to be formally established with your colleagues which will serve as a resource for the entire missions community. Single topic consultations need to be planned which can focus on specific areas of concern. Articles need to be written which will contribute to the creation of a climate for change where change is needed. Common goals need to be established upon which you and your colleagues agree. Plans of action need to be developed to carry out these goals, and you need to identify specific ways in which you can remain active. These kinds of things need to be done today so that the ideas and proposals discussed this week will not die here in Quito when we all leave.

The model of the Missionary Kids Overseas Schools conferences in Asia is one which might profitably be copied in Latin America, Africa, and the South Pacific. Some of the Europe area schools are currently in the organizational stages of this kind of an association, so it might be helpful to get together. It takes time and work to develop cooperative programs but the returns are worth the investment.

These two ICMKs have shown us the rich resources which already exist within the missions educational community. I think they may have also alerted us to the need for our interdependence. Geographical separation has kept us from developing close working relationships in the past but ICMK has changed that. We really do know one another now but we have been working independently for so long it is hard to think in terms of interdependence. We might do well to review I Corinthians 12 when we begin think of ourselves as being self-sufficient and having no need of input from anyone else, or because we are not as large as the Alliance Academy here in Quito we think of ourselves as insignificant.

As we look ahead to the next few years in MK education, there are some areas where we will definitely need to draw upon the collective experience and wisdom of everyone. Staff shortages are becoming critical and almost all of us are facing the crunch.

Since the early seventies we have enjoyed an oversupply of teachers in the United States primarily, but in most other Western countries as well. In 1977 there were over 400,000 more teachers than there were teaching positions open in the U.S. That surplus ended in 1985. In that year the demand for teachers exceeded the supply by 7 percent. The National Center for Education Statistics projects that within five years the supply of teachers in the U.S. will only meet 65.6 percent of the demand. There may be some uncomfortable spiritual implications to this statement but when the jobs are plentiful, teachers for MK schools are more difficult to find.

Concurrent with this teacher shortage are other realities which compound its impact on MK schools. First, the shrinking pool of potential teachers is further reduced by the growing number of Christian teachers who are teaching in Christian schools and see this as the fulfillment of their commitment to a ministry. Note that I have identified this as a reality, not a criticism. Relatively few of our teachers come to us from Christian schools.

Second, the missions community continues to grow and the number of teachers needed to meet the expanding population will also continue to grow. Many of these new missionaries are from countries other than North America, so our teachers should begin to reflect this multinational population. The blending of teachers from a variety of educational systems into a cohesive teaching staff is an additional challenge.

The key to meeting the teacher needs in the future might be to consolidate our efforts on what has, in the past, proven to be the most productive teacher recruiting resource, our fellow missionaries. We need to help them understand the specific needs and then help them refine their ability to communicate effectively with potential teachers. We need to work on a system which will keep them current on which positions are the most critical and which ones have been filled.

We have a potential recruiting force of over 100,000 fellow missionaries who have a vested interest in seeing the teaching positions filled but we must learn how to mobilize them. The Association of Christian Schools International is rapidly becoming an active partner in recruitment, and we need to find ways to increase their productivity and support their efforts.

Coupled with these efforts we must enlist our students, parents, staff, and as many other people as we can to "pray the Lord of the harvest to send forth laborers." That kind of community prayer not only moves the hearts of teachers who are weighing their decision, it also prepares the community to receive that new teacher as God's answer to prayer. That kind of reception has long-term implications.

We all dream of the day when at least eighty percent and perhaps ninety percent of our teachers will be career missionaries. The facts do not support the fulfillment of that dream. Three, two, and one year short-term teachers will continue to be part of our growing team of educators, and in most cases we will continue to fall on their neck and kiss them when they show up, especially if we have been waiting for them for more than three months.

Most of us could cite a long litany of reasons why short-term teachers are problems. You could probably also cite case histories to substantiate most of your reasons for feeling as you do, but the fact remains, we both have and need short-term teachers as part of our staff. It might be more productive to focus on the enthusiasm, creativity, energy, and competence of your best short-term teachers when you are preparing your new staff orientation rather than mingling your gratitude with dread.

Short-term teachers could be one of our greatest sources for career teachers if our perspective toward them were different. Too often they are treated as though they were consumable products. Use them up, burn them out for as long as they are available, and then assume that there will be a fresh supply when they are gone.

When you spot a short-term teacher you would like to make a part of the permanent team, tell him you want him to stay. He needs to be told soon, sincerely, and often that his contributions are appreciated, and that you would love to be able to work with him for the rest of his career. Don't stop there. Let his supporting churches know that you are grateful for the work he is doing and get significant others in the mission to do the same. Find specific ways that you can involve him in decision making. Give him opportunities to minister to students, faculty members, and you. Be creative in finding ways to let him know that he is both wanted and needed. Even if he doesn't stay, he might be the happiest teacher you have.

I almost feel apologetic about making suggestions concerning problems as common as staff shortages but all of us know that it is on this level that most of our time and energies are spent. I think it could be very worthwhile to spend time with your colleagues today exploring ways to identify and contact teachers to fill your staff needs. If this is the level on which we need the most help, then let's not spend our time talking about the philosophy or theology of whether or not teachers are "real" missionaries.

It might also be helpful to work together on such things as ways to keep your teachers professionally current through shared in-service training programs or regional consultations on topics of common interest such as curriculum development or current trends in education. Our teachers must be excited about what they are teaching and how they are doing it if they are going to be effective in the classroom. That certainly comes as no news flash but it is difficult to maintain that currency in most of our schools. The high caliber of students with whom we are working demands that we have the most competent, enthusiastic teachers available.

We have heard a great deal this week about the need to internationalize the curriculum in our schools. Most of us agree, in principle, that this is generally a good idea. In fact, almost everyone has

given it some thought but few seem to be providing us with any concrete models. We need each other as we try to understand the implications of this challenge for our various settings.

If curriculum is determined by what we want our students to be able to do after they have been through it, it is no wonder we are having a hard time putting one together. We were asked if our goals included making a multicultural MK into a monocultural adult. I am not sure if we could come up with a satisfactory answer to the question by looking at what we do in our schools around the world.

Because the body of knowledge to which we have access triples every fourteen years, the curriculum we use in our schools cannot be factually based, but in most cases it is. Things really do not have to be this way. Our students in MK schools are capable of dealing with higher level thinking skills such as synthesis and evaluation. We do them a real disservice by keeping them occupied with knowledge based activities. Short-term and career teachers both need to understand the unique potential of the students they are teaching and develop a learning environment which is appropriate for students who will be the prototypes of the twenty-first-century Christians Ted Ward introduced us to.

If our goal is to help students become truly world citizens, then we need a curriculum which transcends the cultural trappings of any one country's educational system. We should teach them to see the interrelationships of issues and events rather than merely their impact on the United States. We should help students to see cause and effect relationships in the world along with the ultimate purposes of God being worked out through them. We must stop educating our students as though they all viewed success in life as achieving the American dream somewhere near Wheaton, Illinois.

We were challenged with the task of developing a transcultural curriculum by Professor Brian Hill and others at ICMK Manila, but little substantive work has been done since then. I believe we have the people, the resources and the motivation to develop an appropriate curriculum that will prepare MKs to be world citizens, but we must be willing to assume the responsibility, establish a cooperative plan of action and share the risks. These risks include being misunderstood and criticized by parents who want the security of having their children educated exactly as they were educated and colleges who want all transcripts for incoming freshmen to look alike.

Alternatives to traditional schools are emerging in a few places around the world and more will be needed as families work in increasingly isolated settings. We can either continue to view satellite schools, itinerant teachers, various forms of home schooling, parent cooperatives, and other models as threats to our traditional school programs or we can find ways to encourage and support them. This could mean bringing these programs under the school's umbrella by such means as sharing resources and even helping to staff them.

If we are committed to serving the missions community by providing educational services, we need to serve them in ways which respond to and support their changing strategies. We need to serve our students by looking for and implementing some new educational models which will prepare them to take their place in the world community. We should be careful to draw clear distinctions between schooling and education and be willing to risk dumping the institutional trappings of traditional schooling in favor of developing new models of education which are more appropriate for the unique clientele we serve.

Apprenticeships with diplomats, international businessmen, and even local craftsmen are alternatives which might be considered. A diagnostic prescriptive instructional model might be much more productive than group-paced instruction from a textbook which has no correlation with the environment surrounding the student's daily life. We must risk the consequences of deviating from the traditional systems because the circumstances and the potential of our students demand it.

The way we go about providing educational opportunities for MKs will either positively reinforce the differences between them and their monocultural peers and help them feel confident in their identity as world citizens, or it will negatively reinforce the differences and turn these differences into perceived deficiencies.

The state of MK education is "just great" because we have the resources and the vision to make significant contributions to the missions community, the educational community and to our MK students. It is "just great" if we accept the exciting challenges ahead of us that grow out of our willingness to take a fresh look at our task as educators. However, if we return to our schools on Monday morning and drift back into the same comfortable patterns that we have followed for years, then we are setting ourselves up for the trauma of change under external pressure and we are perpetuating the waste of great potential.

2

State of MK Ministry

David Pollock
Director, Interaction, Inc.

The Scripture is filled with people who functioned in more than one culture—Abraham, Lot, Isaac, Joseph, Joseph's nephews and nieces who ended up as third-culture kids in Egypt. There are Moses, Daniel (the patron saint of third-culture kids) and his friends, Jesus, and the two TCKs who became the first two cross-cultural missionaries, Barnabas and Paul. They are all biblical cross-culturalists and internationalists.

A lot of Scripture, and one letter in particular, is written to third-culture people. I Peter begins with these words, "To God's elect, strangers in the world, scattered throughout Pontus, Galatia, Cappadocia, Asia, and Bithynia, who have been chosen according to the foreknowledge of God the Father, through the sanctifying wcrk of the Spirit, for obedience to Jesus Christ and sprinkling by his blood."

These people who had been ripped out of their own culture, out of their own familiar, secure surroundings, found themselves raising their children in communities and cultures very different from their own. After addressing them, Peter immediately begins talking to them about the one who furnishes the stability that allows them to remain consistent in all the experiences of their lives.

An individual who moves cross-culturally experiences chaos at the time he moves. Everything kind of comes unglued. Trivial things seem to become increasingly important and exaggerated. Health becomes a big issue at that particular point.

The individual may have a sense of powerlessness. Refugees often feel this. In a group of refugees who have been moved into a resettlement location, there are often fights and gangs that war against each other. And we ask, "How can people do that? Look at what they've just come out of." But when people feel powerless, they reach for ways to control their own lives. They ultimately end up in little political groups that struggle against each other, and soon there are physical fights generated from their powerlessness.

Peter assures these refugees that there is a God of power who is in control of their lives; they're not at loose ends; the situation is not as chaotic as it looks. In the fifth chapter he says, "Casting all you anxiety upon him, because he, the God of all power, is concerned for you." Peter talks about despair and about the one who has provided hope. He talks about how to survive successfully in that situation.

At the beginning of the fifth chapter, he talks to the elders and tells them certain things that are important in their role as leaders in this cross-cultural flow. That's where you are. As a result of having been here, people are going to ask you, "What did you hear? What happened? What should we do?" You're going to find yourself in the leader role.

What is it that we ought to expect of ourselves as leaders? So often when we think of a leader, we think of somebody at the head of a group yelling, "Charge," and everybody trampling along behind him. But sometimes leaders blend into the group. There are people that are leaders because they wear a badge or because they were elected or hired to that position, and then there are leaders who furnish the real direction. They are the ones that determine where things really go.

Peter talks to the people about being overseers. An overseer is exactly what it says. He sees over. The shepherd can see what the sheep cannot see. He looks over the sheep, across the meadow, and sees the still waters and the green pastures. He sees the threat of beasts. He recognizes that he has to feed his sheep right and bring them to places where they have the right kind of protection.

Peter talks about four basic characteristics of a leader:

Dreamers

Leaders are dreamers — not empty-headed dreamers with visions that never come to pass but people who see what other people don't see.

Several years ago, somebody asked Marge Wyrtzen, "What makes Jack different than other people?"

She said, "Basically it's the fact that he sees things done before anybody else sees them started."

Leadership involves dreaming for other people, envisioning what it is that they can be, and what kind of investment we can make in their lives to set them free to be what God has intended them to be.

We need to dream some dreams for missionary kids. We need to see what they can be, but not force them into a mold, or say, "This is the particular task we think you ought to do." God has something for that person. How do we open the doors?

There are a number of dreams for MKs that I think we could all latch on to. I feel a deep sense of gratitude for people who have invested their lives in developing MK homes. As God moves and works in people's hearts, I'd like to see a network of those homes across the United States where MKs know they can go and be cared for during Christmas or summer vacation, and know it is a place they don't have to feel uncomfortable after the third day of being in the house.

I dream of an opportunity for older MKs to come together in reunions. You just have to get together with some of those people who are part of your mobile home town.

At Urbana at the end of this year, there will be a meeting just for third-culture kids. Next year we'd like to see each school around the world contact all of its alumni, and say, "We're going to have a reunion. Our school, RVA, Alliance, and Faith will each have a reunion, and then we'll have some workshops dealing with careers, marriage, and a variety of other things." That's a dream that has a good possibility of being realized.

Another dream is to see colleges take on the responsibility that few have taken on, to develop some models and do things in order that others can say, "It can be done. We're going to do it in our school as well." I'd like to encourage you to encourage your alma maters to take seriously the issue of caring for third-culture kids.

Another area of interest and concern is the prefield training program for teachers and dorm parents. That started out as a dream. Now Phil Renicks is directing that program in partnership with Missionary Internship. We encourage you to encourage the teachers and dorm parents that are going to be in your school to be a part of that. Part of that program will be cross-cultural preparation; part of it will be interpersonal skills development; and part of it will be how to work with third-culture kids.

What are the things you're envisioning for the future? Don't let go of them. Part of being a leader is being a dreamer. In the process of doing that dreaming, you lay the foundation for getting some things done.

Delegators

The second thing Peter talks about is that the shepherd is a delegator or enabler. By delegator, I don't mean somebody who just gives someone else a job. A delegator enables someone else to do a job. You can't do everything yourself. The leader has to be a catalyst. You may have dozens of good ideas, but you can't give yourself to all of them. What you can do is pass them on to other people. Someone else who has the skill, ability, and insight to latch onto that idea will say, "That's something I can do." Then you find a way to enable him.

Over the years I've found there are two basic kinds of boards or committees. There's the controlling board or committee that thinks that it has to keep the lid on things and not let anything get out of control. Then there is the board that enables.

Several years ago I was asked to be on the board of a Bible conference in New Hampshire. At the first meeting I sat in on, the director said, "Here are some things I think are worth considering."

The board said, "Tell us about them."

He told them and they said, "Let's find out how to do them." Their whole disposition was not, "How do we control it and keep the lid on?" but "If this something worth doing, let's find a way to do it."

An enabler is someone who comes alongside someone else, helps them grasp the vision for themselves, and then says, "How do I help you do it? How do I give you the resources and encouragement to help you move in that direction?"

There are some people around you that need to be encouraged. Don't squash them if they do something wrong once. Give them their heads. Let them do it. Give them the approval. Delegate.

Demonstrator

It's no good to sit there and tell somebody else to do it if you don't invest in it yourself. Peter talks about being examples to the flock – models, demonstrators. What is it that God has given you to do? Are you really doing it? Have you really grabbed hold of it and said, "This is my task. I'm going to do it"?

Defender

The shepherd is also a defender. There are an awful lot of things that can undermine, discourage, and defeat. Part of our task is to defend people against discouragement, to come alongside and encourage them when they're down. Sometimes we need to intervene on their behalf so they don't get clobbered in the process of stepping out and doing something that somebody else doesn't approve of or agree with. If they're doing something worth doing, it is important to defend them.

The whole body of believers deserves our defense. Jesus said to the disciples, "A new commandment I give unto you, that you love one another. By this shall all men know that you are my disciples, if you have this demonstrable love one for another."

Part of loving is to protect the individual and the unity of the body of believers. It has been exciting to be reminded of how many different agencies and groups are represented at this conference.

I haven't heard an awful lot of people saying, "Want to hear how wonderful I am and how wonderful my group is and how exclusively we function?" I've watched people cooperating with each other and recognizing that we have a oneness. With that kind of working relationship, we defend the unity of the body. We do not defend it with strength and power and toughness, but with the demonstration of loving each other in obedience to the Lord Jesus.

Jesus said in John 17, "Father, I pray that they might be one as we are one, that the world might know that you have sent me."

You're a leader. Are you a dreamer and a delegator and a demonstrator and a defender? By God's grace in the months and years ahead, I trust that we will see some fulfillment of some of the dreams that have been dreamt here, not because they're our dreams, but because they're the tasks that God has placed before us.

Part II

COUNSELING AND
DEVELOPMENTAL CARE FOR MKS

3

What People World-Wide Have in Common

Henry Brandt
Psychologist, Palm Beach Atlantic College

I think it is important for us to appreciate the fact that we serve a living, powerful God who will hear our prayers and who will provide us with the strength that we need—quickly. That's been my experience with him.

It has also been my experience to find there are some tremendous similarities in people's response to life. There are a variety of social differences but common responses. For example, there will always be people who are mad at each other. You can depend on that.

One of the things that applies to all of us is that we all have sinned and come short of the glory of God. We realize that what we call sin, some humanists do not call sin. Some folks talk about cultural pressures that create within us the very same things that the Bible calls sin.

Sinful Characteristics

One of the most common characteristics of people world-wide is deceit. We tell people what they want to hear. We say yes when we mean no. We will compliment somebody when we don't really mean it. I would put deceit at the very top of sinful characteristics. We don't call deceit sinfulness, we call it diplomacy. Very often we call deceit tactfulness. Jesus said that these are the products of the human heart. When we talk to people about sin, we need to understand the characteristics that we're talking about.

19

In Mark 7:21-22, Jesus said that these characteristics come out of the heart: evil thoughts, adultery, fornication, murder, theft, covetousness, wickedness, deceit, an evil eye, blasphemy, pride, foolishness. These emotions come out of us. People simply bring out of us what is in us.

Now Galatians 5 talks about the sinful nature. There are seventeen items on that list: adultery, fornication, uncleanness, lasciviousness, idolatry, witchcraft, hatred, variance, emulations, wrath, strife, seditions, heresies, envyings, murders, drunkenness, revellings. Just take a look at that list and you will see responses that all struggle with. We're talking about the nature of the human heart. If a perfect stranger who is telling me about some of his conflicts really lets me know what's going on in his heart, he will come up with some of these characteristics. I will guarantee you that.

People don't take me by surprise. The gamut of responses that people have to life is limited by what Jesus calls the products of the human heart and what the Apostle Paul calls the works of the flesh. We don't have to debate about adultery and fornication and lust and idolatry and witchcraft. But look at some of the things that plague us in our organizations and in our families. I'm talking about hatred and variance. Don't we fight and argue with each other all the time? We would like to talk about diversity, but variance is a fact of life.

Romans 1 talks about the effect of rejecting the knowledge of God. We are not talking about cultural pressure. We are not talking about the effects of society on your heart. We're talking about a faulty relationship to God. This list has twenty-two items. "Wickedness, unrighteousness, fornication, covetousness, maliciousness, envy, murder, debate..." Take the time to study these lists and you will see that they overlap.

"...deceit, malignity, whisperers, backbiters, implacable, unmerciful..." Isn't that awful? We're not talking about some people off in a jungle somewhere who never heard of God, are we? We're talking about some of the things that we face in our hearts, that we are willing to blame the culture for. We're talking about a faulty relationship to God.

"...haters of God, spiteful, proud, boasters, inventors of evil things, disobedient to parents..." Oh, how many parents come to me, "My children are disobedient. What have I done to my children?" Many of us bear a heavy, heavy burden because of the behavior of our children. Maybe one of the things we've done is not impress upon them sufficiently how important it is that they need a Saviour.

I travel all over the world communicating family life principles, but good family life is not a substitute for being saved. A good family life is not a substitute for the ministry of the Holy Spirit in your life. Maybe one of the things that we've done to our kids is to impress upon them how important it is to interact with one another socially, but have minimized the importance of interacting with God.

Dealing with Sin Versus Living with Sin

I used to have a cottage on Lake Michigan, and I had what I called a mile-long office. People would come to see me, and I would say to them, "You've got two miles to get yourself square in life." So we walked a mile along the beach and a mile back, and in that mile a lot of people got squared away. What happened is that they had to come face to face with a faulty relationship to God.

It makes a lot of difference what your goal is when you're dealing with people. I can help you to live with your sins, but I'm not so sure that would be doing you any favor. Better to suffer and face the truth than to find a way to live with your sins, because that doesn't heal you.

One time I had a dry socket. My throat hurt, my jaw hurt, my ear hurt, my sinuses hurt—I was afraid I wasn't going to make it. I called my dentist, and he gave me a pill, and you know what? In a couple of minutes my dry socket didn't hurt me a bit. I still had a bad socket, but it didn't hurt. Just because I dulled the pain didn't mean that I had fixed the problem.

Now you know, I can help you to dull the ache and the pain and the misery of your sin, but I don't think I'm doing you a a favor unless I get to the bottom of the problem. If it's sin, there is no human remedy.

Everybody is looking for the fruit of the Spirit. People want to be loved. People want to have joy in their hearts. We want to be peaceful. Now one way to find peace is to take some drugs. You don't need to straighten out your heart. All you need to do is take some drugs. You can find peace by working off your tensions. You can lose yourself in some music and find some peace. Or you can find some peace in climbing a mountain. But what I'm talking about is not just any kind of peace; we're talking about God's peace, his joy.

So in addition to understanding that we are awfully sinful people, we also need to understand that God will hear our prayers and enter our lives and forgive us our sins and cleanse us of our sins.

That's not a long process. The problem is that we tend to be unrepentant. We tend to excuse ourselves.

I have people tell me some of the strangest things like, "I blew up." College graduates are willing to admit that they blew up. Puff! Folks say, "I broke down." Folks say they are beside themselves. We say all kinds of odd things, but "I have sinned" is not one of them. One of the most difficult things there is in the world to say is, "I am wrong, and I have sinned."

Repentance is rare. But if you confess your sin, he is faithful and just to forgive you your sin (Now that doesn't take long!) and cleanse you from all unrighteousness.

There are nine items called the fruit of the Spirit, and I want to point out to you that they have nothing to do with people. People come and go. Circumstances come and go. Everybody has their share of difficulties and problems and troubles. People let you down. But God is the same yesterday, today, and forever. This is the good news that we have — that you can approach God, and there isn't a human being in the world that can stop you from approaching God. There isn't a human being in the world that can make you approach him either. Not only will he forgive you your sins, he'll give you the fruit of the Spirit.

Now Jesus talked about people who have ears to hear, but they won't hear. And they have eyes to see, and they will not see. Now, whosoever will, can come to the Lord. But the corollary of that is that whosoever won't, doesn't have to. Now that's the sad thing when you're working with people. You're going to watch people break themselves to pieces. You hold the key, but they won't listen. They will even say, "It's all right for you. I see that it's working for you, but it isn't going to work for me."

I used to think to myself, "If I could take another course and improve my skill, I could reach more people. Evidently the reason that this individual doesn't respond is because I lack skill." I think the important thing for you to appreciate is that you need to know the Word of God and speak for him and leave the results with him. You have to face the fact that most folks aren't going to listen.

Some of us have lived long enough to watch tremendous changes in our society, in our country, and in the world, but there are some things that have remained the same. One of them is the nature of man. We've got all kinds of social research and statistical reports and anthropological studies to try to figure out what's wrong with us. I just want to call your attention to the fact that there's a little book called the Bible. It's been telling us all along what's wrong with us, and it's still true.

In the field of psychology, we have found out how to help people get comfortable without God's help. You want to be careful that you are not practicing some of those principles of helping people get comfortable without God's help and doing it in the name of the Lord.

If it's on the list, then you're dealing with sin. If it's sin, you have a very simple problem. The blood of Jesus Christ will cleanse people from sin. You need to be careful that you are not encouraging people to call sin something else. If it's sin, it involves them and the Lord. And if they're serious, then you can see some dramatic things happen. You want to be careful that you don't get your psychology mixed up with your theology. The fact of sin disturbs people, but because it disturbs people does not mean that you need to back away.

One time I had a bad knee. I went into the doctor's office, and he looked at my knee and began to thump it.

He said, "Where does it hurt the worst?" And when he found the spot, he thumped it three or four times to make sure he had the worst spot.

Then he said with a smile, "I'm going to lance it." He went to his cabinet and turned around with a knife. He said, "This is going to hurt." And he cut me open.

I tell you, I never hurt so much in all my life. Now is that any way to treat a basketball player? I hope to tell you it is.

Then he said that I would get better. And I did.

"You upset me. I'm leaving more upset than when I came." That's what people tell me. But they go home and say, "You know, I got to thinking about what you were saying, and you're right." You want to be careful that you are not encouraging people who are dealing with sin, to say it isn't so.

Taking the Consequences for Behavior

Many people do others a disfavor by hindering them from taking the consequences for their behavior.

A lady came to me and said, "My son, who's eighteen has an apartment. He's got three other boys in the apartment, and they're smoking pot. I don't think that he should be there. But my husband and I disagree."

I said, "The first thing that you have to face is that you and your husband are disagreeing with each other. You're at odds with each other. You don't have a parent/child problem.

You've got first of all a husband/wife problem. And before that you have a personal problem because the two of you are so determined to have your own way that you can't function as husband and wife."

So I got a phone call from the husband. "My wife said that you say that we better get together or we're going to lose our son entirely. I agree with you, and I decided to cooperate with my wife. What do you think we ought to do?"

This man owned a company that manufactured a product that was distributed nationally, so I said, "You have a company that functions nationally, and you're trying to tell me that you can't figure out what to do with your son? What do you think you ought to do?"

He said, "Well, I think I ought to go get him."

I said, "Well, that's not a bad idea. Why don't you do that?"

He said, "He'd fight me. I can't do that."

"Well, then don't do it."

"But I think I ought to do it."

"Well, why don't you do it?"

"Because it's going to be too difficult."

"Then don't do it."

"But I ought to do it."

That fellow had sense enough to know that he was not doing right by his son.

He said, "Well how do you think I ought to do it?"

"How do you think you ought to do it?"

"Maybe I ought to take a carload of fellows with me."

"Well, why don't you do that?"

I got a call a couple of days later, and he said, "I got my son home."

"How did you get him home?"

"I took two carloads of fellows with me. We grabbed him and dragged him home. But he's smoking pot in his bedroom. Now what shall I do?"

I said, "What do you think you ought to do, mister. You are smart enough to run this big company. You tell me you don't know what to do about a kid that smokes pot?"

"I know what to do, but I don't want to do it."

"Then what are you calling me for? What do you think you ought to do?"

"I ought to call the police."

"You wouldn't want to do that, would you?"

"Well yeah."

"Well, why don't you?"

"I will." So he called the police.

So I got a call a few days later. "I called the police. Now my son is in jail. And the whole neighborhood is down on me, and so is my church."

"What are they down on you for?"

"Because I did right."

"That's interesting, isn't it? That's a bad, bad thing for you to do right isn't it? Isn't it wrong to do right?"

"No, it isn't wrong to do right."

"Well at least you ought to feel bad about being right."

He said, "No, I shouldn't feel bad."

"Well then, why don't you feel good about being right? What are you going to do now?"

"I'm going to go to jail every day and try to win my son."

He went to that jail every day. His son spit at him and cursed at him, but finally that kid began to realize, "My dad cares about me." And he accepted the Lord in that jail.

This fellow was well-known, so it became headline news that his son was in jail for marijuana. He and his son appeared before the judge.

The judge said to that boy, "I know about your dad, and I'm going to put you on two years of probation in the custody of your dad."

You see, there's a fellow that was prepared to see to it that his son took the consequences for his behavior.

Many of us will do the wrong thing on behalf of our kids in order not to upset them. Joy is not something that you can produce in children. Parents drive themselves crazy trying to keep their children happy. Joy is a fruit of the Spirit, and your job is to do what's right by your kids. Many times, you don't know what's right, so you have to take a step of faith.

You have to appreciate the fact that when you have a good family, you do not take the power of choice away from your children. They still have the power of choice, and there are times when they're going to make some choices that are not in their best interests, in spite of the family.

Your children face incredible temptations. So you had better do the best you can to teach your children to walk in the Spirit. It is the Spirit of God that will sustain them, and not your family.

I'm a great believer in family living and paying attention to your children, but that is not a substitute for the ministry of the Holy Spirit in their lives.

4

Cross-Cultural Implications of an MK's Self-concept

Billy R. Lewter
Henry Brandt School of Psychology, Palm Beach Atlantic College

The heart of a biblical view of persons is that man lives with respect to God in every detail. This is also the heart of true psychology, since the material of psychology (behavior, motives, emotions, thinking, social interaction, etc.) is the very material which is most inescapably and universally related to God. Man is not an isolated being that can be analyzed just in himself. This is the error traditional psychology makes. Man must be viewed in the context of the living God. Paul said it was not man's judgment of him, nor his judgment of himself, but God's that was important (I Cor. 4:3,4). Each person is accountable to God, sustained by God, and judged by God.

The Image of God

It is important to realize the depth of man's problems. The natural man takes a rebellious stand towards God at the deepest level. Paul teaches that the unbeliever worships the creature rather than the Creator (Rom. 1:25). This idolatrous faith is a unifying commitment that provides the deepest meaning for every aspect of the unbeliever's thinking. At the core of his being, man has chosen independence from God. Independence from God is the essence of sin. It is the belief that we can live our lives as though there were no God. It is the suspicion that God is holding out on us, that he really isn't going to meet our needs, that we must depend on ourselves. Isaiah 53:6 says that we have each one chosen to go our own way. The essence of human personality is a rebellious stand against God, a unifying commitment to self.

"Heart" is used biblically in many ways and is never fully defined. It is best defined by context. Basically it is used in a psychological sense as the focus, or center, of man's inner life. The heart, from which "flow the issues of life," is the biblical core of personality, the biblical ego. It is this inner life that must be transformed. The use of "heart" is best understood by simply saying "me." The heart is the seat of everything human, the emotions, the intellect, the intentions or motives, all the vital activities of body, soul, and spirit.

Jesus said the heart, the inner life from which sin and failure come, must be completely transformed.

The heart is precisely that place where man meets or avoids God. Jesus said in John 7:37, "If any man thirst, let him come unto me and drink." The basis of Jesus' appeal was the desire, the craving, the thirst of the human heart. Man's basic problem is his self-serving, desire-oriented motivation. Without a radical reorientation of the heart, the inner person is not dealt with at a level of depth.

Traditional psychology fails to see accurately a biblical view of persons, so it cannot define healthy or unhealthy man, nor can it counsel for deep change in the real problems of life.

A Biblical View of Culture

Culture refers to a pattern or set of traditional arrangements for meeting everyday needs. Culture is a way of thinking, behaving, feeling and evaluating that binds a society together as it seeks to survive and find meaning and motivation. Simply put, culture is the distinctive way of life of a group of people. It is learned, shared and transmitted by the members of a society.

We must also distinguish between Scripture and culture. God's Word rises above cultures and can be meaningfully expressed in all cultures. It is supracultural and is the basis for evaluating the actions and beliefs of each culture. It is difficult to lay aside our cultural biases and practices and to allow the Gospel to become contextualized in another culture. It is difficult to see the world through the eyes of the people to whom we try to witness and counsel, and to respect their point of view. We tend to be a little ethnocentric.

Culture and Personality

We share with all mankind common expressive behaviors such as laughing, weeping, loving, and aggressive responses. There are also psychological commonalities such as the ability to think through problems and learn from experience; the ability to communicate with verbal and nonverbal language; the need for love, belongingness, security, and meaning; the potential for loving or hurting others; and human limitations resulting in anxiety, fear, illness, inhibition, defensiveness, restraint, self-protection, and self-justification. Without such universals, it would be impossible for people in one culture to understand or counsel people in another.

A second level of personality is cultural, and is shared by some, but not all people. This includes the language we use to express ourselves, which influences our perception of the world around us. Language is the most clearly recognizable feature of a culture. Others include family patterns of relationships and child rearing practices, religious beliefs and practices, attitudes toward elders, the physical distance people stand from one another in order to be comfortable, and non-verbal symbols of communication. The existence of the American is a clear example of cultural influence. With a multitude of genetic roots there is a collective personality that is striking to the non-American.

A third level of personality is individual. Each person has unique appearance, possesses a particular combination of strengths and weaknesses, has a personal history like no one else, and has his or her own personal, subjective world-view. No two people are exactly alike.

While we recognize universal similarities and individual uniqueness, we will focus on the impact of culture. There are striking differences between the West and non-West.

Differences between the West and non-West

In the West individualism is a core value. Personal accomplishments and self-improvement are more important than place of birth, family background, or social status. Decision-making and responsibility rest on individuals.

Maturity and self-esteem are related to self-reliance, achievement, independence, responsibility, identity fulfillment, and personal satisfaction.

In the West we make a sharp distinction between the natural and supernatural, between actual events and the unseen world. We consider it almost a right to have private property, to be materially well off, to have swift and convenient transportation and a comfortable home.

We also seek to analyze ourselves and others, and tend to see the world as comprehensible. We plan for the future, set personal goals, and seek to achieve them. We seek personal identity, and as a result our relationships are often weakly bonded. We are time oriented. Life goes on at a frantic pace. Many become workaholics and allow their tasks to dominate their lives to the extent that other people are viewed as a part of the work schedule.

Counseling in the West tends to be one-to-one with the emphasis on an individual's inner difficulties rather than on family, social, or cultural influences. The individual, not the individual in context, is the object of treatment. "Insight" is sought by a slow "working-through" process of self-disclosure. The counselee is expected to talk with a relative stranger about the most intimate aspects of life. The counseling process is future oriented, pragmatic, active, interpretive, and often emotional.

On the other hand, most non-Western cultures suppress individuality. Independence is seen as immaturity. People are not rewarded for initiating change and achieving progress. Self-worth, instead of being based on performance, is based on social status and family background. Maturity, especially in the Orient, is reflected by a satisfying and continuous dependency within family relationships and society. Dependency is not embarrassing to adults, whereas in the West it is often seen as pathological. The family is the primary unit of society, not the individual. Collectivism, or the well-being of the group, is a supreme guiding principle. Individualism is seen as destructive.

In most non-Western cultures when individuals seek counseling, they are in a state of crisis. It is a last resort, and they expect the counselor to be a trustworthy, authoritative advisor and problem solver with immediate, specific answers. They would be upset by someone probing into their family problems. To reveal family secrets invokes guilt and shame, especially in Asia. Insight is not desired. Analytical cause-effect interpretations, personal questioning, expression of deep feelings, or applying confrontive awareness techniques may all prove embarrassing. These violate the limits of self-disclosure and become more terrifying than the original problem.

So, there are differences in the way someone in the West and someone in the non-West see themselves. This creates problems for people who may have parents from the West but who have lived much of their lives in the non-West. There are going to be problems of re-entry if they go back to the culture of their parents.

Western individualism and non-Western collectivism are not necessarily mutually exclusive. Support systems rooted in the culture provide an individual with a sense of community and a network of interlocking relationships and responsibilities. A creative synthesis can draw on the collective elements of selflessness, discipline, unity of purpose, group problem-solving, and supportiveness, while incorporating the individual values of personal responsibility, self-worth and fulfillment. A creative synthesis offers an antidote to the excesses and misdirection of Western self-fulfillment as the goal of counseling.

A Biblical View of Self-concept

Those who study personality have long recognized the central importance of the concept of self.

A self-concept is not something we are born with. It is something each of us develops as a consequence of our experiences with those who surround us. We learn that we are male or female, able or unable, acceptable or unacceptable, liked or disliked, strong or weak, depending on the kind of experiences we have, and our reactions to them.

Self-concept cuts across experiences, beliefs, motives, needs, attitudes, values, behavior and personality and becomes a simple, more central element with which to understand a person. A self-concept, then, is an integrated synthesis of all the dimensions of life.

Self-esteem is the evaluative component of self-concept. It refers to the feelings a person has about himself or herself. There are three kinds of feelings that are especially significant: a sense of belonging, of worthiness, and of competence. Belongingness is an awareness of being accepted and loved. It relates a person to other persons. Worthiness is the feeling of personal significance, and relates a person to his or her own values. Competence is the feeling of adequacy in relation to life situations. All three of these needs can only be met in the final analysis by God. A person is accepted because of Jesus. He is worth the life of Jesus to God the Father, and is competent through the indwelling Holy Spirit.

Promoting the search for high self-esteem has become almost an end in itself in America. This is not common to all the world. I read about an executive of Mitsubishi in Japan who said, "I am not a person except as Mitsubishi defines me as a person." What is needed more than a pumped up self-concept, however, is an accurate appraisal of ourselves.

Two important theological concepts must be kept in balance. Many of the books by Christian psychologists dealing with self-concept deal with one issue only—justification. In justification, a person who accepts God is declared righteous by the atonement of Jesus. More basic than regarding the self as worthwhile is to be declared worthwhile by God.

Many authors fail to see the need for sanctification. Sanctification refers to growth toward righteous behavior. It recognizes God not only as our Father, but as our judge. A sanctified person does not get his or her signals for behavior primarily from what others expect, or from self-centered motives, or unmet needs. He or she is oriented toward growing in Christlike behavior, the only true standard of self-evaluation.

The ultimate solution to a low self-esteem, is not found in increased self-awareness, but in God-awareness. The Christian emphasis should never be high self-esteem but high Christ-esteem. An accurate self-understanding comes only in a proper understanding of our relationship to God. As Christians we know to whom we belong. This gives security, significance, and competence.

We must start a change in self-esteem by concentrating on the spiritual dimension of personality and the need for both justification and sanctification. We need to rationally consider our uniqueness in Christ and his purpose for our life.

We need to examine the family and cultural context of our self-concept. We need to see where the hurts and disappointments and failures have occurred. We need to analyze what we have said to our self about our self as a result of these experiences, and how we have perpetuated these beliefs over the years. We need to examine the contexts, or areas where low self-esteem occurs and to see the threats to our pride that exist in these fearful situations. We need to examine the motives for our behavior. We also need to reach out in love and minister to the needs of others, while trusting God to meet our needs (Isaiah 58:10-12).

Happiness is found outside ourselves in relationship with God and others. Servanthood is the true measure of self-worth.

Much of current psychology, looking out for self, pumping up self-esteem, flatly contradicts what is really needed: relationship, trust, love, obedience to God's Word, ministry to other's needs, and less foolish pride.

5

Developing Healthy Sexuality in the MK and the Christian Community

Dean Kliewer
Link Care

Intentional planning for growth towards sexual maturity may be one of the arenas most neglected in the evangelical church, and in the church generally.

Travel destination

Many of us seem unaware that we're on a sexual growth journey. We don't know there is a destination. On the way, we may be taken with mirages which appear to be an end point. Some of these pseudo-destinations include: a thorough identification with the appropriate cultural stereotype for young boys or young girls; the development of interest in the opposite sex; the onset of puberty at the right time; the initiating of dating activities at the right time; the avoidance of sexual interactions before marriage; lifelong commitment through marriage; a satisfactory sexual relationship with one spouse; a complete loss of sexual interest in persons other than the spouse; the parenting of children, etc. These may all be legitimate way stations on the trip but I don't see them as destinations.

Our goal as Christians is growth into the image of Christ, mature discipleship, the bringing of this part of life under the Lordship of Jesus Christ. Now it's a curious thing that in the contemporary church, that issue is almost never brought up.

In our Christian families we must begin to talk more openly about what we see as our destination in the sexual arena. If this is to happen, we must develop convictions about the meaning of sexual discipleship. I believe that much of our sexual confusion emerges because we haven't done this important work. We need more help from church leadership sources.

Route markers

Let us examine some route markers on the way to mature sexuality. How can we define mature sexuality?

Jesus revealed one evidence of maturity in the attitude He showed toward a flagrant violator of a sexual standard, the woman taken in adultery (John 8:1-11.) Here he seemed less concerned about the accused than he was about the accusers. He didn't even ask the accused for an admission of guilt, or for a promise of abstinence. He simply told her to go and sin no more.

This marker seems to be "judge your own sexual sin not the sin of others." If we see movement toward this objective, we may be on the way.

Loving people, really genuinely caring for other human beings seems to be another marker as one looks at the pattern of relationships that Jesus maintained.

Can I deal openly with my disappointment, my grief, my anger, my fear regarding sexual matters as I interact with people close to me? Or do I have to deny that those feelings are there and say that because I'm a believer, I really don't have those kinds of feelings?

Can I form a lasting bond with another person? Does my affection and loyalty to the person with whom I've made a commitment rise above the interpersonal struggles which bring tension to any intimate relationship?

If I'm married, can I put my sexual needs below the needs of my spouse? Is my primary goal in our sexual relationship to make my spouse happy? Is that where the big joy is, to find another person fulfilled? I suggest that that's a way station. That's something to work toward.

Is unselfishness about need meeting also manifest in my relationships with nonspouse family members and with others close to me? Am I willing to declare my needs and assume that they're OK, but also place the needs of other people alongside those needs and respect them and seek to work toward their fulfillment as well?

Travel tips

How might we expedite the process of assembling information? How can we get better data than what we usually get? Where should one look for tips?

So often we appear to be forced to get our tips from books, from magazines, from locker room bravado, from Dr. Ruth or from the Phil Donahue show rather than from our brothers and sisters in the faith. That seems so backwards to me.

Common sexual fears in the Christian community

1. There seems to be fear that talking about sexual feeling or behavior will increase the likelihood that we'll get into sexual problems.

2. We're afraid of exposure. Most of us as adults still don't know where we stand on sexual matters. We are fearful that others will discover how much confusion we feel about the sexual. It's a fear-based cover-up. I'm convinced that our silence helps us to remain stunted in our Christian walk.

3. Many of us are afraid that we might not be normal sexually. We fear the possibility that we may fail to perform up to our expectations. Will I be capable enough? Or too responsive? Are my sexual interests/needs too weird to be accepted by a partner or too mundane? Fears like these do persist even after marriage. Fears of being judged abnormal help keep marriage partners from sharing with one another about important sexual issues.

   You can have a neat growth experience if you can start talking with your spouse about where you really are. One marker for my wife and me was when I was able to tell her about an erotic dream—a dream that I shouldn't have dreamed, about somebody way back in my history that I never dated. She was interested in it, and we had a neat dialogue. We still don't share everything, but we find ourselves more able to talk about some of those sexual feeling issues than we used to.

4. Fears about our own sexual frailty cause us to maintain a kind of paranoia about potentially uncontrolled sexual impulses in other people. We're afraid of their sexuality. We're afraid that young people will awaken to the sexual prematurely, so we don't talk.

   Deep down I think we feel helpless and hopeless. We can't control what our kids read or see on T.V. or at the movies or what they do in their cars. Our silence is based on a profound discouragement. We shrug our shoulders and shake our heads. Why not risk sharing some thoughts and feelings with people that matter to us?

Observations about Christians and sexual issues

1. Although we have in the Christian community fewer sexual difficulties than in the general population, as far as types and variety of problems, they're all there among us. In some ways sexual matters may be even more troublesome for us because of our uptightness. Many Christians do not seem to accept our vulnerability to sex problems and sexual disability.

2. Any disability is hard to accept, but sexual disabilities are more difficult. We don't understand the contribution of learning to our experience of sexuality. Many of us don't believe that sexual behavior obeys the laws associated with habit and decision making. Neither do we tend to associate sexual arousal with other emotional processes like the processes that lead us to be afraid or cause us to roll with laughter or bring us into a heightened emotional experience. People go wild at ball games, that's legitimate. We can do it there. A lot of people have much more difficulty thinking about going wild sexually, which is part of what can happen between two people that really care about each other. We see sex as something else. We see it as instinctual, inexplicable, capricious. Nature will take care of itself, consequently we don't try to influence it.

3. Many of us seem to think in distorted ways about sexual behavior and sexual feeling. We maintain a kind of prejudice against the sexual in ourselves and in other people. So we tend to be very harsh and judgmental even in a Christian community.

4. We somehow learn to deny our very real need for affection and touch. Denial of needs for sexual touching and sexual communication may be seen as part of this tendency to turn away from closeness, touching and intimacy. People start to get suspicious about a touchy-feely person. Is this person loose? Or is this person simply expressing feeling and willing to recognize genuine feeling with some kinds of touching? Those of you who are involved in other cultures know how healthy that kind of thing can be. In our culture as Americans, we're more uptight about it.

5. We seem to cultivate the fantasy of a light-switch-like change in sexual feelings and behavior at the time of marriage. We want to believe sexual skills emerge as from a cocoon, fully mature. We tend to deny that sexual growth involves a process, a need for rehearsal and practice. For example we

need to learn to accept our sexual feelings, see them as OK, natural, and good, and not be afraid of those feelings; see them as controllable, and find ourselves experiencing mastery over those powerful feelings. Too often we are not taught that there's a need for a sequence of experiences, a necessary behavior-shaping process which enables us to develop skills in coping with sexual feelings and behavior.

6. We may not understand how absurdly arbitrary the stimuli which excites sexual response can be. Just because something turns somebody on, doesn't mean that that's what turns other people on. Whatever I've learned to associate with sexual arousal—an object, thought, or image—can become sexually arousing for me. For example a child might have an experience of sexual arousal in a closet where there are old clothes and shoes and stuff like that. As a result, old clothes, dirty musty places, and shoes can become sexually arousing. It's as simple as that. It's a conditioning process that doesn't have any fancy connections. I'm not saying that that's the only way sexual experiences are learned, but that can be the case.

If some sexual feelings are learned through a conditioning process, it may also be possible to unlearn undesirable sexual associations, and relearn desirable ones. Sometimes believers who are willing to pray about that and are willing to work on it, can see some real change in their own acceptance of that and in their own relationship with their spouses and other people.

6. Most of us do not accept the generality of our sexual response capability. We want to believe that we are capable of responding only to one other opposite-sex person, when actually we have a broad sexual affectional response potential. God made us with tendencies to respond with sexual excitement to a wide variety of persons and situations. Advertisers understand that. On the other hand we may feel bewildered and guilty about it.

Should I desire to feel sexual arousal only with my wife? That does not mean that I will find myself stimulated only when I'm with her. It just isn't the way it goes. I may experience sexual arousal at the most inappropriate times for reasons I only partially understand.

Obviously, I don't need to engage in sexual experience when I feel sexually aroused. Just because I feel turned on by somebody doesn't mean that there's something magical that has to happen there between us, or that my marriage bond is being shaken to it's core. That's why I think it's important that we open up about sexual feeling with spouses. For example it's helpful if I can talk to my wife about situations that turn me on. I can dialogue with her and see her responding with reason. Now not every wife can do that, and not every husband can do that. I don't assume that that's a norm. But I hope we might be able to be a little bit more open with one another about it. It took me about twenty-five years of marriage until I could open up on those sorts of things. I'm embarrassed to say that, but it's true.

7. We may not be aware of the continuity of sexual experience throughout the life span. Sexual experiences start way before puberty. Little boys can come out of the birth canal with an erection, and are capable of orgiastic response long before they are capable of an ejaculation. Peak sexual capability for men and women in our culture comes at strange times in comparison with the kind of expectations we have about sexual behavior. For example, greatest sexual interest and potential for men occurs at about sixteen or seventeen. Women are most capable at an average of thirty-six or thirty-seven. A man is twenty years past his prime when a woman of like age hits her stride. Add in our expectation that the female marriage partner should be younger than the male and you've got a prescription for trouble. Nevertheless we can be grateful that sexual interest and capability can persist throughout old age and although as general physical capability declines, sexual capability also may be reduced, still joy in sexual experiences is not only for the young.[1]

---

[1]Editor's note: A second section on sexual growth as emotional growth ran past the end of the tape. For a written treatment of that topic as well as a fuller treatment of the first section, the book *Managing Sexual Feelings in the Christian Community* by Dr. Kliewer can be obtained from Link Care.

6

Personal Integration: Blending Transition, Learning, and Relationships

John Powell
Professor of Psychology and Counseling, Michigan State University

We don't have to read very far in Scripture to realize that the person, of all the created things, is of supreme importance to God. The philosopher Goethe, in a long discourse about the meaning of persons, simply concludes with this statement: "The person is the one thing on this earth of supreme value."

When we think about the care and nurture of MKs, their development as persons and the processes they go through, we see a blending of experiences that they carry with them.

I'd like to look at transitions, at learning, and then at the importance of community or relationship as a basis for this personal integration.

Let me share with you a couple of ideas about what the integrated person might look like. I invite you to compare these psychological descriptions with what we find in Romans 12 as a definition of maturity.

William Menninger, from the Menninger Institute in Topeka, Kansas, a group that has had a lot of influence on positive mental health procedures over the decades, talks about psychological maturity in this way:

> In positive terms we can state that psychological maturity entails finding greater satisfaction in giving than in receiving (the reversal of the infantile state), having a capacity to form satisfying and permanent loyalties, being primarily a creative contributing person, having learned to profit from experience, having a freedom from fear, with a resulting true serenity and not a pseudo absence of tension, an accepting and making the most of unchangeable reality when it confronts one.

38

A person who exhibits those qualities is probably an integrated person. Notice that Menninger speaks of the satisfaction that comes from giving. That is consistent with the scriptural view of giving. I hope you notice the part that says we're not guaranteed freedom from anxiety. Rather we get to a point where there really is a serenity with an absence of underlying tension. That allows us to cope when anxious experiences and tensions arise, and to accept and make the most of unchangeable reality. That is not to say we are completely free of tension, but we have a solid core.

We can have Christ and not be integrated. Eugene Peterson, in *Toward a Long Obedience*, talks about this. What we want to see in the development of MKs is people who are moving toward this kind of personal integration. They need an internal consistency that forms a base for letting them engage the experiences of life in a balanced way, that will not only bring satisfaction to themselves, but will serve others. That's not something you learn just through adolescence, or even necessarily in young adulthood.

Transitions and Personal Integration

I can't think of very many other occupations or calls where there would be so many transitions as in missions.

I had a very painful experience on the mission field some years ago when I was in a guest house in Asia. There were a lot of people staying in this guest house who were there because they had come in from up and down country to see their children off to school. There were probably thirty or thirty-five parents around the living room area who had just come back from the airport. They were hardly talking to each other. When my wife and I walked in, we both looked at each other because everyone seemed to be stopped.

As we introduced ourselves and got acquainted, we realized that everyone had just come back from seeing their kids off. The striking thing to me was that no one was talking about the tremendous pain that was so evident to us as outsiders.

Any transition we make has tremendous possibilities for loss in it, even normal transitions. If we look at what happens when we accept these realities of life and do something with them, we are obligated to face the pain and sadness, even when we have the very smallest loss.

A few weeks ago I had come home for a quick dinner between leaving the university and going to my private practice for the evening. As I stepped in the house, the phone rang. It was one of the people I see who was in great distress, needing to talk at that moment. I had about forty-five minutes to have dinner with my wife and get to the office and see someone else. Obviously I spent almost all of the forty-five minutes on the phone and felt good about the outcome.

But there was also a kind of sadness and anger about that. I had planned a certain kind of transition between the university and off campus that had been interrupted by another reality that I had to deal with. There was the loss of a nice dinner in the company of my loving wife. I didn't like it.

I was interested in my wife's reaction because she had spent some time preparing dinner. I asked her, "How did you feel about that call?"

She said, "I didn't like it, but I accept it."

I said, "I didn't like it either, but I accept it. Let's get together later." We hugged each other, and I said good-bye, and the transition was made—not the way I planned it, but it was made.

One of the reasons I think it was successful is that right there in the process of the transition we could express our feelings. That didn't leave any backpack of unresolved affect that was going to spill over onto the other people I was going to see in my office that evening. It was taken care of.

If missionaries and MKs don't deal with these transitions in some timely way, they carry some very large backpacks of unresolved grief and loss. They miss the possibility for integration. Any transition can be a relatively good one. A lot of transitions can also be bad.

There are essentially three main points in a transition. If you look back before the transition starts, we have ongoing normal days, both good and bad. Then the information comes that there is going to be a transition. It could be a sudden thing or something you plan for weeks or months like going on furlough.

When the transition hits us, we have a narrowing of focus which says, "Now we have to deal with this transition." There is a change of energy. When we move into this narrow area we become less and less capable of dealing with the broad spectrum of life because we have to give so much attention to the transition. This is what Sidney Werkman calls the engagement stage.

Then we have the transition itself, which is inevitably filled with some kind of disruption of ongoing things. Whether the MK adjusts has to do with three things: (1) the extent to which he or she can understand the transition; (2) whether the transition can be seen as something that is hopeful; and (3) the extent to which the MK is allowed to experience and express his feelings about the transition. If those things go pretty well, then the MK can move into the re-engagement stage and move on with that period of life.

I think transitions by and large are very helpful and growth producing, but too many, too intense, in too short of time, can be really disruptive. The more we can understand the nature of transition as an opportunity for personal integration in this developmental sense, the better the MK will handle subsequent transitions.

Some MKs have a lot of transitions early on and never quite come to terms with those. Later, any transition, particularly a move or a change in relationship, job, or responsibility, causes them to go through that same pattern of anxiety, fear, uncertainty, and loneliness again. It sometimes takes people a long time to cope with that in an adequate way. The positive side is that people who have had the opportunity to process (talk about, feel, think, share with others, understand, find meaning in) have much less difficulty in their subsequent moves and transitions.

We need to be very sensitive to the feelings of a five-year-old going through a transition. Many of his feelings will not be expressed very directly. They will be acted out in some changes in behavior. I think the sensitive parent will be able to help the child express those, perhaps by giving a word for them, or perhaps just by comforting and recognizing that these feelings are taking place.

Allow the child to feel that he or she really is a part of the family, and that this move is part of the family commitment that has been made. I realize that is idealistic, but I have seen it work.

I think the idea of hope is difficult for the five-year-old. If there is a favorite object, even though it may cause some extra expense or difficulty, the child ought to take it along. If you give a younger child a sense of participation and allow him to bring something that has constancy, then you are preparing the child to recognize that constancy does not rest necessarily in a place, but more ultimately inside the person. Anything that makes transitions easier really builds the prospect that later transitions will be somewhat easier. Again, there are a lot of individual differences.

There really has to be a sense of family unity that is developed through a lot of communication, a lot of sharing, a lot of affirmation, a lot of tenderness, so that there is a base for an understanding of the commitment. That means time, but that time saves hours and hours later on. A good family system becomes the core that is still there when moves and transitions are made.

As parents assisting in transitions, we want to look so much to the positive side to give children hope that we don't let them take the time they need to process the transition. They are going to tell us some things we don't want to hear. We are going to hear them hurt, but that's the best thing one can do.

Start as soon as possible to help the MK say some complete good-byes. If the child has done some things that he feels guilty about, let him get that straightened out. If he has been mean to a teacher, let him go and talk to that teacher and get it dealt with. Let him leave as cleanly as possible with good, complete, resolved good-byes.

I would suggest that in this process, you also begin to give the child realistic information, not pie-in-the-sky information, about your new situation. There will be times when he doesn't want to receive it. One has to be sensitive and talk about it whenever the situation might permit.

Share your feelings about leaving. Moms and Dads need to talk about their feelings and let the kids hear them.

Learning and Personal Integration

There are three critical kinds of learning for the MK. We have talked about the formal, classroom, organized part of learning, and that is important. But the other two have an equally important role in personal integration.

The second is an informal learning about life—the way the child sees life practiced. If there is anything that the child, and even more so the adolescent, is keen on, it is seeing the inconsistencies between stated values and behaved values. If transitions are not made well and the child sees tears pushed back and denied, you have taught the child that feelings are not to be expressed, at least in polite company.

There is a third kind of learning, a cultural learning. Let me suggest that there is a kind of third culture that is the subculture of the mission group within which the child is growing up. A tremendous amount of learning that is critical to personal integration takes place, but it may not be easily transferable even to other mission groups or to churches at home. There is also the learning which takes place within the culture.

My colleague Dave Wickstrom told me about an experience he had when he came home on a furlough from Nigeria at about the age of ten. In Africa when they were waiting for someone or waiting for a bus, they would hunch down in the African style. So, when they got waylaid in an airport somewhere, he got tired and hunched down in that style. That was very natural in his culture, but pretty soon there were people looking and pointing at him. He still remembers how embarrassing that was and how much he felt "out of it" because it was not acceptable.

While we can readily identify that as host culture learning, it may be harder to identify some of the ethos of the mission subculture that we also take back. The children have to do something with it before it is integrated.

Importance of Relationships in Personal Integration

In this whole personal integration process the key experience is that of relationships. I was recently asked to remember someone who had been important to me. A man I had worked with one summer when I was about fourteen delivering Coca Cola to some of the surrounding communities came to mind. I hadn't thought about him for years. But as I thought back on the long conversations we had about male-female relationships, about what it meant to have a job, drive a truck, and have a family, I realized that old Vern Burkhart had been a very important person to me, someone I had trusted and admired.

If we think back, considering our own sense of where we are, particularly in our Christian development, we find that God in his tremendous grace has provided us a number of relationships like that, each one putting in just the right amount for the recipe of our personal integration.

It is critical that the MK have a set of relationships like that, and also that within the set of relationships there are some that are absolutely constant in their availability over time.

Sometimes on the university campus I ask, "Who has been important to you?"
Students will think for awhile and say, "Grandmother."
"Where does Grandmother live?"
"In California."
"How often do you see her?"
"Only once every three years."
"How could she be so important?"
"Because every time I see her, I know that she loves me. And even when I don't see her, I know that she loves me."

Over time they internalize those images of people that they know love them. When they feel worthless, unloved, and in pain, or sad because they have lost someone, many times God in his mercy vividly brings back to their mind that person. They know that some place there is that person who loves them.

It doesn't matter so much if the person is actually present, if personal integration has been successful up to that point. What is important is this internal sense of caring—what has been given to them in those relationships that they can draw on to build other ones in new situations.

Studies of people who are well-integrated show that it is probably better to have a few relationships of some depth than it is to try to have a lot of relationships that are somewhat more superficial. This will vary in terms of individual differences. You don't need to worry about whether the MK is a social person or tends to be more introverted and prefer solitary activities as long as a few relationships are being nurtured in that person's life.

Life Stages

Late childhood is generally the third phase of psycho-social development, ages six to twelve. Social roles are largely defined as being a student, a helper, a big brother, or a big sister. The developmental tasks in that six year span of late childhood generally involve being able to take initiative, having a sense of industry and planning, and having an influence on what happens to them in terms of a broadening scope of responsibility, and learning such basic skills as reading, math, and fundamental social skills.

The coping behaviors are manipulating and having positive control over his environment in increasing ways. The child learns value-oriented behaviors and puts more energy into productive work activities. Either in the boarding school or at home, there is a richness of resources beyond what the child would have in the home country.

The fourth stage, organization, is from ages twelve to fourteen, early adolescence. Here the roles shift from the family-oriented status to a peer-oriented status. They learn about heterosexual roles. The developmental tasks have to do with identity, developing a sense of person, learning to be masculine or feminine, and refinement of a value hierarchy that allows them the beginning development of a sense of purpose in life and an internal guiding behavior system. The coping behaviors are social behaviors, sex appropriate behaviors, and achievement-oriented behaviors.

I think this is the point where some MKs begin to slip in terms of how much they stay on track developmentally. For one thing, they probably do not have the same latitude for heterosexual exploration that they might have in larger settings where there are greater possibilities. The counterbalance is that there is usually a lot of opportunity to talk about what male-female relationships mean relationally. Thus they are better prepared in terms of values and ethics than their counterparts at home may be. It is a trade-off.

The last stage I want to talk about is exploration, which is later adolescence, ages fifteen to nineteen. There is a refinement of peer roles, much more development of heterosexual roles, and the taking on of more socially responsible tasks such as having a job and taking on serious school projects. The developmental tasks are: establishing identity as a worker; learning to develop intimacy in both same and opposite-sex relationships; learning to be a member of a group in a constructive way; and coming to terms with one's value system and often one's spiritual or religious commitment. The relevant coping behaviors are learning much more about reciprocal behavior, learning tolerance for what may be seen as deviance in other people, learning cooperative behavior, and learning much more about mutuality.

Because of the nature of much MK learning, there is probably tremendous precept teaching in these areas, but a paucity of experience. They may know a lot about it, but in terms of having grappled with some of the hard ethical questions, they probably have not had the opportunity to do that in the same way that their home-country counterparts have. They may have some real difficulties, and we may see a regression of their spiritual values, particularly if they are hit with too much too soon.

What we mean by integration is the pulling together of all we are in terms of who God gives us to be and what God has given.

Autonomy, management and enjoyment of emotions, identity (including sexuality), interpersonal freedom (including intimacy), values development, sense of purpose, sense of competencies, and cognition are dimensions to look at in how missionary kids may be helped in learning, transitions, and relations. They need to integrate these so that they become whole, mature persons with characteristics that honor Christ and make them productive in his Kingdom, and also give them a joy that might be full, as the Lord told us.

I'd like to distinguish between handling the transitions more easily and experiencing the transitions more easily. As a parent I do not experience the separation from my children more easily even though I have been doing it year after year. I hope I am mature enough to be handling it better, but it is not easier.

7

Ministering to Maturing MKs

Alice Brawand
Wycliffe Bible Translators Counseling Department

Troubled MKs see their past as a barrier to growth rather than as a strength on which to build. Based on research and interviews with approximately one hundred MKs, I am going to suggest ways to understand and encourage troubled MKs by helping them reframe their view of their background.

The focus of this presentation is that the past life of maturing MKs needs to be faced and better understood. Only then can MKs truly use those experiences to benefit themselves and the world around them.

Usually, without any prompting, the MKs interviewed began to unfold a struggle or a need they had faced. They expressed both positive and negative aspects of their experiences in growing up. It was obvious that most of these needs had been resolved, but a few were not. One middle-aged married MK who wields a strong influence in her leadership responsibility, exclaimed, "Oh, these are still live issues within me!"

One twenty-eight-year-old man unexpectedly exclaimed, "Oh, this is so good—I mean just to talk like this with someone who is interested." Another well-adjusted, happy MK mother, upon hearing my topic, excitedly remarked, "Oh, good, you're dealing with the adult MK! They are a forgotten people."

The interviews substantiated findings of others, namely that MKs' needs fall into three main categories: social adjustments, personal factors relating to self-esteem and identity, and re-entry needs.

Social Adjustments

Since MKs have been exposed to two or more cultures, some MKs feel confused as to which culture they most directly identify

46

with. This causes problems in personal identity which affect social adjustment.

On the foreign field MKs may find personal acceptance by being who they really are. Then suddenly they feel like they don't really belong when they return to the homeland of their parents. Like any teenager, MKs have a strong need to fit in, to belong, to be a part of the culture in which they find themselves.

How do teenage MKs adjust socially when their parents and all that is familiar to them are far away? This separation causes some MKs to become involved in a relationship with the opposite sex prematurely. At times there are premature sexual experiences during the adolescent years which may result either in an early marriage or, in some extreme instances, even suicide. These MKs long for security especially in the area of friendships.

Personal Factors

This second area of needs involves self-esteem and personal identity. A contributing factor to this area of need is the early separation from parents resulting in unresolved grief.

One married MK in her twenties spoke of her dad as a "phantom father" who was emotionally removed from his wife and children. Another spoke of his dad in this way:

> Daddy thrived on a hectic schedule, finding the constant demand on his mind and body exhilarating.... In many ways Daddy felt more at home with the people he served than he did with his own family.... Daddy's work was far more his baby than I was! ... Daddy was away so much that there was a constant aching loneliness in my heart.... I lost touch with my parents; there was no soul-level relationship.

Trauma of premature separation from parents can bring a sense of too-early, new-found independence. This can be a contributing factor to personal problems.

Overly strict parents who do not share their own feelings and needs and yet have very high expectations for their children may cause problems in the lives of their children.

"It seems I am always trying to measure up to an unreachable standard.... Although never vocally expressed by my parents, I feel I am to be an example of perfect behavior and flawless upbringing. It is my responsibility to reflect my parent's righteous life."

Some parents practice a twenty-five-year-old morality which adds confusion and strain on their maturing or adult MK child.

One maturing MK was asked, "What would be freedom to you?"

She replied, "Oh, to have my ears pierced!" Imagine the new-found freedom and joy when shortly thereafter her ears were pierced!

At times missionary parents may place unrealistic expectations on their maturing children. Recently a forty-eight-year-old MK told me, "Just the other day my parents asked me, 'When are you going to the foreign field?'" This adult MK was feeling a sense of strain and pressure for he is fulfilled and happy in his present work in the U.S. Such unrealistic expectations held by parents may cause tremendous struggles within the maturing MK's own personal identity.

At times, MKs feel like foreigners wherever it is that they are living. Recently a high school MK sobbed as she told me her story. "It's all different now. It has all changed since I was here in the U.S. three years ago. When I return to Africa it will all be different there too!" Now, about a month later, she is accepting this change as inevitable. She is learning new customs, styles and the current slang. Now she is reaching out to make new friends.

There are numerous needs returning MKs encounter upon re-entry to their parents' homeland. For example, in Manila, MKs cannot drive until they are eighteen. In the U.S., as we know, the age is sixteen, and a sixteen-year-old may even own a car.

Re-entry needs

MKs in high school or college sometimes wonder where to go during vacation time.

Sometimes what brought a feeling of acceptance and status on the foreign field does not bring the same result in the U.S. When MKs lived abroad they were considered to be wealthy and a part of the upper class. This upper class status changes when they return to the States where they are more likely to feel they have low to middle class status.

At times, those ministering to MKs feel overwhelmed by the number of needs MKs face relating to personal identity factors, social needs and re-entry concerns. It is only when needs continue to be unmet that they become problems. The results of these interviews show that for most MKs their needs are probably not long-standing, but that they use their needs as stepping stones to live secure, steady, successful lives by God's grace. Having successfully adjusted to numerous situations in life makes MKs all the stronger as they face the challenge of the future.

Responding to the Needs of MKs

Personal prerequisites

- A positive attitude. Gentleness, vulnerability, and reliance on God are desirable qualities to develop.

- Training and experience. God not only uses training and experiences to better equip one in working with MKs, but he also uses personal trials and struggles as preparation for this special ministry. Have you ever known anyone who was an effective people-helper who had not gone through deep personal struggles and trials? If you are facing these, rejoice. God has a plan for you.

Suggestions in relating to MKs

- Listen with the heart.
- Accept them just as they are.
- Take time with them.
- Accept doubting as real and valid.
- Encourage MKs to deal with feelings of guilt.
- Allow tears to come.
- Mourn endings in order to celebrate new beginnings.

MKs and their parents

- Encourage them to spend time with their own parents. While it is true that MKs cannot "go back" in time to the growing up stage and situations they experienced, still they can "go back" in imagination with their parents.
- Encourage the physical touch.
- Resolve hurt feelings. Reliving a painful experience with one who cares can promote healing of memories.
- Promote understanding regarding MKs' life's work. Yes, MKs must realize and be made to feel it is okay to have a secular job.

MKs and others

- Promote bonding with other MKs.
- Encourage the deepening of friendships.
- Encourage a close relationship with the Lord.

Suggested activities

- Drawing a chart of their life. Using peaks as high points and valleys as low points in telling their life story may serve to enable them to have a better understanding of their own life.
- Listing benefits in being MKs.
- Writing about past, present and future accomplishments.
- Writing their autobiography. Such an assignment enables them to put their own life into perspective and to better understand their past.
- Making their own scrap book.
- Revisiting the place where they grew up.
- Adopting an "aunt" or an "uncle."

Preventive Measures

What can be done to help prevent certain problems in the lives of MKs? It is true that there is no perfect living situation anywhere in the world. There is no "sterile" environment. However, there are certain preventive measures which can be taken.

Role of parents

- The attitude of parents is crucial. Personal interview and research indicate that it is crucial for parents to maintain a positive attitude toward both cultures.
- The missionary father has a key role. The implications are that the father needs to be an involved parent, especially in giving supportive warmth and firm control.
- Children need to be a part of their parents' ministry. This brings far-reaching benefits to the missionary family and to the people they serve.
- Parents need to be good models. They need to express appreciation and praise to each other and to the children.
- Parents need to trust children. As MKs mature, parents need to trust their children's decisions, even if these decisions may be wrong. This trust will help build the MKs' self-confidence and self-esteem. There comes a point when parents need to stop "parenting."
- Parents should encourage interdependency, which will help them develop a support system for all of life.

Conclusion

Maturing MKs need to be given plenty of freedom to be themselves and to serve God in this world in whatever capacity God is calling them. Let us cheer them on to success! God needs His witnesses everywhere. Where they serve does not matter. What matters is whether the Lord is the Lord of their lives for now and for all eternity.

8

Developing a Caring Core on the College Campus

Richard Gathro, Christian College Coalition
Dave Pollock, Interaction, Inc.

Dave Pollock: Unfortunately over the years not a great deal has been done in the area of caring for the third-culture kid on the college campus. He's been considered an interesting individual, but there has not been a great deal of concern on his behalf in terms of how to meet his particular needs. However, during the last couple of years, we've found a growing concern on the part of Christian colleges to address the issue of the third-culture kid on their campus. We've been particularly delighted with a relationship that has grown with Rich Gathro, who is the Associate Director of the American Studies Program for the Christian Colleges Coalition. He works in Washington, D.C., and has expressed a very keen interest in the ministry to third-culture kids.

Richard Gathro: The Christian College Coalition consists of seventy-seven schools that are Christ-centered, accredited, and liberal arts oriented. They must have a strong Christ-centered missions statement, and must hire only faculty that are committed to Christ. There is a lot of desire to do things for missionary kids, but a lot of just plain lack of knowledge. I have tried to make our student development people aware that there are communication problems with financial aid and admissions. For example, one college kept insisting that the MK take the Test Of English as a Foreign Language. I also let them know that there are re-entry seminars that they can send their students to.

As you're developing a relationship with these colleges, don't be hesitant to ask them, "What are you doing for MKs?" They are interested in having your kids. Sometimes they just need to be made aware of some of your needs. There is a wide diversity of what these schools are offering MKs. Some of them are doing a lot, and some of them are doing nothing. Hold their feet to the fire. On most campuses it's a buyer's market. They want your students.

Survey Results

Before coming to this conference, we conducted a survey of our colleges. Forty-five responded.

Some of the survey respondents that have larger numbers of MKs were Azusa Pacific, Biola, Bryan, Calvin, Bethel (in Minnesota), Eastern, Evangel, Goshen, Houghton, Messiah, Nyack, Southern California College, Seattle Pacific, Taylor, and Westmont. A third of these schools are on the West Coast. Almost every campus has 4 or 5 percent of their student body made up of MKs. The highest was Warner Pacific with 8 percent.

Twenty six out of forty-five have programs specifically to meet the developmental needs of MKs.

Special financial assistance seems to be growing. Correspond with the colleges you're interested in to encourage this. As a result of strong encouragement about the special needs of MKs, Bartlesville Wesleyan in Oklahoma now has a tuition-free package for MKs. The only requirement is that the MK be a U.S. citizen.

Places like Southern California College have developed specific orientation programs for the MK. They and seventeen others of the forty-five have MK advisors, and the number is growing.

Point Loma has an Aunt and Uncle Program where the MKs are adopted, in effect. Roberts Wesleyan has different homes in the community to be homes away from home for the MK.

Houghton College is developing a video for MKs. Sixteen others also have videos promoting their campuses. You now can have a video library which will provide your MKs with a chance to visualize a particular campus. I imagine most of these videos are free.

One of the greatest needs pointed out by the survey was the need for student development people to have special orientation and training. Only ten campuses have student development people who have had any kind of special training. The numbers are about the same for having a special re-entry program, although one college in the "no" category doesn't have such a program because their denomination has one for their own MKs. Only eleven are encouraging re-entry seminars.

I think those are two of the more glaring needs—developing increased sensitivity among student development officers and making our colleges more aware that re-entry seminars are available.

Fourteen colleges said they have plans to develop additional programs. Some are in process of writing MK manuals. Two schools specifically mentioned that they have MK manuals—Gordon College in Massachusetts has one written by MKs for incoming MKs. The other was Nyack College.

Schools that consistently had the most extensive programs were Azusa Pacific, Grace, and Houghton. Those are the leaders we can look to for models. Grace College wants to establish a bonding program. They are aware of the need for developing a sense of belonging and relationship. Azusa Pacific is now developing a cross-culture kind of course offered for credit for MKs.

When I was at Trinity College as admissions director, we asked the MKs to identify themselves to help us with our international students. They were invaluable in terms of doing some cultural communication with our international students. We had one situation where a particular international kept insisting that his roommates were his servants. We managed to get an MK who had grown up in the same culture, to explain that just because a person was in the same room did not mean he was a servant. This is a state-of-the-art situation.

I want to re-emphasize that there's interest on the part of our colleges, but we have to bear in mind that there is turnover in our student personnel staffs. One of the tasks of the Christian College Coalition and of Interaction is to keep working at the communication and education process. One of your responsibilities is to hold these colleges responsible for the development of these kinds of programs.

Having been an admissions director, I know that they are very responsive to letters they get asking, "Have you developed a special orientation program for MKs?" If they say no, they may want to know how. Maybe you can point them in the right direction.

Pollock: It is exciting to see the change and development that's taking place on college campuses. One of the first to respond was Grace College. They ran the first of the two-day consultations that we offer to our Christian colleges called "The Care and Feeding of Third-Culture Kids and International Students." We spent two full days on their campus meeting first with the President's Council and talking to them about their interest. We feel it is very important that there be a top-down awareness and interest, lest the people at the grass roots become very frustrated when they ask for funding. People at all levels have to be demonstrating a concern.

What We Do in a Two-Day Training Session

1. Orientation to the seminar—exchange of basic ideas and expectations with the key people who have invited us to the campus, usually the student development people.

2. Introduction to the issue of third cultureness and a profile of the third-culture kid.

3. Flow of MK care—things that can be done by the community for the missionary kid and the third-culture kid. Pinpoint the things that colleges can do.

4. Flow of international student care.

5. General exchange and discussion with third-culture kids.

We spend a lot of time in discussing the needs of third-culture kids and internationals, and having the college people raise issues that are of concern to them. We help them identify things that they're already doing. Sometimes people are doing the right thing, but because it's done accidentally it doesn't become a pattern. A professor on campus may be doing some great things for international students, and as long as he is there, everything is fine. He goes, and the program comes to an end.

We spend time with the faculty as a whole, talking about third-culture kids. We spend time with the development people on the issues of counseling. When there are career guidance people on the campus, we deal with them in relation to career guidance for third-culture kids.

We spend the last half day with as many people from the staff and faculty as possible, looking at what is being done, what ought to be done, what can be done, and what they're going to do. We come out with an end product. I heard about six months later that Grace had put everything into effect that they said they were going to do.

Depending on staff and depending on the corporate attitude of the international students and the missionary kids, the success in any given year may fluctuate. You may have one year when things go great, all the pieces come together, and it seems like everybody's needs are being met. Then you have another year when everything seems to bottom out. It takes time to put together a program that is going to be effective.

We try to be sensitive to the fact that a college is not made up entirely of third-culture kids and international students, so a tremendous amount of funding and large numbers of faculty and staff cannot be committed to the task. But there are things that can be done that do not cost much and are easily put into effect if you have a few people on campus who are sensitive and concerned.

What Schools Can Do

Some schools, Houghton being one of them, have hired a director of cross-cultural programming, who is to be the coordinator of this kind of a program. That happens to be the spot that I fill.

Identifying the TCK is often a key issue, especially if his parents are home on furlough at the time he applies for school. There are certain TCKs that slip between the cracks simply because their home address is in the United States and not overseas. However, there are some things that can be done without having a spot on the application form that says, "Are you a TCK?" One is to check the SAT or ACT test. The school code will give you some clue as to the location of the school where the test was given. When you find out that it's in some other part of the world, you probably have a TCK.

Make sure you understand the difference between a TCK and an international student and don't hound the TCK about taking the TOEFL test. That tends to be a little aggravating.

Air mail early. It is very uncomfortable for an individual to be applying from a school overseas and receive forms that should have been sent back three weeks ago. Catalogues certainly cost less to send by surface. However, if a person gets last year's catalogue, it may be a little hard for guidance counselors in an overseas school to do much with it.

One key issue is the big brother/big sister program. In any adjustment process, the key issue is having a mentor. Upperclass third-culture kids are in the best position to be mentors. They can be the initial contact.

If possible, contact with the big brother/big sister should occur before the third-culture kid ever gets on campus. Meeting him at the airport just adds to the relationship.

The older TCK may delight in finding a younger TCK to whom he can say, "When I was in Ecuador..." and the other one says, "When I was in the Philippines..." and everybody feels good about saying "When I was there..." Nobody's threatened. Having an older TCK as a mentor gives the freshman a natural entree into an age group where he is more comfortable. Third-culture kids are far more comfortable with juniors and seniors when they are freshmen than they are with other freshmen. They can relate better to faculty members. We need to recognize that they are more comfortable and have more social currency to exchange at that level. Finding ways to usher them into that older level is a major help in adjustment.

The big brother/big sister program is not always put into practice because some people say, "That was stuff that happened years ago. That was fun and games back in the old days." It may not be so important for the monocultural kid, but it certainly is a key tool as far as the third-culture kid is concerned. Sometimes it's not called anything. It just happens. They say, "Will you take care of that person?" The terms *big brother* and *big sister* aren't a problem for most MKs. They've been involved in big brother/big sister relationships in the dorm overseas before, and it's not necessarily a negative thing.

We've found that some of the upperclassmen are delighted to have the chance to have someone to talk to, especially if it's somebody from home.

MKs do not want to be isolated and segregated so that they become a separate entity that cannot interrelate with the rest of the school. But being in the same home, especially if it's labelled an International House as opposed to a mission kids house, has some real possibilities. The promotion of the program has to have a low profile. If you start putting posters around saying "Third-culture kid seminar is going to be held at such-and-such a time," you lose an awful lot of people just because they don't want to have to wear a label that will segregate them. Word-of-mouth promotion and individual invitations in their mail boxes usually take the onus away so they can participate without fear.

At King College, MKs started an international club a couple of years ago and drew in the international students and other kids who wanted to be participants. This is an interesting way to get around the issue of being segregated as a strange group of third-culture kids. Have an international club that welcomes everybody—international students, TCKs, and monocultural kids. This puts them in a place of being of service to the college campus.

That was basically the way my relationship with third-culture kids began. There were a whole bunch of them who were kind enough to let me be included in what I wanted to be a part of. I wanted to be a third-culture kid. My parents weren't cooperative.

There has to be sensitivity to group dynamics. There may be one year when the international students and the third-culture kids get along great and the leadership works out, and another year when it doesn't. You have to be prepared to flex with that. When you find an unhealthy situation, rather than having the whole thing be destroyed, back off.

Re-entry seminars. The re-entry seminar is not a cure-all. It is part of a process. Re-entry is not an event; it's a lifelong process. The re-entry seminar is there to let the individual know what he's going through and what he can expect. It is there to give him some tools to work with and to give him some orientation so that re-entry can be a learning experience rather than a traumatic experience.

We need to contact the retention officers on campuses. There's a good possibility that an individual will stay on a campus longer if he has been helped to understand that his tendency will be to move. Certainly colleges are very interested in retention, so we may hit a nerve there and get them to send people to re-entry seminars.

Guidance counseling

Make sure that career guidance people are aware of certain aspects of the third-culture kid's life. We need to remind ourselves that the third-culture kid has eighteen years of unique input. We tend to look at him as we do the monocultural kid and say, "Here's what you got on your SAT's; now let's take a look at what your career is going to be." With the third-culture kid, we have to look at his language acquisition, his overseas experience, his cross-cultural skills, and say, "Those are not just cute and interesting. That is the kind of stuff that a career can be made of. Let us help you think through how you might include that in your future career."

One TCK said that until just about a year ago he had not realized that his third-culture-kidness had anything to do with where his life was going and what he could do with it. He was thirty-three years old. [See chapter 41, volume 1, "TCkness: Impact on Marriage and Career"]

Several years ago at Houghton, an MK had appendicitis, and if I recall correctly, it burst. The fellow was in real trouble. Don Monroe, who is the head of the biology department, spent nights with him in the hospital and called long distance to his parents every day to give them an updated report. I don't know about you, but if I was that parent, I'd be a bit appreciative of a faculty member that cared that much for my kid. Those are the sensitive things that a college can do that are really critical.

Gathro: That's one of the advantages of a Christian college. Largely there are those kind of people on those campuses. I am a lot of what I am because of a certain faculty member who took interest in me.

Please encourage your students to "squeak." So often students are overlooked because they don't let their needs be known. I would suspect that a lot of MKs are fairly independent and need to be encouraged to get to know people. Visit the financial aid advisor; visit the student development people; let their needs be known.

Pollock: Also teach them how to squeak for each other. Often they won't squeak on their own behalf. You have to go to some other MK and ask, "Is there somebody who doesn't have a place to go for Thanksgiving?" You have to work the network and get them to report on each other. They'll often be willing to tell about somebody else's need. They may have the exact same need themselves, but, "Hey, you learn how to take care of yourself." You don't want to tell on yourself.

Bob Purdy from Camp of the Woods in the Adirondack Mountains in New York has expressed an interest in mobilizing camps and conferences to (1) promote available jobs to missionary kids for the summer, and (2) to make that camp home base for them. Someone who doesn't have a place to go could consider going to a place like Camp of the Woods where they have marvelous facilities. We have to bear in mind that even though a home may be open, it can be pretty uncomfortable for more than two or three days. We need to have places where an individual knows, "It's OK to be here. I'm not inconveniencing anybody."

There are also a few homes around the country that are open for kids during vacations. I think this is something we can begin to promote, as college people. We can encourage other people to open their homes in the community. Then the TCK wouldn't have to worry about dormitories closing down at Christmas time.

The Value of the Third-Culture Kid to the Campus

There's a flip side to this whole issue, and that is the value of the third-culture kid to the campus. All too often third-culture kids spend four years on a campus and the campus never benefits or benefits very little from them. I'm not saying we ought to grab hold of every third-culture kid and say, "You're going to speak in chapel tomorrow," or "Tell us all you know about Guatemala."

Faculty members need to be aware that they may have some people sitting in their classes who have something rather unique and very important to share. I know of one situation where a student from a Central American country made a comment in disagreement with something a professor said. The professor was furious and told him later he'd rather he didn't make those comments in class. That's an awful waste of a marvelous educational opportunity.

The third-culture kid's experience becomes valuable currency when he is given leadership in cross-cultural experiences, whether it's taking somebody back to his home country or into a Hispanic part of the community, where his Spanish suddenly becomes very important.

Matt Hess at Houghton College is going to be bringing a group down to Ecuador. He has done this on his own. There's a foreign student from Sri Lanka who's going to be taking a group of kids to Sri Lanka this next summer. Our hope is to mobilize the third-culture kids and international students to take leadership in the cross-cultural experiences of other students. All of a sudden people are wanting to hear things that nobody wanted to hear before. You've got a group of five or six people who are saying, "Tell us about Sri Lanka."

9

The Art of Encouragement

Lareau Lindquist
Barnabas International

I want to list six assumptions, concerning the ministry of encouragement. I come to you basically as a pastor, and what I have to say will be a biblical Christian presentation which I'm convinced is philosophically and psychologically sound.

1. God is the ultimate encourager.
2. The Bible is our greatest source of encouragement.
3. All people need to be encouraged. Every one of us needs encouragement. The healthiest one in the crowd, the smartest one in the crowd, the most gifted one in the crowd—all need encouragement to do better, to be more than we've ever been for God. We always need this.

   It's easy for us to think that those in high office are doing fine. But I can tell you as I travel around the world with leadership, I find they desperately need encouragement.

   All of us need encouragement. I want you to remember this. Those that you sit with on the plane, those that you meet in the store, those that you work with on your campus, MKs—all need encouragement. Beyond the title that might confuse you, under the mink stole that might throw you off, is always a person that needs to be encouraged.

4. All Christians are to be encouragers. I believe in spiritual gifts, but encouragement has very little to do with spiritual gifts. I know Romans 12:8 says that one of the gifts is encouragement. Other gifts are giving and mercy, but that doesn't mean that those who don't have these gifts don't give, or don't show mercy. The call for you to be an encourager has very little to do with your spiritual gift. It has everything to do with your obedience.

Let me give you some clear exhortations. I Thessalonians 5:11, "Encourage each other and build up each other." Hebrews 10:25, "Encourage each other especially as you see that day approaching."

5. God uses people to be encouragers. In Scripture there are a number who were explicitly called encouragers—Titus, Barnabas, Paul, Tychicus, Silas, Philemon, Judas. There are many others who illustrate the principle.

II Corinthians 7:5-7, is an excellent paragraph on encouragement. It talks about the variety of pressures that Paul had. He specifically talks about physical discomforts, harassment, external pressures, and inner fears. In verse 6 he says, "But God used Titus to encourage us." In verse 7 he says, "And you Corinthians encouraged Titus, and now he's encouraging us."

6. The Christian community is to be a society of lovers, encouragers, builder-uppers, lifters. William Barkley says that the family of God is to be a band of brothers. Bruce Larson in his book *No Longer Strangers* gives us a basic life principle: we are to convey to the world that Jesus cares. If Jesus lives in me, I must be known as a caring person. Romans 1:11 and 12 talks about mutual encouragement.

There are three levels of communication. There's mouth-to-mouth, where all we pass on is words; there is head-to-head, where we are communicating content; and there is heart-to-heart, which is the deepest level of communication. We communicate life and reality at that level. It seems to be a major missing ingredient in many of the Christian community's fellowships. Many of our mission stations, many of our churches, tend so often to isolation, distrust, friction, loneliness, insecurity, anger, fear. We're afraid of each other, we are strangers to each other. How well are we modelling to our MKs what we want God's society to be like on earth?

Characteristics of the Christian Encourager

To encourage means to strengthen on the inside; to build up inner resources; to infuse that which is positive into the inner core from which a person lives and moves.

Another definition that I got from a Christian psychologist is "to nudge them toward Christ." I think if you put those two brief definitions together, you've got pretty much where we're coming from in the Christian context.

This is not a definitive statement, but I submit to you the Christian encourager is characterized by the six following things. I'm putting all of them in the present tense so that you and I realize we're always to be on the growing edge in becoming an encourager:

Experiencing God's encouragement

The Christian encourager is experiencing the reality of God's encouragement. II Corinthians 1:3-4, "God is the encourager who comforts you so you can comfort others." In other words, the encourager is one who has personally and is personally experiencing God's encouragement. Not hearsay, it's know-so. If you enter the ministry of encouragement, you will have a great dosage of hurt and pain.

You will know more valleys, pain, frustration, failure, self-doubt, insecurity, and guilt, than perhaps your neighbor. I observe that Christian leaders, those who are uniquely used of God seem to have a greater measure of pain, variety of affliction, than others. It's a common thread. Many will come to you as a leader in their time of trouble and will ask you for help. You must personally be able to know God's sufficiency to make it known to others.

C.S. Lewis said, "I hate pain, but I will never argue with those who insist it is God's best way of building character." Pain will come, and you will have heavier dosages than many.

Martin Luther said, "The best book in my library is the book of affliction." And Charles Spurgeon commenting on Luther's comment said, "And the best page in that book is the darkest page of all." Very few know the darkness through which Spurgeon traveled. The months on the bed of affliction, the self-doubt, the deep depressions, and out of that he wrote so richly to encourage others who were hurt and in pain.

Somebody said, "God will not use you mightily till you have been bruised mightily."

I want you to know that I have known the joy of mountain peaks and the despair of valleys. My daughter did everything you hoped your child would never do: dropping out of high school, running away from home repeatedly, finally, drugs and the whole thing for a long, long period of time. We know what it's like to have sleepless nights, and to pray, "Lord, by the first of the week might everything be back to normal." "Lord, by the first of the month?" "Lord, by the first of the year?"

We know what it's like putting demands upon God, and then waiting, and waiting. There is nothing quite like that pain. But she returned and finished school, went through nursing, is dating a fellow preparing for ministry, and is marvelously alive in Christ and often says through teardrops, "I thank God for the valley and for the pit. I would never today have the ministry or care that I have, had not I walked through the pit."

We can say that no matter what the pit, no matter what the mire, God in his creative redemptive power is able to take the worst and make something very beautiful out of it.

As you experience the valleys, you will come to know God's sufficiencies. He says, "My grace is sufficient." You will experience that first-hand. Strength available one day at the time. You'll experience that. For Jesus says, "I'm with you always." No matter where you go, you'll experience that. Have you ever noted that after all the problems Job went through, he said, "Once I heard all about God, but now after all that, I've seen him with my eyes." All you and I might travel through as pilgrims and strangers here is so we might come to see that God is really everything that he said he is in his Word. And we need to be able to model this to the world and to our students.

Personally vulnerable

The Christian encourager is willing to be personally vulnerable. There's a need for authenticity, to be open, to be honest, to be a learner, to be a struggler, to let people know you're en route.

Ephesians 4:15 says, "Speak the truth in love." That is not a text which gives you permission to tell each other off "in love." That text in Greek tells you that you are to be truthing in love. It has very little to do with telling the truth to somebody else about them. It has everything to do with telling them the truth about you. That's truthing in love. It's taking off the mask; it's being open; it's being honest. David was so brutally honest. Paul repeatedly says, "I'm not what I used to be, but I'm certainly not all that I ought to be."

You and I try to give the impression to each other that we've got it together. Some years ago as a pastor I learned that as long as I preached with the idea that everybody but me was struggling, I wasn't helping anybody. I had to let them know that I, too, was struggling along the way.

The world says that you lead best through strength. Get the title, get the position, get so many under you, and be strong. But I believe that we lead best from weakness.

Our MKs see through us. They know they're struggling, and they assume we must be struggling. We had best let them know that we're in journey.

Believing in people

The Christian encourager is always believing in the worth and potential of the individual, always believing in people. I point you to the life of Barnabas. If there is anyone in the New Testament you and I could be like, it is Barnabas. Acts 4:36 tells about a guy who's name was Joseph, but the disciples gave him a nickname, and the nickname stuck. He is never called Joseph again, but always Barnabas, which in Hebrew means son of encouragement—*bar*, son; *nabas*, encouragement. Let me encourage ladies by saying the female equivalent is Batnabas, woman of encouragement.

There are two illustrations in the New Testament of the difference he made in the lives of people. The first one deals with the Apostle Paul. Paul was converted on the Damascus road. He went to Damascus and began to share about his new-found faith. He was kicked out of Damascus. In Acts 9:23-27, it says that Paul thought, he'd go to Jerusalem where all the Christian leaders were. When he got there he tried to join the disciples, but they said he wasn't really converted and rejected him. Verse 27 says, "But Barnabas...." Barnabas took him in, put his arm around him, tutored him, started a missionary team. Barnabas was the head of it. Paul was the new guy on the block.

"But Barnabas...." Have you ever thought how gutsy that was of Barnabas? All the church leaders rejected Paul. They said, "He's not real; stay away from him." Barnabas didn't care what the official leadership said. He had been touched and lifted by Jesus, and he realized that he was now to lift others.

I've often wondered, would there have been half the New Testament authored by the Apostle Paul, had there not been a Barnabas in Paul's life? Speculation. The dynamic difference that a man made because he believed in the individual.

What about the illustration of Barnabas and John Mark? Remember, John Mark was the guy that went with Paul and Barnabas on the first missionary journey, but he dropped out. We have no idea why—homesick, physically sick, lonesome? He just dropped out as soon as the journey started. Some years later they were ready for another missionary trip, and Barnabas said, "Let's take John Mark," but Paul said, "No way, he was a drop-out."

Barnabas said, "I think we ought to give him another chance."

Paul said, "Nope."

Incredible isn't it? Paul, who had been befriended and believed in. How quickly we forget! We don't pass on to others what has been passed to us. Some years later Paul evidently recanted, because he wrote and said, "Send John Mark, I really need him."

The thing I love about Barnabas is that sure, John Mark had failed. He had dropped out, but did that mean that he was to go on the shelf forever? Barnabas was a man who believed in people, who forgave people, who had hope, who lifted, who accepted, who gave a second opportunity, and a third, and a fourth.

All of us could be a Barnabas. No way could we all have the gifts of a Paul, but all of us could be a Barnabas or a Batnabas. What a difference he made in John Mark's life!

There's an antique shop that has in its window this motto, "No piece of pottery broken beyond repair." God has that sign hanging in heaven. Your life is not broken beyond repair. You have never yet met a person broken beyond repair. You could be the difference.

Developing the discipline of listening

A Christian encourager is developing the discipline of listening. He doesn't have all the answers, he doesn't do all of the talking, he has his spiritual and emotional and psychological antennas tuned to words, feelings, body language. He gives full attention. Don't you hate to be talking to somebody you really wanted to say something to, and they're looking over your shoulder at who's going by? You're going out of the church on Sunday morning when you stop to say hi to the pastor, and he looks you in the face for a minute and then while he's still got ahold of your hand, he's looking at the next guy. Learn to be a listener. Scripture says an awful lot about that.

Delivering a word of hope

A Christian encourager is always delivering a word of hope. In every situation, there's always a word of hope. When the preacher preaches about hell and judgment, it's not with glee, but with a teardrop and with a message of hope for all in the crowd. When you're speaking about divorce, there's still a message of hope. In counseling, in living, in parenting, there is always a message of hope. The Bible says so much about saying the right word at the right time.

Developing a servant's heart

The Christian encourager is developing a servant's heart. If there is one thing the evangelical world of our day needs, it's a re-discovery of servanthood. The church in America is developing stars, and status seekers. The mother of James and John came on the scene saying, "Jesus, my boys have worked so hard, and they're such good boys, give them a little special status." Remember what Jesus said? "That will be given to servants." It's not arbitrarily handed out. It's given to servants.

Barnabas discovered Paul. When you read in Acts about them, the first few chapters always talk about Barnabas and Paul. Acts 13:43 talks about Paul and Barnabas for the first time. Thereafter it's mainly Paul and Barnabas. How do you like that? Barnabas starts the organization, he discovers Paul, and all of a sudden Paul's in charge of the organization. I want you to know that's fine with Barnabas, because a servant is not so interested in status or stardom, as he is in service. He's not looking for glory to self, but glory to God. And that's illustrated all the way through the life of Barnabas.

I close by asking, "Are you an encourager?" You are beckoned to come and be an encourager.[1]

---

[1]Missionaries who want to be on the mailing list for Barnabas International to receive free newsletters and a devotional letter can write Dr. Lindquist at the address in the appendix.

10

Counseling Models for MKs

Nancy Duvall, Biola University
Dean Kliewer, Link Care Center

Dean Kliewer: When we talk about models, we're really talking about ways of thinking. A developmental model helps us understand what's going on with a person at different times of his life.

A systems model is usually used to think about a process that's complex and has a variety of components. A systems model may be seen as a model that can be superimposed over other models. In a systems model, components are considered mainly in the light of the whole. In other words, there's a clear concern about a whole that's bigger than the part that one is examining in one given situation or time.

Let me give you two illustrations of a systems view. The first is the wind and sun wager. Remember that old fable about when the wind and the sun got together and bet each other that they would have control over the man with the coat?

The wind said, "I think I can get the coat off the man." He blew very hard and the harder the wind blew, the closer the man kept his coat. The wind failed in getting the coat off the man. The sun on the other hand simply came out, shone on the man, warmed him up, and the man voluntarily took off his coat and threw it down.

It's a rather simple systems illustration. The sun and the wind had different concepts of the system. The wind was taken with his power and his ability to blow, but he didn't consider how he worked with a person. He also didn't consider one other aspect of the system, and that is the persistence and stubbornness of a human will. Just because someone is blowing doesn't mean that another will yield. The sun understood the whole system, so in a sense he had a better view of a systems model.

Another example of the systems situation that I like to use is the World War II Merchant Marine problem. Material was not being delivered to the European sector where the battle was raging because the Merchant Marine was having difficulty getting across the Atlantic. There was fear of the Axis and their submarines. There was concern that the Merchant Marine would be sunk as they traveled with their material. So the Merchant Marine began putting canons on their boats, carrying depth charges, and chasing submarines, and pretty soon the materiel ground to a halt. Various persons who where managing the overall war effort began to say, "Hey, we've got this wrong, the job of the Navy is to protect the Merchant Marine. The Merchant Marine should get about their job of getting the materiel across, and let the Navy protect them." Getting the systems concept straight allowed a job to get done.

I'd like to give you an example that illustrates the need to think beyond the present problem to the broader systems issues.

I'd like us to look at Elwood, age fourteen, who's caught with cocaine at the Island School for Missionary Kids. Elwood is a hub person. The other hub person at this moment is Mr. A.J. Howary, the principal of the ISMK. There's the local community, which happens to be the mission school. There's the larger community—the parents especially, and their mission groups—even though they might not be there physically. You can't just think about Elwood and Mr. Howary. You've got to think about all of them. The main question is, "How does A.J. respond?" What are his options?

The model that I want to use is an extremely simple model. It's a Participants System Actualization model, which I've adopted for my work with clinical problems.

First, the model presumes that, if possible, all systems participants be heard, considered, or represented in any kind of solution that's contemplated. The system is the underlying focus, not only one or two participants. We really have to keep the whole system in mind. We can't have the luxury of dealing with only one part of the system.

The basic assertion that we make in this model is that problem solving among people raises systems actualization questions. The goal in counseling is to actualize the system—to see the system fulfill its promise. I think you might find the PSA model useful as you consider ways of looking at problems. I use a little slogan, "Dream, check, move." We dream fearlessly, check thoroughly, and move confidently.

There is a dream and a status. What we mean by the dream is ideals, goals, and objectives that we're moving toward. What we mean by the status is the reality as it exists. A.J. has a dream for his school that it be drug free. Now his dream is being spoiled. He has a tendency to get pretty angry about this, and he's pretty concerned about Elwood. But he has to check the status. He doesn't know whether or not the cocaine was planted; he doesn't know whether Elwood has used the cocaine; he doesn't know where Elwood got the cocaine. He's got a lot of checking to do before he makes his move. If he makes a move that's unwise, if he doesn't check with the participants, if he doesn't check with the faculty, if he doesn't know Elwood very well, he's in big trouble.

Most of our pain is involved with discrepancies between how we see the dream and what we see as a status. Consequently, we have to resolve that in terms of our move. After we make an intervention, we check to see whether the difference we saw between the dream and the status is now reduced.

The systems model that I'm suggesting is one continuous series of dreams, checks, moves, dreams, checks, moves. It's helpful for me to differentiate components of a problem by identifying them as dream components, status components, or intervention movements.

Nancy Duvall: If you have ever said "I think this student needs some counseling," or "They aren't doing as well in school as they ought," you have at the very least a crude developmental model of where someone ought to be. In the intellectual realm, we have IQ tests for finding out where a person is, compared with others of his own age and culture. We're working on trying to be more precise about that in an emotional way. Somewhere in your head you have some norms about how things ought to be. What we're going to talk about today is a way to be more precise about those kinds of norms.

Another crucial issue is the context of relationship. We know that relationship is absolutely critical. How do we know this? God in his providence and wisdom made human beings the most dependent creatures on earth. When we're born, we're absolutely dependent. If there's not someone there to relate to and to take care of us physically, we die.

Developmental Issues

When I dialogue with somebody whether an adolescent or an adult, there are three things that I look at to see where he is.

One we call ego strength or the ability to deal with life, to handle stress, to make judgments, to think, to regulate life and problems.

The second would be his relatedness to others. What kind of relationships does he have? Two things point it out: (1) The ability to relate to others even though they do some things he doesn't completely like. (2) The ability to maintain a relationship even though he doesn't see the other person as perfect.

The third issue is interdependence. Not only do I take care of and respond to other people, but I let other people respond and be helpful to me.

Where are they on these issues? Are they about where they should be? Are they adequate in one area but not in another?

As I think about their ego strength, their relatedness to others, their sense of themselves and their ability to regulate their self-esteem, I think about where they are developmentally and how they are coming along with those issues.

A seventeen-year-old MK

Let's take a couple of scenarios. One might be a seventeen-year-old named Sue. Her family is home on furlough. Sue has started talking about maybe not going to college next year, but maybe going back to the field with the family. The mother isn't sure what's going on here, but Sue is talking like she wants to stay with the family. There's a sister, Betty, who is a couple of years younger. Betty seems to be having some struggles. She's not as bright as Sue, and she's not as popular.

Sue's mother is concerned. She has noticed that Sue has seemed depressed lately, and she's even heard Sue make some comments that might seem that she's thinking about suicide. Sue would never say, "I'm thinking of suicide." That would be too blatant. But Sue has said things like, "Maybe life would be better if I weren't around." This mother cares a lot, and she has been sensitized to some of these issues. She decides to go check things out and see if something needs to be done.

She brings Sue in to me. As I talk with Sue, I find out she's bright. She's doing OK academically—A's and B's. I find she's got some friends, and they seem to be of a pretty good sort. They're not trying to get her into trouble. She's involved in some extracurricular activities and seems to really enjoy them. In one way it is sad, though, because her younger sister isn't as successful. Sue is aware of that and feeling some qualms about it.

It is my responsibility to check out the suicide issue because it can be serious. I ask her about it, and she says in essence, "Yes, I've thought about it, but I'd never do that because it wouldn't please God." That's a good sign. It also tells me about her relationship with God. She goes on, "Besides, I'd miss my family." That's telling me something about her relatedness and her connectedness, and that there's some caring.

I ask her, if she did commit suicide, how she would do it. She says she's never thought about any way she could do it. (You take it more seriously if they tell you a specific plan.) My worry about the suicide is abating. By the way, I notice she dates some, and it sounds as if the guy is a pretty good guy. She says her mother isn't completely happy about this, and worries and won't let them be together an awful lot, and this kind of thing. I like her and she seems to relate to me. She begins to open up and talk to me about things. "I'm afraid it would hurt Mom if I were gone, and I'm also worried about my younger sister."

Then I interview the mom, a strong lady, been through a lot, probably an excellent missionary, cares about the kids a lot, has very strong ideals. She isn't aware of how her daughter feels about these issues. She says, "I want my daughter to be independent." But on the feeling level there's a lot of "I'm going to miss her." I get the sense that the mother doesn't know how the daughter feels, nor even how she herself feels.

Let's look developmentally at what's going on and what needs to be done. Ego strength? Excellent. This girl is doing fine.

Relatedness to others? She's got a good peer group. She's beginning to relate to boys and is having some dating relationships.

Sense of self and self-esteem? Pretty good. She's a little worried about her mom and her sister, and that gives me the click. Now if we look at what a seventeen-year-old adolescent is supposed to be doing, she's right on the button. In other words she's not behind. She's really working on an issue that's appropriate for her, which is the separation from family. She's having a hard time, though, because Mother is having a hard time giving her up. She's having a hard time because she really cares about her sister.

I would probably spend a few sessions with Sue, talk to her about how hard it is to leave home and about how hard it is to worry about Mother. I might spend some sessions with Mother too, talking about what she really feels about the daughter being gone and the daughter separating from her. I might even have some sessions with the daughter and the mother together.

An adult MK

Now I want to talk about an adult MK. Bob is twenty-six years old, not married yet. He's got a master's and is working in Christian education in a church. He comes in and says, "I know something is wrong. I don't know exactly what it is. I'm not sure, but I know I need something."

As I interview Bob, I get a history of great achievement, super-competent person, well-liked, has a number of friends, dated, but has not felt comfortable. His social and work relationships predominantly are taking care of other people—supporting them emotionally, helping them move, or whatever. He's skilled academically. He's a good sportsman. He's a committed Christian, although he tells me, "You know, I don't feel as close to God as I used to." In fact he's the kind of guy that every mother in this room would love to have for a son-in-law. He looks super.

My reactions to him tell me a lot. I like him. I'm a little worried about him being a workaholic, and I wonder if he can really relax. I notice he's not aware of his feelings. When I respond to what I think he's feeling, he leaves. He gets cognitive.

In this paradigm, if we look at our developmental goals, this guy's ego strength is great, too great. He's too good. He's always taking care of others. In terms of relatedness to others, great friend. You couldn't want a better guy. He'd be committed to you and help you out. In terms of self he's got some sense of identity because he's got enough achievement, but he can't keep it. He feels like he's got to keep working. If he isn't taking care of people, they won't like him. To be overly simple, he's got a problem with intimacy. He's got a problem of really trusting that he is OK. He feels OK as long as he's doing what he thinks people want him to do, but inwardly he's scared.

What would I do? I would want to use psychotherapy in a long-term relationship. I'm not talking about a couple of sessions. I'm talking about a kind of reparenting where he goes back, and in the relationship with me, learns it's OK to feel; it's OK to be dependent; it's OK to get in touch with who he is; it's OK to mess up; it's OK to not take care of me.

You think parenting the first time is hard. The second time is harder because he's got scars. Whenever he gets close to feeling, he closes over, leaves, or gets cognitive. So I have be very tender and say, "There's a scar here," or, "You just felt something but you want it to leave because it was scary or painful." I not only have to understand his feelings, but I've got to feel with him and help him grow out again.

Parenting and Reparenting

In the developmental process it is crucial that the child feel the bondedness, the connectedness, the security. And then it is crucial that the child separate in a way that is not too overwhelming. That does not mean you have to be the perfect parent. If you met every need and they never had any frustration, they would never learn frustration tolerance. Winnicott says you have to be "good enough."

What do you do if you didn't have "good enough" parenting? As an adult I began to realize that I wasn't as secure as I wanted and needed to be. I didn't have "good enough" parenting in some ways, because parents aren't perfect.

I remember my great delight one day when something caught my attention in Psalm 27:10, "If my father and mother forsake me, the Lord will take me up." I looked at another translation. It said, "*When* my father and mother forsake me, the Lord will take me up."

I thought, "God are you saying that if I didn't get what I needed, if symbolically I was emotionally forsaken, you will take me up and help me have that "good enough" reparenting that I'm going to need so that I can really feel good about myself, so that I can relate to others without being scared, so that I don't have to be afraid of separation?"

Lo and behold, God's Word said it, and he did it. That verse is true. For those of us who haven't had what we need, if we allow him, God will provide what we need to have healing and reparenting so we can become healed, whole persons.

One of the early church fathers said, "The glory of God is a human being fully alive." That's our goal.

11

Therapeutic Community:
Its Application to the MK

Glen Taylor
Director General, Yonge St. Mission, Toronto

First I'd like to share with you a definition of therapeutic community which was developed in social psychiatry some years ago. Therapeutic community is a self-consciously created community designed to maximize the total resources of the community. I suggest that we design our MK schools so that they accomplish the purpose for which they exist.

Total Resources of the Community

Resources that are inherent in the staff and the patients

One of the things we do in a therapeutic community is a strength identification of all of the staff within the organization. Unlike most psychiatric hospitals, we look at the patients and we ask the question, "What are the resources the patients are bringing to this therapeutic community which can be used in maximizing their treatment and the treatment of others within the community?" That is a tremendous departure from traditional psychiatry. In traditional psychiatry the patient is considered to be totally dependent, irresponsible, and often unresponsive. Therapeutic community says every patient is first a person. Every patient brings abilities and relational skills that can be maximized in facilitating the health and care of the rest of the patient community. That's a very important resource, which raises a question in my mind: What are the resources that the students we serve in the boarding school bring, and how do we maximize the resources they bring to accomplish the goals and purposes of the school?

Organizational structures

What is the impact of the way in which a superintendent of a school relates to the staff in terms of the educational purposes of that school? How about the relationship of the assistant principal to the teachers? The teachers to one another? The administrative staff in relation to the staff who maintain and care for the building? Those dynamics that make up the organizational structures must be looked at in terms of how they either facilitate or inhibit the purpose of the institution.

Staff relationships

In a therapeutic community, one of the criticisms that is sometimes registered is that the staff spend more time dealing with their own problems than they do dealing with the problems of the patients. The modelling that the patients see in the staff relationships either facilitates or inhibits the experience of health of the patients. That means that the quality of relationship between teachers in a boarding school may in fact inhibit immensely the goals and purposes of the school.

I do a great deal of family counseling. Rarely am I interested in working in a counseling relationship with a child unless I can also work with the parents. I have discovered that the quality of the relationship that exists between parents is the single most significant factor influencing the well being of a child. I would make that as a categorical statement. Research has established that you can generate or you can retard the manifestation of illness in a child by altering the relationship that exists between the parents.

When we think of the educational context, we have to seriously consider the relationship between the teachers, between the teachers and their spouses, between the house parents and the teachers, between the husband and wife who may be house parents together, as well as between the staff and students. Those relationships either facilitate or inhibit what we're trying to accomplish.

Emotional climate

Have you walked into a dorm and as you walk in, you sense something? You're not sure what it is, but these antennae pick up something. The air is charged. Can we control that emotional climate? What can we do to make that emotional climate facilitate treatment?

Physical environment

The physical environment becomes a very crucial consideration as well. Let me give you one illustration. When Dr. Maxwell Jones went to the psychiatric hospital I was involved with in Scotland, he discovered that the dining room was the site of the most conflict and where riots generally occurred. This dining hall in Scotland was a very large room. It was what I call a hard room. It was a castle-like structure, with a lot of stone and a big tall ceiling. It had long rows of tables that stretched from one end to the other with benches where people would sit.

When you came in to eat, there were great big, burly guards who would shove you in the appropriate direction. After all, they were dealing with very sick psychiatric patients who obviously couldn't take charge for themselves. They had to be pushed through the line where they would pick up a tin plate and someone would slop some food on it. Then they would scrape back a bench and sit down. The din in the place would rise to a horrendous height as they tried to communicate with one another along these long rows of benches. If you weren't crazy when you entered the dining hall, you would be shortly after you got in there.

When Jones arrived, he decided that was the first thing that had to change. So they altered the physical structure of that room. They put drapes along the walls to deaden the sound. They put some indirect lighting in. They took out the long tables and benches and put in round tables. If you sit at a round table, you can communicate more quietly to six or eight people, than if you have to shout down the length of a long table. They put tablecloths on the tables. They put up dividers with nice plants, flowers, greenery, that would guide the flow of traffic. They put dividers up among the tables so that there was some visual discontinuity between groupings of people. Do you know that just by changing the physical environment, they eliminated all their problems in the dining room.

The physical environment that we create for doing our thing either facilitates it or inhibits it. In Bible colleges, and in the schools for missionaries' children, I think physical environment needs to be one element we look at.

Patient organization and activities

When I went to work at the Bible college in Toronto, one of the things I discovered was that the student organizations, the student council, and related organizations had set themselves up following the pattern that characterizes our government and judicial systems in North America. That's basically an adversarial system.

One of the things that really confused me was why would we, in a Christian community, set up a similarly adversarial judicial system that has proven itself ineffective in our secular community. You see, the student organizations that we create say a great deal about the kind of relationship that we assume should exist between students and teachers, between students and administration. We suggested in the Bible college setting that we should reevaluate the student activities and organizations in the light of God's Word. Is there no guidance there? Must we go for an adversarial system? We had to call those things into question because they were inhibiting our purposes.

Total Community as Treatment

In the therapeutic community, the total community — everything and everyone — is treatment. Nothing within the community is looked at as being unrelated to the goals and purposes of the organization.

Blurring of Role Distinctions

Secondly, role distinctions are blurred. For example, when you walked into the psychiatric hospital in Scotland, you discovered that the nurses could not be differentiated from the doctors, nor they from the psychologists, nor they from the psychiatrists. In fact, the staff could not be differentiated from the patients. Those differentiations were blurred. Why? Nurses were not permitted to wear little white uniforms which identified them with their subculture. Doctors were not permitted to run around with stethoscopes around their necks just to convince everyone that they were doctors. Psychologists were not permitted to wear turtle neck sweaters so that everyone would know that they were psychologists. And so on.

Why do you want to blur those distinctions? The philosophy is this: In this hospital we relate to one another in terms of our primary similarity, which is people relating to people. First of all, you are a person, and you must relate to patients, to fellow staff, to administration as persons relating to persons, not as one role relating to another role.

You see, we tend to hide in our roles. When we use our roles to insulate ourselves from one another, we are moving in a counterproductive direction as far as therapy is concerned, according to this particular philosophy.

Let me just transfer this into Christian thinking for a moment. We all stand on level ground before the cross. Are there no role distinctions? Absolutely, but all the role distinctions and functions that we have within the body of Christ say nothing about us in terms of our value as persons.

All the differentiation that we have by virtue of our gifts, our roles, our functions within the body of Christ are an exercise of God's grace, and we are gifted with those functions in terms of our capacity to serve. They don't bring status, nor do they bring control. They bring the opportunity to serve. There is a great similarity between therapeutic community and Christian community in terms of this phenomena of blurring role distinctions and insisting that people function in relation to people as people, not simply as professionals. We are people first. We're only professionals or patients secondly. This egalitarian focus generates tremendous openness.

Patient Responsibility

Patient responsibility was another theme within the therapeutic community. It didn't matter whether you were a schizophrenic or a manic depressive. Every patient was encouraged to look at his responsibility for himself and his own well-being, and for the other patients with whom he related. Patients were involved in the treatment process.

For example, I recall one lady who was sent to the hospital by the court. She was somewhat mentally retarded. She had been there only a few days when she said to one of the nurses, "I would like to have permission to go home on the weekend."

The nurse said, "I'm sorry. That's not my decision to make. If you would like to raise that possibility at our group meeting tomorrow, you're welcome to do it. But it will be the group that will decide."

In that group of twenty patients, there was probably also a psychologist or two, a social worker, and a psychiatrist. The next day, part way through the group meeting, this lady indicated she wanted to raise her question. But she was very nervous and didn't communicate well, so she said, "Would you explain what I want?"

The nurse said, "No, you'll have to explain that."

So in her stumbling way, she said she wanted permission to go home on the weekend.

One of the patients immediately said, "Well, I don't know why you're here. How can we know whether it's OK for you to go home if we don't know why you're here."

There was a silence. The lady looked to the nurse and said, "You tell them why I'm here."

The nurse replied, "No, that's your information. You share whatever you feel free to share with the group as to why you're here."

So she said, "Well, in my community I got into some trouble. The trouble was with men."

One of the ladies who was also a patient said, "Boy, that was my problem, too."

Somebody else said, "Yeah, who ever knows how to get along with men?" And so this conversation traveled around the room.

Pretty soon she was explaining the kind of trouble she was having with men. Really it was men taking advantage of her because of her being mentally retarded.

Finally one of the patients in the room said, "Do you think it's safe for you to go home this soon?"

Somebody else said, "Yeah, it'd be good if you waited for a few weeks."

Another patient said, "You know, the first time I went home, I took someone with me. Maybe you could take someone with you when you go home."

Over a period of fifteen or twenty minutes, the patients in the group helped this new member of the community go through a process of sorting out the fact that it probably wasn't a good idea for her to go home, perhaps for a few weeks, and then when she went she should take someone with her. It wasn't an authority saying, "You can't go home until you've been here a certain length of time." The patients were involved in the treatment of another patient, and in this way became responsible for one another.

Culture Carriers

Social engineers are those people who intentionally design a community by creating the culture they desire, to facilitate treatment. Within that culture they identify people who they describe as "culture carriers." They are the ones who communicate that culture to newcomers. The culture carriers are those who know how the institution operates. When patients came through that front door of the psychiatric hospital, they were met by another patient. This culture carrier showed the new patient through the hospital and explained the philosophy of the treatment.

Social learning was a focus. Permission was given to experiment with new behavior. The focus was upon changing behavior rather than upon the psychoanalytical approach to treatment. Patients were given opportunity for reality testing and encouraged to experiment with new behavior. There was an attitude of permissiveness, of acceptance, and confrontation. Putting it simply, I suppose you could say this: you were permitted to do almost anything that you wished to do in the psychiatric hospital. You would not be rejected because of what you did, but you would be held responsible for what you did. Patients, regardless of how ill they were in psychiatric terms, were not relieved of responsibility for their behavior.

I think this is a key issue in schools for missionary kids. When new children come in, how do we help them realize what the culture of that educational community is? How do we introduce them to the ropes? We set up a program in Bible college where we identified students who had been there at least one year. We called them Resident Assistants. It was their role, during the first week that students were at the college, to take a group of eight or ten students and to communicate the culture of the college to those students. Then over a period of eleven weeks, they met with them on a weekly basis to help them understand why we did things the way we did, who was what in the organization, and so on. The students can play a tremendous role as culture carriers.

Staff Issues

The last point I want to make is that the staff must deal with their own issues. That became a very important part of the community. The patients saw that staff were dealing with their own issues. "Wounded healer" is a significant phrase to me. I think as we work with people, we do so as fellow pilgrims who are moving along in the Christian life and seeking the growth that we are encouraging others towards.

Christian Community

Christian community, I suggest, is also a created community. It is created by God, intentionally designed by God, to accomplish the purposes that he has in mind for it. It is an organismic community. There are distinctives in function. We are members of the body. There is interdependence, but there is equality before God. If we can include the students as part of that organismic community, then I think some of these implications have application. The community is a community of grace in ministry. We are responsible for one another. Our goal is maturity in Christ.

The culture that the Christian community is to manifest, if we study the Scripture, is characterized by love, acceptance, forgiveness, and reconciliation. Our goal is to edify, comfort, and confront.

Healing relationships are for the purpose of growth, and growth in the New Testament is perceived to come through relationships.

One of the things that has got us into great difficulty from a Christian point of view, it seems to me, is that we have taken the rugged individualism that has characterized our North American culture and we have imposed that on Scripture. We have lost the sense of community that the New Testament and the Old Testament have so much to say about.

Man can only be man in relationship to God. Man can only be man in relationship to man. Man in and of himself is never perceived as a complete entity in the New Testament or the Old Testament. We make a personal decision in response to Jesus Christ, but that must be worked out and manifested in relationships. Relationships are what the word of God is all about. We experience healing; we experience growth; we experience the practice and development of gifts in community. I would suggest that we have to create opportunities in our schools for young people to experiment with new behavior, to discover the gifts that God has given them, and to practice those gifts.

Self is revealed in behavior. In the Bible college (I think you might apply this to an MK school in some ways), my philosophy was this: I wanted the students to be free to behave in a way that was a true expression of who they were. Now that created a lot of negative behavior. You see, we're sinners. Bible college students are sinners. I wanted the Bible college students to have the opportunity to sin. Does that sound terrible? It's only terrible if I do nothing about it when I've given them the opportunity to sin.

How can I know them and how can they know themselves if we don't give them the opportunity to sin. But how can we be responsible before God, giving them the opportunity to sin? We can create an environment of unconditional acceptance and love where we let students manifest who they are and then respond to them in ministry. I discovered that Bible college students who were permitted to sin didn't like their sin. So I would come alongside of them and say, "Look, you have done this." Never deny their sin. Never pretend that they didn't sin. That's a terrible injustice.

What we often try to do in Bible colleges in North America, and I'm sure in MK schools, is outlaw sin. We make it illegal. We set up a legal system which forbids people the opportunity to manifest who they really are. We minister to an illusion. We minister to people who are playing games, who are pretending not to be sinners, or pretending not to hurt. How can you respond to a hurt if you don't give a person the opportunity to manifest his hurt?

Although we don't have a large list of rules and regulations and the outlawing of sin through a legal approach, this does not mean that we don't have standards and values. I think we have to clearly articulate the values that we represent as part of the culture of the community. That has to be very overtly understood. For example, your commitment to the stewardship of time would be part of the culture or curriculum of your community. I would define it as such.

The first time a student is late, you don't hang him in the nearest tree, but you don't ignore it. We seem to feel that if we have values, we must constantly hammer people with them, or they are going to think those values are not real.

Let me put it in another context which I think illustrates it more clearly. When a person comes to me and indicates that they are involved in the taking of drugs, I don't have to constantly tell that addict that in my value system, or in the value system of the community I represent, the use of heroin is not appropriate. I don't have to constantly hammer away in order that he know that. I would deal with him in terms of, "You use heroin. How does that help you in your life? How does it get in the way of what you want to accomplish." I am teaching values around that.

I wouldn't deal with the student who is late for school by simply saying that the law says, "Thou shalt not be late for class, and the punishment is thus and thus." To administer justice and to try to teach values in that way is quite ineffective. Rather, as a teacher or as a principal, I would sit down with the student and say, "Look, I see you're having difficulty getting to class on time. Is that a problem for you?" In other words, I'd try to enter into the experience of the student. Maybe he's had the example of his father being late for everything he went to. Maybe that is part of the peer subculture he is moving in. We need to get to understand his reasons and to deal with tardiness, and the inappropriate use of time that the student is experiencing in his own life. As I work with him, he will understand that I, as well as the total community, am committed to the stewardship of time as a value, but I want to help him deal with his problem.

The important thing is that we develop the skills to come alongside of a student who is wrestling with the values that the community represents. Now, we all have to deal with that because we all get in trouble with the values that we are committed to as Christians. None of us live up to the standard. So it is as a struggler, as a fellow sinner, if you like, that I enter into that student's life.

A legalized system outlaws sin and automatically and impersonally applies the law. The person being punished loses dignity. Hostility is generated. You remove that person from the community and push him into a subculture. This is what happens to delinquents.

Sometimes people have to be removed from the community. I never asked a Bible college student to leave because they had broken one of the laws or one of the values, of the Bible college. That didn't create a problem for me. The only time I had to ask students to leave was if they breached those values and then willfully perpetuated their behavior and proselytized others. As I explained this to them, it was a case of removing themselves from the community by virtue of that behavior.

On a number of occasions I did have to ask students to leave. When I did, I always left the door open for them to return when they decided that the pattern of life they had entered was not effective, was not leading them to fulfillment in their life, or accomplishing the purpose God had for them. When they wanted to work at changing and reevaluating those things, they could return and we could work through some of that. This is a redemptive approach to discipline.

12

Counseling at the Elementary Level

Diane Morris

What does an elementary counselor do?

Sometimes when people ask me what I do, I say, "My main job is being an attention giver."

I stand outside my office and I pass out hugs to the children as they go to class, to the playground, and to lunch. I am there for them to say, "Can I see you?" or for them to tell me something that just happened to them, "Daddy's away," or "Mother's sick."

I'm not an in-depth counselor. In terms of problem solving, the elementary counseling program is mainly a preventive measure. This is true not only in working with the students themselves, but maybe even more importantly in working with the parents. I help parents see needs that are present or impending and suggest some ways in which they might take care of those problems now, so they don't become serious later on.

One of my greatest goals is to help the children apply scriptural principles to their little fights on the playground, to their struggles in class, or to their loneliness, and to help them see that the Lord Jesus is interested in those things and has a way of helping them. The counseling office can become a laboratory for the application of scriptural principles.

Aid to teachers and students

An elementary counselor often

- Supervises testing procedures.
- Assists in placement of students in classes.
- Acts as a liaison between students and teachers, teachers and parents, students and parents, teachers and teachers.
- Provides an additional moral support for individual students.

- Helps students work out interpersonal and other kinds of problems according to scriptural principles.
- Provides a "time out" spot, where kids can catch up on work or where they can go because of a behavior problem. They don't need discipline. They just need time out and a place to go.
- Provides a place of quiet and comfort during times of stress. I've held little boarding kids on my lap when they were lonesome and told them, "It's OK to cry. Probably your mom and dad are crying too, because they miss you a lot." It's important to have a place for both the boarding kids and the day kids to go.

Aid to the principal

- The counselor can help the principal with some of the public relations things like giving campus tours, and by answering parental questions that don't have to do with school policy.

Prekindergarten screening

Prekindergarten screening is another major area of involvement. We've found that helping the kindergarten teacher and the principal evaluate prekindergarteners as to their readiness has prevented a lot of retentions later on.

We set aside several weeks during which the kids who are planning to enter kindergarten the next year can come and have a practice kindergarten one day a week. This gives an opportunity for the kindergarten teacher, counselor, and principal to observe them. This observation is the most important evaluation.

We do give a formal test. We have used the ABC Preschool Screening Inventory. The Gissell Institute has probably the best preschool screening device. At the end, we have a conference with each of the parents and share our observations and our recommendations. Our school year begins in July, so our kindergarten students must be five on or before September 1. We've been pretty rigid on that as through the years we've observed the value of it.

During prescreening the key thing we watch for is emotional maturity. We look at physical, intellectual, and social maturity. A child who's emotionally and socially mature is going to experience more success. The intellectual part will come. Probably our greatest problem is with children who are intellectually advanced. They would be able to handle the material, but physically they are immature. We have a full day kindergarten, and there are a lot of physical adjustments for a child. The family of an intellectually advanced student has a harder time accepting the fact that it would be better for the child to wait until other areas catch up. However, almost without fail, when we have told a family we recommend their child wait a year, even though he might be the right age and advanced intellectually, that parent comes to our prekindergarten session the next year voluntarily to say, "We're so glad we waited."

A counselor provides benefit to parents by:

- Being a sounding board for parents to share areas of concern.
- Providing resources for finding help with discipline, schoolwork, abilities, disabilities.
- Providing guidance in preparing the family for major changes that are coming in their life.

How can we do all these things?

- **Family interviews.** Usually we conduct an interview with the family when the family first applies to the school.
- **Class time.** The counselor can be scheduled in the classroom. This gives the teacher a break and a chance to sit in to observe the children in a different kind of setting. I usually structure this time either with a story or a question and then let it go from there. Sometimes we just share together. We discuss events that have happened at school, again according to scriptural principles.
- **Informal gatherings.** I invite the kids in when they have a birthday. They can invite two or three friends. We just start talking, and it's a time for them to share. Sometimes I call them in individually. New students come in to get acquainted. Returning students come in to help settle back in.
- **Referrals.** Teachers, parents, boarding home parents and missions sometimes ask us to see children, when they observe special needs that the kids have.
- **Student requests.** Students themselves can say, "Can I come in to see you?"
- **Parent group meetings.** I wish we held more parent meetings where parents of primary children could come together and share the kinds of concern that they have. The counselor could share some things that might be helpful and there could be prayer together. It could be organized by age groups or by interest groups.

- **Student group meetings.** Another area of help we can provide at school is to have small group meetings with students. Get all the boarding students together, and let them share how things are going. Get all the new students on campus together at the beginning of the year. Let them share how they are feeling and what they are struggling with. Students coming back from furlough, get them together to share what they are feeling.

- **Keep in close touch with the boarding parents.** Teachers, I can't encourage you too much on this. The boarding parents want to be in close touch with the school.

Aid to families living in the provinces.

- When our provincial parents are in the city, we make an effort to be available to them, because they need to talk to school people.

- We offer to help them evaluate the teaching that they are doing at home and see how their kids compare with those in the classroom.

- We make standardized testing available to them.

- We offer prekindergarten screening evaluation to them. We let them know that we are available to listen, and that we care what they are experiencing. We can give them curriculum advice. Sometimes they need some enrichment in particular areas. We can make provision for our provincial students to visit class when they are in the city.

- I think a key thing that schools could do would be to release a teacher from time to time to visit parents when they are in provinces.

Problem areas

- In the Philippines we have a growing number of students from many different countries. We have Dutch, British, Korean, Chinese, and Japanese MKs. We have a responsibility to meet their needs, and their needs are unique. How can we help those kids to feel an important part of a school where seventy-five per cent of the students are American? They aren't only adjusting to the Philippines and their own culture that they brought with them, but they have to adjust to this Western culture that they are in and all these other cultures that are there too. It's hard for these kids.

- What about the ones that come to us and don't know very much English? We don't always have an ESL teacher. How can we help those kids? How can we help them so that they can understand what's going on in the classroom? These kids need special emotional support too.

- What about our special ed students? We have a learning disabilities program for kids — the definition of learning disabilities being kids who have normal or above-average intelligence but have learning difficulties in particular areas. We can offer help to those kids.

- But to what extent can we help students who come to us with severe learning disabilities? This is something we're really grappling with. If a missionary family is coming to the mission field with a child who is severely handicapped, we have a responsibility to them. Yet we have no expertise. We don't have facilities; we don't have the materials that those kids need; we don't have people who know how to meet their needs. What about our mission policies? Should our mission policies take this into consideration? What about our recommendations to missions, in these areas? What responsibilities do we have as a school to help our mission leaders become aware of these areas of need before the family leaves for the field?

- What about our gifted students? Are we making provision for them?

What if you have no full-time counselor?

- Every elementary teacher is also a counselor. Counseling is going on effectively in every elementary classroom where there's a sensitive teacher. I believe that with all my heart.

- A teacher with a special interest in this area could be asked to consider teaching part-time, and being available for counseling part-time.

- Principals with a sensitive spirit can and should be able to meet some of these needs. The disadvantage here is that counsel and discipline should not have to go together, although some counseling should go along with every disciplinary act.

Conclusions

There are important counseling needs at the elementary level. We may not see dramatic changes like we sometimes see with older children, but perhaps we will be able to prevent some of these children from needing to consult the secondary counselor or the marriage and family counselor later on. Serious needs that develop later might have been prevented at an early age.

Discussion

What is the most critical problem with elementary students, and what strategy do you have to work with it?

I would say that a child who feels that he's not loved and cared for is the most critical problem. A child needs attention.

However, let me balance that statement. In counseling, in the area of child development the big word has been *self-esteem* or *self-concept*. We have hit it, and hit it, and hit it. I'm just sharing my observations now. This is not based on research, but in the past two years I've observed our kids at Faith Academy becoming more and more selfish and self-centered. I'm deeply concerned about it. They need to be taught they're special, but what we're forgetting in the process is to teach them that the other guy is also special. That's my burden right now. Kids' greatest need is to feel loved and cared for, but we also need to teach them the responsibility to care for others. It can be in little ways. It can be you teachers, every day in your class, touching every child in your class in some affectionate way.

Are there any guidelines for dealing with a child who is below his grade level emotionally and socially?

We try sometimes to bridge that gap at furlough time for these students. If they are going to make a change anyway if they are going to a different school in a different place where they are not known, we've recommended to the parents this might be a key time to help their child get back on track with his emotional or social level. Sometimes those kids are struggling academically too. Sometimes they've been advanced because they are academically advanced. Sometimes they naturally seek their level on the playground. They'll play with the younger kids. We can help the family to understand what's going on and not to blame the child. We have to help meet those emotional needs by helping him feel cared for, but the most specific thing to do if they are changing schools is to give them a chance to go back and catch up.

Can you address the issue of abuse and neglect at the elementary school level?

The kind of abuse that we're seeing has been experienced mostly by our adopted kids coming into the missionary community. Those children have sometimes experienced extreme abuse and neglect. Because of their background they often have had nutritional deficiencies which have affected their mental processes. Some are brain damaged. We're struggling with that because we don't have a resource for that level. We can help in the area of neglect only in terms of support: emotional support and physical support. Right now on campus we do have a family counselor who can help in those areas on a deeper level. We even refer out into the community, if there are resources beyond what we have. But what do we do as a school?

We get a tremendous number of adoptions in our area. These kids often come to us with severe learning disabilities, but the family is already on the field when the child comes into the picture. They may have a long-standing ministry. One teacher at home right now who has discovered that her adopted daughter is severely learning-handicapped. Does she come back to the field now if we don't have anything to help the daughter? We haven't answered her yet.

How much pressure are MKs under? Can you identify the pressures?

I can share the pressure that I see the most at Faith Academy. Our missionary families mainly come from college-trained backgrounds. They come with superior academic qualifications. They are top-of-the-line people, and our students tend to be highly competitive from Day One. They are perfectionistic, and this becomes a great burden to them. The competitive spirit is good, but it needs to be trained and channeled. As a school one of our greatest needs is to help our kids become more caring and less "me first," and "I got the answer; how come you didn't get it?" and "You mean you're only finished now? I've been through a long time."

13

Comprehensive Counseling: Part of the Caring Community

Donald R. Fonseca
Counselor, Stony Brook School

Recently I did surveys of forty-some schools in the United States — Christian schools, public schools, and private prep schools that are non-Christian. Only two had what you would call a counseling program. Now, I'm not saying that those other thirty-nine or so don't have good counseling. Not at all. What I'm saying is, that they don't have a coordinated program. I found that this person was doing some counseling, and so was this person, and so was that person, but counseling cannot be hit or miss.

Preventive counseling

Counseling, as much as possible, should not be remedial. It should be preventive. As counselors we try to evoke change, because the very nature of counseling means that change needs to take place. Maybe it's an attitude. Maybe it's an emotional disturbance.

The first priority in any counseling program has to be the desire to honestly help. Do you really want to help, or are you trying to have an ego trip? Some teachers will say, *"I'm* talking to this kid. I'm not going to let someone else take care of this kid. He came to *me."* It becomes a personal thing; it becomes a conflict. Perhaps that teacher is not capable of helping that particular kid, but instead of passing the kid onto someone who can help, they hold tight. That's not good. The good of the student must be first and foremost.

I've been made aware of how important care is within the counseling program, honest caring.

I talked to an MK we have at our school from Dakar, Senegal. I said, "Kristen, you've been at Stony Brook for a little over a year. You seem to be happy all the time. How have things gone as far as your transition from Dakar, Senegal, to the Stony Brook School is concerned?"

She said, "Terrific."

I said, "No problems?"

She said, "None that I'm aware of."

I said, "Why?"

She said, "Because everybody likes me." She has a big smile. She's a senior this year.

One hundred percent of our faculty are involved in the counseling program. It's a structured program. We have about four hundred kids at our school and nearly sixty full-time faculty. Our entire student body is broken up into groups of from six to ten students. Each group has a counselor. The counselor who may be a teacher who has never taken one course in counseling, meets with those ten students biweekly for about forty-five minutes.

The counselor will sit down with his group, and they may discuss the honor code at our school, rules at the school, the commitment statement at the school, and things like that. Primarily they talk about academics. "How are things going? Grades coming along OK? How are things going with your teachers? Do you like your classes? Are you doing well? Anybody having a problem?"

The teacher or counselor in each group can do whatever he or she feels needs to be done at that point. We do give ideas to the teachers that they can use if they wish to. For instance we might say, "Today we're going to talk about student load. Are some of our students overloaded with classes?" That's the subject for the day, but do they have to do that subject? No.

There's a form that the teachers can hand in if they have something to put on it. If they don't, no one says, "Hey, where's your form?" But if in that group meeting, the teacher does find a problem, something he's not sure of, he fills out a form, and it goes to the grade chairman.

This makes sure that no kids fall through the cracks within the school. Sometimes even kids with problems will not go to anyone for help. When you talk to kids who have had problems, they may say, "There was nobody I could go to," meaning, "I didn't know what to do." We try to ensure that there's going to be a place for those young people. Out of these group sessions very often come individual counseling instances. The student may come up afterwards and say, "Hey, I've really got more of a problem than I wanted to say there. Can I talk to you privately?"

If an individual meeting takes place, that teacher has the right to keep it to himself, to come to me, or to go to someone else about the problem that might be taking place.

A kid comes up and says, "Mr. Fonseca, I need to talk to you. It's about a really severe problem. It's going to shake you up. But I'd like to talk to you about it. Is that OK?"

I say, "Sure, come in."

He'll sit down in my office and say, "Now one thing. This has got to be totally confidential. You've got to promise me that it's totally confidential."

What do you do? Do you say, "Right, Johnny. Just you and me. We'll keep it to ourselves"? No way! You're putting yourself into a bind. That kid may tell you something that you've got to tell, not only ethically or morally, but perhaps legally.

"I'm going to burn down this building tonight."

"Oh, well let's just keep that to ourselves." No, you're going to go to someone and say, "Johnny's going to burn the building down."

Then Johnny's going to say, "You're a great guy. You gave me your word." Of course Johnny goes to everybody else and says, "Don't go to him. He doesn't keep his word."

I've had kids walk out of my office when I've said, "No, Johnny. If you have enough trust in me to come to me in the first place, then you've got to trust me that I will be circumspect in how I use the information you give me. I might have to say something about it."

I've had Johnny get up and say, "Thanks. Let me think about that." Of course you never see Johnny again, and that's sad. That's upsetting to a counselor, but that's the way it has to be.

Is there a policy that obligates you to report to the school whatever comes to you?

The Dean of Students would have more of an obligation because the Dean and Associate Dean deal with the discipline. But if someone comes to me, I have to use my discretion as to what I do with the information that's given to me. I try to do that with all the integrity and expertise I have.

Obviously when a kid came to me and said, "I've been stealing in the dorm, I can't help it and I don't know what to do," I could not keep that to myself, because it was a school situation where other kids were suffering. I had to go to the deans and discuss it with them. We brought "Johnny" in and talked to him. We got the parents involved. We got a psychologist involved. Johnny is now getting treatment, still within the parameters of our school at this point. How long that's going to go on, I don't know.

If it's a serious breach of a school rule I will probably do something about it, because I feel I have an obligation to the school. That child is my first priority. I want to help him, but I can't destroy a bunch of other people for one student.

When I first brought up this approach to counseling in a faculty meeting, a hand would go up. "I'm a math teacher. I'm not a counselor. You do your job and I'll do mine."

We had to educate them. "Are you teaching just a math brain sitting in your front row or are you teaching a kid? That kid is not just a mathematics student. He bleeds, hurts, cries. If he's got a problem in your class, it's your obligation to help that kid. Now you may not be able to follow through on helping, but at least you've got to start the ball rolling." We have no faculty members or administrators or dorm people who do not teach. I'm the advisor for the seniors and I teach two classes. The other advisors are full-time teachers.

I had a faculty person come to me just this past October. "Hey, I'm not sure where to go. There's a junior girl sitting in the second row of my class with tears splashing on her paper. I didn't know what to do with the girl; whether to stop the class. I didn't want to embarrass her. What should I have done?"

So we had a chance to talk about it. I didn't go to that girl. I didn't say, "Let me handle it. I'm a counselor." No way. I said, "What I would suggest is that you go to that girl. Find her at lunch. Sit next to her. Say, 'Hey, Janet, how are things going? I think you were a little upset in my class this morning. Everything OK?'"

He said, "She may say, 'It's none of your business.'"

I said, "That's part of the problem of being a counselor, isn't it? But she may just say, 'Let me tell you.'"

And that's what happened in this case. She was waiting to tell someone what her problem was.

I have fifteen minutes at the beginning of every faculty meeting and Headmaster's Forum to try to help the teachers who have not taken any counseling courses, to give them some techniques and ideas.

I want to get everybody involved; get them behind the program; help them to realize that they are indeed helpers, every single one of them. The first year we did this was rough sledding, but it works beautifully now.

Academic counseling

I want to show you how we integrate the academic counseling into the overall counseling program. I am not *the* counselor in the school. Kids are not sent to me. Kids go to whomsoever they wish to go. My basic job as director of counseling is to coordinate the program and see that the program runs well.

The key to academic counseling is communication. We try to keep totally on top of the student's academics on a regular basis. Every three-and-a-half weeks during the school year a comment slip with a grade on it goes home to the parents. Every three-and-a-half weeks the parents have an upgrade on what their student is doing in addition to a comment from each of the student's teachers. If a teacher says, "Johnny's having a rough time," he'd better follow that comment by saying what he or she is doing to alleviate the rough time. You don't just say there is a problem and let the parent dangle. You tell them what you are doing to meet the problem.

Why does that come under the counseling program? Because we find over and over again that when a kid is having a problem with a grade, it's not academic at all. We had a boy a couple of months ago whose grades took a terrific tailspin. The teachers came to me and said, "He's not working; he's not trying."

"Wait a minute. That's a terrific change of grades. Let's take a look at this."

We did. What had happened? The father had left the mother some time ago. We knew that. But we found out that he was living with another woman. No one knew that. We also found out that the mother, because of this, had become an alcoholic and for the last six weeks had been in a hospital trying to be rehabilitated from alcoholism. Guess where this tenth grader was living. He was living at home by himself. And they were wondering why his grades had gone down? He had an academic problem. No he didn't. Its manifestation was academic, but that was not his problem. We're dealing with that problem from a totally different perspective now.

Each marking period, every three and a half weeks, each of the teachers reports any academic problems to the grade chairman. Then he or she will immediately take those and decide what has to be done. It may mean a parent conference or a teacher conference. It definitely means a student conference. I'm the academic advisor to the senior class. I set up their schedules. I work with them if there's a D or an F. They come into my office. We talk; we find out why they are having a problem if we can; we document it; then we get the parents and teachers involved and try to resolve that problem. Sometimes we can't, but most of the time we can.

The whole point here is communication. We know what's going on. We know what's happening with those students. If the problem isn't academic, then we take the proper steps to try to help the student so that he can get back on top academically.

We have one chairman for each of the grades seven through twelve. Every three-and-a-half weeks I get a stack of notes from the teachers saying, "Here's a problem I'm facing with this student." The goal here is to help the student keep his grades up and to get all the help he can possibly get.

We have a student tutorial program. This program is run by an academic prefect who is a student. This student will arrange for ten or twelve bright students from the senior class to tutor other students. If there is a kid who is having trouble with precalculus in tenth or eleventh grade, a student tutor who is good in calculus will spend maybe two hours a week tutoring him. That program fits in very nicely within the overall academic counseling program.

Every student in the school has to work half an hour a day at some job, whether they're day students or boarding students. That also is supervised by a prefect. Tutoring is considered a work job.

Peer counseling program

Not all students will go to an adult when they've got a problem. However, many of those students will go to a peer.

We have a board of prefects made up of ten seniors who are elected by the students and the faculty of the school. These prefects work very hard, and the student body realizes that they're there to help them, to be their liaison between faculty and students.

I meet weekly for an hour and a half with this board. Some of the other prefects in the dormitories may also attend, along with any other students who wish to come. At any given time I probably have fifteen to eighteen students in this session. I do the same with them as I do with the faculty, only on a little different level. I give them some counseling techniques and a little bit of training as to what to do. How do you handle confrontation? How do you handle your status in the dormitory now? It's easy if you're a senior and an eighth grader steps out of line. You just grab him and say, "Hey, shape up." There's no problem. But your best friend does something wrong. What do you do?

Where do you draw the fine line between a kid referring some-one for help, and squealing. ("Yeah, I know I should have said this to help him, but I didn't want to get him busted.")

We try to help them deal with topics such as how to be a pre-fect without losing your status; how to confront without being a goody-goody; the signs and symptoms to look for in the dorm. For example, one of your classmates is sleeping every free moment. When the kid has a free period, he habitually goes back to the dorm, crashes for fifty minutes and then rushes back to the next class. That's something to take note of. He might be on drugs. He may be getting up at 2 AM and going out for a little toot on the town and not getting enough sleep during the night. Something may be taking place that has to be addressed.

I tell these kids, "You're not a counselor in the sense that you're going to be solely responsible for a kid with a real problem. You're going to see if you can help, and then try to get the help that that kid needs, but in a way that won't break your relationship with him."

We had three suicide attempts this past year at our school. Two girls were very unhappy with their home life and wanted every-one to know about it. They tried to cut their wrists with a blunt instrument that couldn't have broken the skin. But we knew they were trying to tell us something. The other one nearly died. Fortu-nately she did not, but she is out of the school right now. She had very severe problems at home having to do with incest—a very tragic problem. This girl would have graduated probably number two or three out of a hundred seniors. Brilliant girl. She's in a school in New Jersey for emotionally disturbed young people trying to get some education and getting psychiatric help. Most of these things come to my attention from the kids.

> One of the prefects came to me just a few weeks ago and said, "Mr. Fonseca, you were talking about anorexia in our peer counseling meeting."
> "Yeah?"
> "You know what you said about kids hiding food at the table, stuffing it in their pockets, making believe they're putting it in their mouths and dropping it down their shirts or blouses?"
> "Yeah."
> "I know a girl who's doing that. But I don't want to cry wolf, Mr. Fonseca. Maybe I'm not really observing right."
> But he was right on. This girl was pre-anorexic. We're trying to work with her at the present time.

To have a counseling program without involving your students is like having a well oiled wheel with a cog missing. We need to involve the kids for our benefit as well as for theirs; to help them realize they do have a responsibility within their school community.

If a student does not want something to come to me, he will not go to a prefect, because he knows that if it's serious enough, I will hear about it. Usually the kids still come. They're fully aware of what the peer counselors are doing.

College placement

A hundred of our seniors every year go to a four-year college. I start in September of their junior year, and work with them for two years on college placement. During the senior year from September to March I meet individually with each senior an average of fourteen times. I help them with applications, give them some ideas, and answer questions.

This year our hundred students made 810 applications. I read all of them, and I filled out nearly that many secondary school reports.

Why is this considered part of the overall counseling program? Isn't college counseling different from all the rest? The answer is no. Many schools make it different, but they shouldn't. I find that as these seniors come to me on a regular basis, I deal with more personal problems within the college counseling situation than I do in many others.

I had a kid come in the other day and hand me a bunch of crumpled, messed-up applications.

I said, "What is this?"

He said, "I don't know how that happened. I just went to get them, and I don't know if my roommate got them or what."

I knew what it was after talking to him. He was afraid. That transition from high school to college is a rough transition. He was afraid he was going to be rejected. So we had a talk about that, and I gave him another batch of applications.

I have meetings with the kids when the rejection slips start coming in. I tell them, "Hey, look. It's not a reflection on who you are. It doesn't mean you're bad because you didn't get into Northwestern. Georgetown rejected you? OK, let's get on with life." These are very difficult things for some kids to handle. Many students have sat across my desk and cried because they didn't know what to do about the whole college situation.

College counselors should be doing a lot of personal counseling, if they're not, they're missing an opportunity to help young people.

Crisis counseling

Probably the most time consuming aspect of my job is dealing with young people in a state of crisis. Parents are always involved in crisis counseling.

I think I spent about forty hours in a three week period dealing with the girl I mentioned who would have graduated up at the top of the class. I spent even more time with the father and mother going through all of the mud, muck, and garbage that this girl was trying to deal with seven years after it all took place. She was seventeen years old and beginning to realize what had really happened back there, and she couldn't handle it. A 4.0 student became a 1.6 student, failing almost everything. This peaceful, calm, model student, became aggressive, and angry—physically fighting with other girls. Because of our co-ordinated program, we recognized a broken behavior pattern.

I was at a fine prep school in New Jersey and I asked, "What if a kid runs away or attempts suicide at your school? What happens?"

No one could answer the question.

"We hope that . . . "

"No, you can't hope. What happens?"

The answer was, "We don't know."

If a problem occurs in a coordinated program, immediately things begin to happen. People know what to do. A kid in the dormitory attempts suicide or falls apart, the dorm people know what to do. They call me. Does that mean I have to handle it totally and completely? No. But I have to get something started. Someone should be able to do that even if it's two A.M.

Who contacts the parents? Where does it go from there? So often kids are not helped as they should be, because nothing is done when it should be done, or someone sits down with the kid and tries to give them tender love and care. I'm all for that, but there are times in a student's life when that is not enough.

What do we do with crises?

Prevention. Let the dorm people know what to do when they observe certain signs and symptoms. A kid is giving away all of his stuff, stuff that he really likes, his stereo. Or a kid was having an angry time and all of a sudden he's happy and he goes into an upswing. What do you do? Do you rejoice and say, "Ah, everything's fine now?" You better be careful, because that's one of the major symptoms of a kid who is going to attempt to take his life. Now he's decided. "I'm going to end it all. Everything's going to be

OK. My problem will no longer exist." We've got to watch for those things, know the signs and know what to do.

Intervention. When something does take place, get yourself in there and do something about it. Do you know how to handle a kid who has just attempted suicide? What you do may dictate whether or not that kid tries it again the next night as soon as you go home.

Postvention. You've solved the crisis, temporarily at least. Things are going pretty well. Now what do you do with that kid in your school. Do you kick him out and say, "Sorry, we can't have you here"? You might have to, especially if it's a disruptive situation. But if you keep that kid because your school is the best place for him, you're going to have to have a strong school. "What will the constituency think if we have a kid in our school who has taken drugs?" You've got to be able to handle that. For whose good? For that kid's good. We rarely ask the question, "What's good for the Stony Brook School?" or "What's good for the parents?" We do sometimes, but rarely. First of all it has to be, "What's good for that young person?"

Refer, refer, refer. Many counselors feel that to refer is a sign of failure. It isn't. You show me a counselor that refers when someone needs to be referred, and I'll show you a good counselor. The bad counselor is the one who hangs onto something that he can't do, either because he doesn't have the time, energy, expertise, or because unfortunately, he doesn't care.

Regular meetings. Lastly, you've got to have a time when everyone who is involved with student activities gets together on a regular basis. We meet every Monday at lunchtime. Monday is not arbitrary. Monday follows the weekend. Ten of us meet—four dorm heads, two deans, the chaplain. I chair that meeting. We sit down and talk about students. We don't gossip about them. We talk about them.

I might say, "A teacher told me that Johnny's having trouble in his class, and he thinks it's more than just what it seems.

Then one of my staff might say, "I'm glad you brought that up. I've noticed ... "

Then another one may say, "Right. You know, in the dorm I've been wondering ... "

And before we know it, that one little thing that was brought to me becomes a composite, and we see a problem. This may even be an attitude problem. Attitude is just as important as action.

What do we do? We don't just say, "Tsk, tsk. We'll have to keep an eye on that." That is the most dangerous thing you can do. That means no one will do anything until the crisis comes up.

What do we do? We say, "OK, we see a problem. Who knows Johnny best?" It may be one of us in the room, but it may be someone outside, another teacher. We'll go to that person and say, "We'd like you to go to Johnny, ask him how things are going, see if you can find out something."

Folks, this is the key to a preventive counseling program. The number of kids we have prevented from getting into a deeper problem through this Monday meeting is incredible. It makes me want to cry because I'm so happy with that situation. We know what's going on. We know what we're doing, and we know what is happening within our school.

Finally, you did not notice a category called spiritual counseling. You're probably asking, "Aren't you a Christian school?" Yes we are. What makes a Christian school? One thing and one thing only—not textbooks, not praying before classes, but the fact that you have a totally committed Christian faculty. That's all you need for a Christian school. Some of our students are not Christians.

By design, we do not have a category called spiritual counseling, nor do we ever want to. As Christian educators within a Christian school situation, if everything we do is not from a Christian perspective, and if it is not of a spiritual nature, forget it. We're doing something wrong. When I sit down with a kid in peer counseling or college counseling, I am counseling spiritually because I'm a believer, and that affects all I do.

14

MKs, Are They in Their Right Minds?

Ed Danielson
Christian Heritage College

Missionary kids who grow up on the field may see things differently than those who moved overseas and learned a second language as adults. The MK may have different learning styles and a slightly different value system. This might be due to the environment which affected the development of brain systems and functions. MKs may use the right hemisphere more than their parents. Some research seems to support this, but more research needs to be done if we are to answer the questions which arise.

Using the right hemisphere is neither superior nor inferior, just different. God has given each one of us certain abilities and has allowed us to develop in unique and special environments so that we can serve him more efficiently.

The more we learn about MK learning styles and outlook, the more efficient we may become in educating and counseling them.

[For a technical discussion of bilingualism and hemispheric lateralization, write to Dr. Danielson for a copy of his presentation.]

15

Stages of Spiritual Response in Children

David C. Greenhalgh
West Bay Christian Academy

The relationship between the developmental stages of children and their concept of spiritual truth is important for parents and teachers to understand. Work done by Piaget, Erikson, and Kohlberg can be valuable in helping those who work with children to know how to present God's truth in age-appropriate ways. Mr. Greenhalgh provided an overview of these developmental theories paralleled with James Fowler's *Stages of Faith* (New York: Harper and Row, 1981).

For a complete treatment of this subject see "Developing Spiritual Values in Young Children on the Mission Field," by David Greenhalgh in the 1984 Compendium of ICMK-Manila as well as the following sources cited by Mr. Greenhalgh:

Bonnidel, Clouse. "The Teachings of Jesus and Piaget's Concept of Mature Moral Judgement," *Journal of Psychology and Theology*, Vol. 6, No. 3, Summer 1978.

Edwards, James. "Faith as Noun and Verb." *Christianity Today* 29.11, Aug. 8, 1985.

Kilpatrick, William *Psychological Seduction: The Failure of Modern Psychology*. 1983.

Kleinig, John. "Moral Education in a School Setting," *Journal of Christian Education*, July 1982.

Shelly, Judith Allen. *The Spiritual Needs of Children*. Downers Grove, IL: InterVarsity, 1982.

Radcliffe, Robert J. "Spiritual Growth: A Developmental Approach," *Christian Education Journal*, Vol. 5, 1984.

Richards, Lawrence. *A Theology of Children's Ministry*. Grand Rapids, MI: Zondervan, 1983.

Ward, Ted. *Values Begin at Home*. Wheaton, IL: Victor Books, 1979.

Part III

ADDRESSING CULTURAL ISSUES IN THE MK SCHOOL

16

MK Education in a Cross-Cultural Context

Thomas H. Moore
Wycliffe Bible Translators

The Cultural and Communal Context of Education

Although we usually conceive of *education* as the learning of specific skills which will enable the student to realize specific life goals (e.g. enter college, get a job, be a good citizen), our larger hope is for our graduates to become well-integrated human beings, reaching their full potential as world citizens.

The place of schooling

All of community life involves education. Therefore, we should distinguish schooling from education, and set schooling in its context of the community.

Although school, church, work, social life, entertainment and recreation all contribute to a child's education, his parents are the most significant influence. The communal base of education, i.e., the Christian family, in active fellowship with a spiritually alive church, seeking to honor Christ in all areas of life, provides a firm basis for the Christian education of children. Christian education is mostly enculturation to the Christian culture of the community.

Along with specific skills, all schooling seeks to transmit the culture of the adult generation to the students. This may or may not be a conscious process.

Culture

Man is specifically commanded to apply his creative activity to God's creation (Gen. 1:28): "Be fruitful and increase in number; fill the earth and subdue it." This command has been called the "cultural mandate," since the uniquely human, social response to it results in the creation of culture. Therefore, a biblical definition of *culture* would be "the uniquely human task and accomplishment of developing God's creation."

From the dawn of recorded history, people have been aware that different societies have different cultures. Geographers note that physical circumstances (raw creation) account for some of this variation. Historians chronicle the development of culture, accounting for more of the variation. Christians would propose that the gods a people worship will also mold their culture considerably, as men subdue and rule creation in the service of their gods. In fact, culture in itself is essentially religious in two ways: it humanizes us, and it is experienced as god-like.

When we use the term *culture*, we are referring to the mind and personality we share in our humanity. If we see culture as more than this, we tend to mystify it and see it as a superhuman force. In fact, this is what we do in everyday life.

Perceived as a superhuman force, culture takes on the attributes of God. It is omnipotent in that it determines most of what goes on in society; it is omniscient in that all knowledge comes to us through it, and omnipresent in that it is in all of us; immanent yet transcendent. Our tendency is to uncritically accept the idols of the national, secular culture along with our God and his teaching.

Christian culture

Christians are commanded to live in this world without becoming part of it. They would seek to influence their culture in a godly way without paying homage to its idols. They do this with varying degrees of success. My observation is that those who form communities based on mutual faith are more successful than those who live as isolated individuals in the wider, secular culture.

Ethnocentrism and ethnism

Ethnocentrism is commonly conceived as the application of one's own cultural standards in evaluating another culture. Every enculturated being is ethnocentric by definition. However, when one's culture is viewed not only as the right way to live, but also as the righteous way in an absolute, religious sense, I will describe this sentiment as *ethnism*.

We would be quick to apply (and rightly so) the ethnist label to the Islamic fundamentalists; yet it also applies to common sentiments found in Christian subcultures. While this may be a problem in producing well-integrated graduates in North America, it is a far more serious problem if exported to the MK school.

Theories of social evolution were popular in the nineteenth century. Such theories usually culminate with one's own culture standing at the pinnacle of cultural development and sophistication. While these theories have long been discredited by social scientists, many Americans hold similar views regarding their own culture—its Christian origins and its mission to spread righteousness throughout the heathen world, not only with Christian missions but also through international economic and political activity.

This view of American culture has serious implications for all missionary activity, including children's education. Along with Christ, a Western, individualistic, materialistic way of life is brought to the host country. The expectation that the people of the "underdeveloped" world will view "developed" culture as superior to their own leads to the feeling that we have nothing to learn from them. People from the industrialized world are the cultural teachers rather than learners, and this ethnist attitude will probably be reflected in their education programs.

Patterns of Adjustment

In an earlier study, I found three typical patterns of adjustment to the cross-cultural situation: the foreigner role, biculturism, and the third culture.[1] The foreigner role requires the least modification of personal lifestyle. It would almost always be a short-term solution. Of all the patterns of adjustment studied, this was by far the least successful. In the long run, Americans tend to exhibit two distinct adjustment patterns: biculturism, and the third culture.

Bicultural individuals have actually adopted two cultures, either by living in a bicultural home or by adopting a second culture through immersion. They are fully capable of participating in either culture with facility, understanding, sympathy, and acceptance.

---

[1]Moore, T. "Americans in Ecuador: A Study of Adjustment." Ph.D. dissertation. Department of Sociology, U. of California, Berkeley, 1974.

The third culture is an adaptation which lies somewhere between the foreigner role and biculturism. A third culture is constructed by visitors from the first or home culture as they strive to live in the midst of the second or host culture.[2] Wherever foreigners are established, a third culture is likely to thrive. In my experience, more missionaries are part of third-culture social groups than are bicultural.

The Path to Biculturism

I would predict that, for the missionary as an individual, biculturism would help develop a richness and depth in personality, an ability to identify and articulate different points of view, and the capacity to separate what is biblical truth from what is cultural heritage. This experience should produce a closer awareness of, and liberation from, his home culture. The anthropologist Ralph Linton writes "those who know no other culture than their own cannot know their own."[3]

My research suggests that the path to biculturism comprises three distinct phases: evaluation, information, and personalization.

Evaluation

Everyday evaluations of home and host cultures are the key to unlocking the potential of bicultural learning experiences. As the host culture is experienced, what evaluations are placed on it? At first, it will be a stereotypical, caricatured version. For example, foreigners "know" that Latins are lazy, emotional, dishonest, stupid, and slow. By American standards, they may well be! However, by Latin standards, the American is stupid, materialistic, unfeeling, disloyal, selfish, totally lacking in manners and social graces, loud, and conceited. Both caricatures are due to cultural ignorance, and when the attempt

---

[2]Useem, J. et. al. "Men in the Middle of the Third Culture: The Roles of American and Non-Western People in Cross-cultural Administration," *Human Organization* 22:1963, pp. 169-179. I am using the term *third culture* as it is commonly used in our missionary community to refer to the home culture as it is affected by its foreign location. This is the most common adjustment made to life abroad, which the Useems call the "second culture." Their term *third culture* refers to what I've called *biculture*. While this may seem confusing, I believe it more closely follows our everyday use of language.

[3]Linton, R. *The Cultural Background of Personality*. London: Kegan Paul, 1947, p. 81.

is made to understand the culture of the other in its own terms, healthy attitudes, conducive to biculturism, can grow.

We must distinguish between two kinds of truth in order to make valid evaluations of both home and host culture. Absolute truths are true because they "just are." Consensual truths are true only because a human authority (the government, community, etc.) says so. For example, the absolute truth that murder is wrong is a fact similar to "water boils at 100° C." On the other hand, our language and which side of the road we drive on are true because of consensus—we agree that they are true. Ethnism confuses these two kinds of truth, absolutizing consensual truth.

So the first step in overcoming ethnist evaluations of the host culture is to become wary of absolute truths presented by either the host culture or our own culture. Ethnist evaluations are not easily laid aside. In order to begin to appreciate another way of life, one must be willing to question the absoluteness of every previously held belief and value. This involves not only a decision to begin to do so, but a continuing, life-long exercise.

Information

The second step seems the most obvious: one must acquire a good deal of knowledge about the host culture—its history, values, ways of doing things, and so forth. This requires the eradication of ethnism, mastery of the host language, and considerable contact with local people of all sorts.

Personalization

Since mind and personality are largely cultural, then biculturism will result in alterations and additions to the individual's ways of thinking and characteristic approach to the external world. The host culture becomes part of the person. This does not require the destruction of a person's native culture (although it will be evaluated differently), but is, rather, a valuable addition to it.

Missionaries are typically from American and Northern European cultures, living amongst tribal and/or third-world cultures. At the risk of oversimplification, I will attempt to present a rough sketch of the modifications in personal values and thinking that would be associated with this kind of biculturism (or, indeed, worldmindedness).

Individualism is the key to understanding American culture. "We (Americans) believe in the dignity, indeed the sacredness, of the individual. Anything that would violate our right to think for ourselves, judge for ourselves, make our own decisions, live our lives as we see fit, is not only morally wrong, it is sacrilegious."[4] On the other hand, traditional cultures are family and community oriented, stressing group identity and achievement, economic levelling, cooperation, and sharing; rather than consumerism, personal ambition, and individual achievement.

The bicultural person would be comfortable with both individualistic and communal values and be able to participate in either culture with personal sympathy and understanding. It would be natural to retain a dominant cultural identity. I do not mean to suggest that biculturism is an amalgamation of two cultures into a third or an obliteration of one's identity. Rather, it is an expansion of mind and personhood.

Third Culture

Changes in a person's circumstances of life are stressful. The TC is a mechanism of adaptation to a stressful situation, and in that light can be seen as analogous to the psychological construct of defense mechanisms. Stress can be a healthy mandate for change, growth, and maturity, although it can be temporarily avoided through unhealthy defense mechanisms. A person suffering from the stress of "culture shock" may endeavor to deal with the root problem by learning a new culture, or may seek a system of defense. The TC is a culture of defense offered to him by those having come before. It is not exactly like the home culture, but it is enough like it to make its adoption far easier than adopting the host culture.

Both the home and host culture are essentially human responses to God's command to inhabit, subdue, and rule over creation. Just as one learns another language and becomes fluent, so one may also learn another culture. The TC is an attempt by uprooted people to modify the pre-existing home culture so they can comfortably exist in non-home-culture surroundings and provide a home for those who are unable or unwilling to learn the host culture. Therefore, the TC is not a real culture; it has not developed in response to God's command, but rather, for man's convenience. It does not unfold creation any more than a phrase book communicates a foreign language. It is a temporary expedient which suffices until the displaced person is re-united to his home culture.

---

[4]Bellah, R. et al. *Habits of the Heart: Individualism and Commitment in American Life*. Berkeley: Univ. of California, 1985.

In the long run, the TC may prevent persons in the cross-cultural situation from becoming fully human—students and parents alike. The Brazilian radical educator Paulo Freire distinguishes between mere "adaption" to one's environment, and "integration," which is the "the capacity to adapt oneself to reality plus the critical capacity to make choices to transform that reality." For Freire, the "integrated person" is a subject, while the "adapted person" is an object. "Adaption is behavior characteristic of the animal sphere; exhibited by man, it is symptomatic of his dehumanization."[5] In our terms, Freire is speaking of a situation not unlike the TC.

The implications for missionary families are serious. First-generation entrants to a new culture may rapidly become bicultural in their ability to function in both home culture and TC. Failing to learn the host culture, their children are very likely to become monocultural TC objects who lack the equipment to move in either home or host culture with any facility! Their understanding of both cultures will probably be seriously deficient since they see only highly selective representatives from each—home culture professionals who live upright, moral lives, and host culture "sinners," those with whom the missionary works. This tendency would be exacerbated by the missionary's concentration on those most open to the Gospel, which usually tend to be from the lowest classes of the host culture.

While the bicultural person may have an identity problem, the TC kid has a more serious problem: his very selfhood is culturally dependent on an artificial construct. The TCK will be a misfit in any genuine culture (and experience culture shock), not only because of a faulty education or lack of experiences, but rather because of what he is as a person. Therefore, he can never reach his potential as a bicultural individual. Research on detribalized Africans and American Indians indicates that cross-cultural experiences in which a community loses its old culture without replacing it with a viable alternative may have serious effects on personhood.[6] This may often be the case for the MK.

---

[5]Freire, P. *The Practice of Freedom*. London: Writers and Readers Publishing Corp., 1976, p.4.

[6]Honigman, J. *Culture and Personality*. New York: Harper, 1954, pp. 413-16.

Educational Implications: Bicultural Education

Many who work with MKs observe that, for one reason or another, the MK fails to reach his potential to take his place as a leader both in his home country and in the international community. It has been my position that the cause of this failure is not individual, but cultural.

A study of overseas-experienced Americans (including MKs) lists factors which build world-mindedness: living in local communities rather than the American overseas community (the TC), language fluency, and interaction with local people.[7] Significantly, all of the factors found important in building world-mindedness were associated in my study with biculturism rather than the TC. Sixty-four percent of the MKs responding to another survey desired more contact with national peers, and none desired less.[8] MKs appear to seek more host culture experience than we currently provide.

I have argued that all education is a function of the community, and that schooling should reflect the wider communal enculturation of the child. In the cross-cultural context, missionary families live amidst an alien culture and religion. That is, after all, the reason they came! Schools for MKs are viewed as enculturating institutions, if only to prepare the student to enter university back home. Bicultural education, then, would be an exercise in bicultural enculturation. MK schooling would accurately evaluate host and home cultures, avoiding ethnist stereotyping. It would incorporate host culture materials into the curriculum. Its ideal product would be the MK who has integrated these cultural experiences as a bicultural person.

We shall now survey the potential for bicultural education in existing options for MK education. These options are monolingual national schools, bilingual schools, and TC schools.

Monolingual national schools

Isolated missionaries who live immersed in the host culture should be able to raise their children biculturally. Many send their children to local schools, providing the English portion of the curriculum at home. Children from this kind of environment, I would assume, would be likely to become bicultural, providing that sufficient

---

[7]Gleason, T. *"Social Adjustment Patterns and Manifestations of Worldmindedness of Overseas-Experienced American Youth"*. Ph.D. Dissertation, Michigan State U., 1969.

[8]Gross, C. "Missionary Children's Contact with National Peers." Seminar paper, Graduate School of Missions, Columbia Bible College, 1975.

furlough time is spent in the home culture, and the parents do not have an ethnist attitude toward the host culture. One study found that MKs value national schools just slightly less than mission schools, and more than correspondence or U.S. public schools.[9] It also reported that there were more "spiritually aware" MKs attending national schools (88 percent) than those in mission schools (56 percent).

Bilingual schools

Bilingual schools may provide an excellent opportunity for bicultural enculturation. However, since they are designed for the host culture, primary language immersion would not be in the national language, which diminishes the value of the program. Further, if a British curriculum is used, Americans may not find it suitable after the fifth or sixth grades.

Third-culture schools

Most MKs are educated in TC schools such as those operated by mission boards (boarding or day), or American schools in foreign cities. These schools are largely staffed by foreigners who themselves adapt to their cross-cultural situation by joining the third culture or remaining foreigners. In this situation, bicultural experiences other than "outreach" would be minimal. Enculturation in such schools is to the TC.

TC schools are part of the larger missionary support network. The more remote missionary support becomes from evangelism and discipleship, the more it takes on the character of lifestyle support. Support services tend to isolate missionary families from the host culture, diminishing valuable cross-cultural learning experiences while fostering ethnism. For example, "nationals aren't capable." An extreme example of lifestyle support would be the missionary compound, where barriers to bicultural education may be insurmountable.

Shifting to a Bicultural Approach

The TC school's path to biculturism would be the phases of evaluation, information and personalization. We begin by evaluating existing programs to see if they include ethnism, but the information and personalization phases also involve evaluative processes. All

---

[9]Smith, W. "Planning Your M.K.'s Education." Th.M. project, Dallas Theological Seminary, 1975.

three factors constantly interact. Therefore, a shift to a more bicultural approach involves not only the desire to do so and incorporation of more host culture information, but also a change in our habitual ways of evaluating our own culture (and the host culture) along with changes in educational methods and major school policies. Specifically, a bicultural approach would increasingly use the host culture language, personnel, methods, and materials.

Language: The key to bicultural integration is language. In my previous study, there was a .52 correlation between language facility and biculturism. The bicultural school must be thoroughly bilingual. However, since many missionary families come to the field with older children, a second track program would need to be offered, with an effective second language program at all levels.

Personnel: The whole school would employ both home and host culture personnel. Ideally, they would all be bicultural. Since this is probably not possible, all personnel would at least need to have a thorough commitment to biculturism. National teachers would teach as many subjects in the national language as possible. This would provide an excellent foundation for biculturism while reducing the financial burden on the church for missionary teachers. It would also contribute to the local economy and build bridges to the host community.

Methods: Research has shown that students from traditional Mexican culture learn differently than Anglo-Americans.[10] Anglos tend to favor a "field independent" cognitive style, in contrast to the Mexican's "field sensitive" style; a distinction which parallels the general contrast made between American and traditional cultures. For example, Anglos prefer independent work, competition, and individual achievement, while Mexicans prefer to work with others to achieve a common goal. Teachers also exhibit a preferred cognitive style which is reflected in their preferred teaching methods. The bicultural program would make use of both teaching styles, which would result in a more bicognitive learning style and ultimately in personalization of a bicognitive approach.

Materials: National curriculum materials should be incorporated into the program as much as possible. It would also be wise to limit importation of school supplies, using locally purchased ones wherever possible.

---

[10]Ramirez, M. and Castaneda, A. *Cultural Democracy, Bicognitive Development, and Education.* New York: Academic Press, 1974.

Although every area of curriculum should be bicultural, the social studies would perhaps be the most natural area of integration. From kindergarten on, materials incorporating an anthropological approach to social studies (such as *The Social Studies: Concepts and Values.* Harcourt, Brace, Jovanovich, 1970 series) would be useful. Of course, the amoral stance taken by these secular materials should be replaced with Christian values.

Ethnocentric social studies materials should be avoided. In their place, the teacher would include material more relevant to the school's location, while maintaining a Christian perspective. Unfortunately, what passes for "Christian" in U.S.-produced educational materials for social studies may actually be more American than Christian.[11]

Problem areas in bicultural education

Some object to bilingual education on the grounds that students educated in a non-mother-tongue language — especially during primary years — have suffered academically. Research indicates that this occurs only when the national language is viewed as "superior" to the "inferior," ethnic minority tongue. On the other hand, when both languages have social value and relevance, then the second language is "additive" rather than "subtractive". Additive bilingual children "show definite advantages on measures of cognitive flexibility, creativity, and divergent thought."[12] Not only is another language learned, but along with that language, another approach to thinking. Bilingual bicultural students also become bicognitive, which should lead to the kind of world-mindedness we are seeking.[13]

Educational researchers find that additive bilingualism and bicultural education appears to be a healthy experience. "These studies suggest to us that there is no basis in reality for the belief that becoming bilingual or bicultural necessarily means a loss or dissolution of identity." A summary of French-English immersion programs in Canada concludes: "There is no evidence at all that acquisition of a

---

[11]Noll, M. et. al. *The Search for Christian America.* Westchester, IL: Crossway Books, 1983.

[12]Lambert, W. "The Effects of Bilingualism on the Individual: Cognitive and Sociocultural Consequences," in Hornby, P. ed., *Bilingualism: Psychological, Social and Educational Implications.* New York: Academic Press, 1977.

[13]Ramirez, M. et al. *New Approaches to Bilingual, Bicultural Education.* Austin, TX: Dissemination and Assessment Center for Bilingual Education, 1974. Manual 6.

second language and interaction with members of the related ethnic group under the immersion conditions in any way threatens these children's native language or culture."[14]

One might object on the grounds that the French-English community is already somewhat bicultural in Canada, and therefore Canadians have a head start towards biculturism. This objection emphasizes my earlier point that the educational program will only be effective to the degree that it is an outgrowth of the Christian community. The move to biculturism begins with parents in community. Without their support, the educational program will be less effective.

Summary and Conclusions

Much of what I have written here will be well known to those living abroad. My contribution to the conventional wisdom is (1) a cultural contextualization of education and schooling, (2) a cultural conceptualization of personality and cognition, and therefore (3) an awareness of the deep roots of cultural forgery which we may be fostering in our missionary children through TC enculturation.

I have described two typical adjustments missionary families make to the host culture: the "third culture" and "biculturism." Both have advantages and disadvantages. For short-term workers who are there for only one or two years, I think the third culture would have tremendous advantages. But from the MK's point of view, I would predict that the longer he resides in the TC, the less successful he'll be in adjusting to any real culture. He also misses significant learning opportunities offered by the host culture; learning which transfers far beyond biculturism.

I do not mean to suggest that current attempts to help MKs adjust to a difficult situation are not valuable. However, I do suggest that current attempts miss the root cause of the problem, which is not simply one of individual psychological or social maladjustment. Nor is it due to faulty education in the field. Rather, it is a problem of enculturation, whose roots will not be easily eradicated by an additional course in school, superficial modifications in family lifestyles or school curricula, or two-week seminars in the U.S. Following the example of the Savior, missionaries should evaluate the place of host culture in schools, families, and personal lives, and pray God's strength for the opportunity for growth and maturity he offers, if not for the adults' at least for the children's sake.

---

[14]Lambert, op. cit.

17

Principles of Curriculum Development for a Multinational School

Peter M. Blackwell
Rhode Island School of the Deaf

There are several major conflict areas in multinational curriculum planning which we need to address.:

Entrance requirements to post-secondary program

In some countries there are fairly rigid entrance requirements to post-secondary education (e.g. O and A levels in Great Britain, HSC in Victoria, Australia.) There are a variety of procedures that kids have to go through either in the last year or two of their secondary school experience. My niece from Australia has been living with me for the last six months. I've been struggling with the issues of her going back into the eleventh grade in Australia and what that's going to mean. I've also learned a lot about what's changed since I went through that process some years ago.

Parent perceptions and concerns

I've found that there is a great deal of concern on the part of parents the further they get away from their home country and the longer they've been away. They often have a whole set of unrealistic expectations and generally fear-related concerns that they want the school to address. I strongly believe in meeting with parents on a continual basis. That includes discussing curriculum. I think that's the only way you are going to help them. I've enjoyed going out to various missions and working with parents to try to bring them down to a comfort level. I try to encourage the school to address many of those concerns. The parents are unaware of what has changed back in their own country. The longer they've been away, the less they're in touch.

The American school these days is no longer the white Anglo-Saxon Protestant suburban school from which most of the teachers in mission schools have come. When I get materials from Australia, I see the number of multinational and multilingual issues that the schools there are dealing with. In Stockholm, for instance, there are fifty-two languages in the schools. We understand Sweden to be that pure Nordic, Viking-oriented kind of population, but when you're dealing with fifty-two languages within the school system of Stockholm, you realize that something has changed. The schools in those countries are becoming more and more multinational. That's happening all over the world. In every country, I'm dealing with a rapidly internationalizing situation. If parents have been away for twenty years, they've lost the perspective of what their school situation is like in their home country.

You cannot bring about curriculum change without those parents understanding what you're addressing.

Curriculum content

History is one of the courses in which I find the greatest dissonance among the various national groups. Most people value their own people's history. Most governments require kids to have a knowledge of their own history and literature. If your kid doesn't grow up learning British history or British literature, and you're planning to go back to Britain, you have a problem.

The content is going to be much more critical in some areas than in others. If you're going to change a curriculum, you need to make sure your parents understand what's going to work for them in those weighted areas.

Curriculum style and structure

There's also an issue of style, which often gets mixed with the issue of content. There's not a great deal of difference in the content of mathematics, but there's a great deal of difference in the style in which mathematics is done. It's not a content issue. It's a style issue.

You need to sort that out for parents and for teachers and for yourselves in the curriculum process. I've just developed a new math curriculum for my own staff. I found that my elementary school teachers were very uncomfortable teaching mathematics and very poor at doing it. It was primarily because they themselves had had lousy experiences in math. I find that important. If teachers have had bad experiences themselves, you've got to do a lot of in-service with them to enable them to become successful in those areas. I went through each of five curriculum outlines from various countries and said, "What do these people want kids to know by the time they finish grade six?" I actually could reduce those systems to five areas of concern. They wanted the kids to know how to measure things. They wanted kids to know you could organize this world into sets of things. They wanted kids to know how to apply a whole bunch of mathematical procedures to these sets — multiply, add, subtract, and so forth. They wanted kids to know about time and money. That's it. That's what every curriculum wanted the kids to know. Now some started with sets and some started with measurement. They did it in different ways. It was the style of doing it that was different, not the content. I found absolutely no difference in the content between K and 6 in the math curriculum. When you get into the secondary level, it does get a little more complicated.

Standardized testing is a very big issue and very value-laden. Americans, as you well know, are very big on testing of all kinds. In Sweden, it's illegal. If you've got Swedish parents and you're testing their kids, you are hitting them in a very sore spot. We have spent the last five years convincing the people we're working with in Scandinavia that what we're doing is evaluation, not formalized American testing. If it was, we would be in trouble.

Teacher awareness

Major differences between teachers are in their training experiences, their dependence on textbooks or other systems, their knowledge of other educational systems and their world-view.

I find the issue of maps very interesting. My view of the world is that Australia is in the middle, because that's what the maps were like that I studied. I've been in the States for twenty-two years, but I still have this view of the world. Americans see the United States as being in the middle, and I'm sure the British see Britain in the middle. It's just the way we are, and it's no small issue.

Issues for Successful Cross-Cultural Planning

The more a curriculum is geared to a fact-oriented syllabus, the greater the problem in meeting the needs of a multicultural population. Textbooks are primarily fact oriented. If you remove the textbooks, you're going to have a very uptight bunch of parents as well as an uptight bunch of teachers.

This year the city of Lancaster, Pennsylvania removed textbooks from its system. I think that was very courageous, and I'm interested to see what happens. The first question from the teachers was, "What do we teach?" That's a very good question for teachers to ask. They very rarely ask that. Normally they just ask you at what page they should start. They have made no judgments whatsoever in terms of what should be in the curriculum.

The more dependence on curriculum decision-making by publishing companies (from Scott Foresman to A-Beka) the greater the risk of intercultural dissonance. The more you have a culturally weighted decision on curriculum made by publishing companies, the greater are your problems in terms of a multicultural population. Textbooks and materials should be chosen last in curriculum planning.

It's very interesting for me to watch local schools go about curriculum planning. What they do first is bring in all the publishing companies. They have this great room set up and all the publishing companies come in with their textbooks, and the teachers have a day off to go look at all of those materials. That's the process of curriculum planning. It's a catastrophe. Those teachers have absolutely no criteria to decide whether the material is good or not. It comes down to superficial issues by which they choose the curriculum.

I'm arguing for a concept-oriented curriculum, which I believe is a supra-cultural curriculum. We don't want to develop a curriculum that serves as the lowest common denominator. That's what textbook companies have done in the United States, and those texts don't even meet the needs of local communities. There's a real textbook crisis developing in the United States.

What we need is the framework of a curriculum that doesn't deny the individual differences of curriculum, but becomes a supra-curriculum organizing process. It turns curriculum differences into advantages.

If you happen to be an American administrator and you've got a bunch of Australians, you can be very tokenistic to those parents and say, "We value your curriculum. We're going to try to fit it in when we can." It's not going to sell. What you're saying is "This is what our program is, and we recognize that you're there and that you have a work to do, and it's sort of a pain, but we'll try to meet your needs."

The supra-curriculum makes the curriculum very exciting. It encourages integration. It is goal-oriented. It's motivating. It's a more efficient curriculum. It's more able to meet the special needs of missionary kids.

What you have in most missionary schools are high-achieving kids and then one or two kids that are really very normal but who are regarded as abnormal. They would be perfectly normal in grade three in South Kingston Elementary School, but the mission school teacher thinks, "What am I going to do with Charlie Brown? He's only reading at the grade three level in grade three." Even if he's reading at grade two level in grade three he's well within the norm. You've got to have a two grade level difference.

This curriculum has a built-in teacher growth process. I'm very interested in the issue of teacher burnout. Most of my teachers in my own school have been with me at least thirteen years. We are constantly involved in teacher training. We have a professional growth process going all the time. I take them to Europe with me. I send them to South Africa. We publish their materials. We are constantly working on curriculum. Every teacher, every six weeks, is in the curriculum planning process. The more complicated the kids they're working with, the more often I meet with them.

What Is a Conceptually-Based Curriculum?

Jerome Bruner's term *conceptually-based curriculum* refers to a network of inferences that grows out of the process of categorization.

For example, there's a factual set of statements. Australia has a history. Captain Cook discovered it in 1770, although Dutch explorers had touched part of the country. It was colonized in 1789 partly due to the loss of the American War of Revolution in 1776.

If you answer the question, "When was Australia discovered by Captain Cook?" you're either right or you're wrong. That's what a lot of curriculum orientation is. It's a set of factual information the kids are expected to know. I have problems with that as curriculum for any kid, let alone a multinational.

Move that into conceptual statements, the supra-curriculum. "All nations have a history." I need several illustrations to really develop that concept. I cannot generalize that all nations have a history from one example.

For a missionary school in Peru I would want to include Australia, the U.S., Sweden, and Peru, if I had those nationals. The combination is arbitrary. The supra-goal is for kids to understand that all nations have a history. If I ask you to give me the facts of the history of Denmark, and you can't, does that mean you had a lousy curriculum? Does that mean there's a whole body of knowledge you should have in your curriculum that you don't have? Of course not. If, however, I move to conceptual terms and say, "From your knowledge of anybody's history, what might be true of the history of Denmark?" then we can start talking. "There's a history of governmental change. There have probably been a series of wars. There has been a series of economic developments. There you have the conceptional level functioning. That's our goal. The greater the diversity, the more the possibilities for generalization.

"They were often discovered by explorers. Sometimes several explorers found the land at different times. The establishment of nations was often motivated by problems elsewhere." These are general statements. All I've done is take them from my factual statements and raise them to a higher level.

What I've got is a framework in which I've got to say, "What set of facts best illustrate and build this understanding for my kids?" If I've got a group of kids who happen to be Dutch, it makes sense to use that history to help illustrate that all nations have a history. It provides a process of categorization and a network of inferences.

For the purposes of discussion I chose Grade 8 in the United States, Form 2 in Australia, and Högstadiet, the higher grades in the Swedish curriculum. Most curriculum outlines require history of that particular nation to be taught at about this level. The content requirements are usually very general.

Sweden specifies the following guidelines (Läroplan för Grund-skolan, 1980):

> Something on historical sources and methods. Something on various historical ideas and concepts. Work and life in pre-industrial and industrialized society. (The issues of social democracy, very value-laden in the Scandinavian curriculum, are probably very uncomfortable for American conservative evangelicals to teach, but if those issues are not properly addressed, the needs of Scandinavian kids will not be met. Those kids are going to go back having some real problems understanding the ideological issues of Scandinavia.) Development from the middle 1700's in Scandinavia, in some leading world power and in some developing country: commerce, change, people, ideas.

One U.S. school has the following course outline (South Kingston Junior High School, Rhode Island, 1986-87):

> During the first quarter all students will study American History from 1900 to the present. The following mini-courses will be offered during the second, third and fourth quarter . . . . Consumer Economics, Civics, Career Education. (This overlaps, interestingly enough, with the Swedish curriculum.)

In most countries there are only guidelines in the curriculum. Teachers and schools have a great deal of latitude. I've tried to stay with the guidelines for the purposes of this workshop.

Course Development

When I go through this process with teachers, I push teachers to make the statements in sentence form. If a teacher says, "We could do industrialization," I say, "Fine. Give me a statement about industrialization." It's rough.

I find that it's helpful if in the conceptual statements there are quantifiers such as always, usually, never, all, most, some. You can't say "Captain Cook usually discovered Australia in 1770." Quantifiers push you to the larger level.

Look for shared ideas, not facts, in the data, to identify possible organizing concepts. When I looked at the three curriculum outlines, I had pre-industrial and industrial change in the Swedish and American curriculum. That was an idea I could latch onto and turn in to some conceptual statements.

At least three examples are usually necessary to develop the conceptual relationships.

Course outline

This is a possible course outline for a missionary school in Peru:

1. Changes in a nation's history are often most evident in its government and commerce/industry. (I gathered that idea from looking at both the U.S. and the Swedish curriculum. And then when I looked at medieval history I began to find that the same sort of thing took place.)
2. Such changes often are tumultuous and involve great discord.
3. Change may be motivated by new knowledge, new ideas, leadership, or causal events.
4. Similar change processes and motivation may have totally different results. (You may finish up with a republic or a constitutional monarchy.)

Teaching modules

We have forty weeks in our school year. We work on about six weeks per module of teaching. Here are three modules.

1. Commercial and industrial change

a. Medieval (the feudal system), eighteenth-century Swedish and U.S. economies were largely agrarian. (Compare the agrarian economies.)

b. The medieval feudal system changed largely because of the rise of the commercial middle class. (Marco Polo, Italian; the Lombards, Dutch; Calvin Swiss; etc.)

c. U.S. and Swedish nineteenth-century economies changed largely because of industrial revolutions (Reasons for industrialization, major inventions and inventors)

d. These changes brought hardships for people, often resulting in revolt and reform.

Both curriculum outlines wanted these topics included. There's value in comparing and contrasting.

2. Governmental change

a. Early governments were usually absolute monarchies, such as in medieval Europe.

b. The first changes were in the form of monarchy with parliamentary government, often brought about by force. (Magna Carta)

c. Some nations became constitutional monarchies. (Great Britain, Sweden.) How does it work?

d. Some nations rejected the monarchy and become constitutional republics. (U.S.) How does that work? (There's your civics program.)

Contrasting the two forms of government is a much better way for kids to organize that information than just trying to remind them how a bill passes the legislature.

3. Nations in change

a. What is the economy and government of Peru?

b. What are the similarities and differences between the constitutions of Peru, the U.S., Great Britain, and Sweden?

c. What do people have to know and be able to do to function well in a complex industrial constitutional society? (That gets back to your civics. It also gets into consumer education, and deals with a developing country.)

My teachers deliberately choose to teach something that they don't know anything about. It forces them to do research on it, and that keeps them from burning out.   Textbooks never did that for them.

Chaucer said, "And so I would teach.   And so I would learn."   I find the more my teachers are learning, the more excited they are as teachers.

Another course outline

I started with the Swedish curriculum which wanted the kids to know something about the sources of history and the views of history. It's a little higher level.

1. The history of nations involves an interaction between events, ideas, and people.
2. We know a great deal about history because:

   a. Events are recorded in various ways.

   b. People write about their ideas.

   c. The lives of people are recorded in many ways.

Teaching modules

1. How do we know about the medieval period of history?

   a. Documents: *The History of the English Church and People*, by Venerable Beade, (Penguin); *A Treasury of Early Christianity* (Mentor), a collection of early church documents, poems, and creeds. (I'm responding to grade eight kids. I don't want to have them sitting there listening to me. I want to have them digging in the documents. When we take our grade eight kids through the museum, we give them a page in which they have a set of things to be looking for. We do not take them through and sort of expose them to the museum.)

   b. Tapestries: The Bayeux Tapestry (*National Geographic*)

   c. Castles, churches, monuments, etc.

2. In similar way we study Sweden and the U.S. looking at the fact that the more recent the history the more complete the history and the more varied the resources. (When I gave my kids hundred-year-old documents from our school, they began to recreate the history of the school. They learned. That project taught them a great deal about historical sources.)

3. What are the recorded documents of history that affect the way I live? (Constitution, laws, charters, etc.)

4. Some records in literature (prose or poetry) add color to the facts of history. (Dickens.)

5. How do people view history?

   a. Random cause and effect. That's taught in most Western textbooks.

   b. Cyclical. It goes back to Mesopotamian or Canaanite views of history. That's why Abraham had so much trouble when he moved and why he had to go down to Egypt. He was cyclical in his training and God wanted him to be different in his historical view of the world. It's inherent in philosophical views of people like Spangler and Schopenhauer. It's in the writings of some historians such as Arnold Toynbee.

   c. Spiritualized. Cause and effect plus God. God is sovereign in history, and aren't we glad?

   d. Eschatological. I believe our kids should be trained to understand that they are eschatological. That's the lesson Abraham had to learn. There was only one event in history and he was moving toward that, the city whose builder and maker is God. Augustine picks that up nicely in *The City of God*. Jacques Ellul does in *The Meaning of the City*. You get some fantastic stuff that I'd love to see in a curriculum for kids that is eschatological in its view of history.

6. How does a view of history affect the way I live in this world, in this country, in this school, in this house?

How do you achieve this in a school?

It is a tough process. It's taken me twenty years to get my own school where I wanted it to be. Now when I go into a program, I do it over a period of one week. I go for one or two teachers that will take the risk and go with me on it, and eventually they become the resource for those who are more insecure.

That's what we've done in Scandinavia. I started in 1980 with the first week-long workshop with three teachers from each school for the deaf. We worked for three summers. They tried it the first year. Then they came back and we went through what worked and what didn't work and why. We patched it all up and they did the second year. By the third year they were feeling pretty confident. We used a lot of them to teach the next group of teachers that came through.

18

The School That Internationalizes – Reducing Limitations on the Gospel

Ted Ward
Trinity Evangelical Divinity School

There really isn't any such thing as a perfect school. All schools are defective, but your task as an educator is to make a defective environment somewhat less defective. There are three alternative views of what a school is for.

Purposes of a School

To serve kids

Many institutional educators will tell you the most important thing that a school does is to serve kids. You find a tremendous amount of emphasis, especially with the American-style school, on basically a kid-centered approach to education. They are concerned with the needs of kids, the development of kids, the future of kids, and the perceptions of kids. All of that is fine. The only problem is that as a frame of reference, it's not quite large enough. But it is characteristic of much that we think of as American education.

To serve parents

Now, overseas schools are to some extent different in that they have another strongly developed notion of their purpose. They tend to see themselves in business to serve parents. I ask people what the purpose of their school is, and quite often missionary educators, mission boards, and people working in such school environments, will tell me that one of the major things they're concerned about is making it possible for the parents to be missionaries. In other words, they take the responsibility for ministering to those children in order that the

129

parents can minister to the purposes of the gospel. We also find this, interestingly, in the overseas dependent schools of the Department of Defense and in the international schools.

Overseas parents tend to develop a kind of paranoia about their children. There's an anxiety that is very common among Americans overseas. There's a tremendous preoccupation about the possibility that the kids are going to be harmed by the experience. The parents are overseas making big bucks for the oil company or doing God's work in the mission field, but they are not sure that God really wanted their kids out there. I always find this a very interesting view of God—kind of a schizophrenic God. He wants the parents out there but somehow isn't quite big enough to cope with the problem of the kids being out there. Therefore the parents have a guilt thing that says, "In order to do what God wants me to do, I end up feeling guilty about the part that God hasn't spoken to me about."

In a secular society, I understand it largely in terms of the good old American habit of buying insurance. If you can't be sure of something, buy insurance. If you really can't be sure that you're doing the right thing by your kids, you buy insurance. You buy insurance by paying insurance premiums to an American school. The American school gives you a kind of policy on your kid that says, "When this kid is ready to repatriate, he'll make it." There's a kind of insurance policy mentality among some missionaries also, which quite often works against educational values.

One of the things that we educators sometimes do is default on our responsibility. As I see it, our whole responsibility is to develop people, not simply to pander to the whims and emotions of parents. We have responsibilities to the educational process and to the community that are larger than just those obligations to parents.

In the United States, parents don't pay directly for public education; they pay taxes. When we find ourselves working in the private sector, we tend to use what I think of as a department store mentality that says you've really got to make sure you please the customers. The customers are the people who pay those insurance policies.

Notice I'm beginning to tie together those two metaphors now. You have people who are paying money on insurance to a big department store. The people in that department store run it as if their customers were always right. That's a good notion if you happen to be in business, but school people can get blown over by this. On the one hand, there is a terrible problem if we ignore the interests and concerns of parents and kids. On the other hand, there is a terrible problem if we pander to those instincts and feelings.

I find quite often the school people will take the anxiety of the parent and play to it by saying, "Let us take a look at this. We'll help with that. Then you won't have to worry about it." As a matter of fact, what we ought to do is sit that parent down and say, "Now look. What you're talking about is really not that different than what everybody who has a girl or boy that age runs into, and here's how you have to cope with it."

One of the problems that has beset the missionary schools in the last few years is a very young faculty. Of all the overseas international schools, the missionary schools tend to have the youngest faculty. They tend to have faculty people who are in their first, second, third, or fourth years of teaching and who often do not have enough know-how, experience, and moxie to know what life is all about. Therefore it becomes very easy for them to be sucked right into that department-store syndrome.

To serve society

There's a third purpose of education, which we have to think about as a late-century rediscovery. Early in this century, one of the concerns in American education was the place of schooling in a free society. In that era, the emphasis on individual differences and the new testing movement that came out of World War I made it possible to think of kids as individual units. They began thinking more in terms of a child-centered curriculum. In that particular period of debate and philosophical discussion, some of the strongest positions advocated, and some of the clearest and sanest, pointed out that in the final analysis schools have to serve societies. It is not good enough simply that schools serve kids or that schools serve parents. There are bigger questions.

In various societies schools are allowed to serve organizations, political organizations, or world-views. Generally in a democracy, education is asked to serve the world-view. The building of a democratic society by preparing people through schooling to cope and competently function in a democratic world is the whole notion behind the American educational system. But it is very difficult in today's curriculum and in most of the ethos of American education today to find much of a clear-cut residue of that commitment to a free society. Instead, schooling has become largely a kind of service station, simply pumping out whatever gas is currently the fad.

Now let me consider with you the possibility that a missionary school has an organization to serve; it has political entities to serve; and it has world-views to serve. I think you have to make some choices here. Ultimately you have to ask the question, are we serving a society or parents or kids? What is our priority?

Serving the Kingdom Society

I would argue that the business of being in a Christian community and developing Christian competencies in persons is really a world-view issue. The Christian school can do nothing if it is not doing the job of developing a Christian world-view. That is a far bigger task than simply teaching an odd assortment of courses and calling it a kind of curriculum. If we are to take our responsibilities seriously, then, we must raise the question of the purpose of the school. Are we there merely to serve kids? Are we there merely to serve parents? Or, is ours a responsibility of serving a very particular kind of society, the kingdom society, and through that society to serve the world to which it has been called to minister?

I would like to suggest that this service of society, the Christian perspective with a Christian world-view at its center, could easily become one of the consequences of this new enthusiasm about looking at the missionary community and about looking at the missionary educational problem and about looking at the missionary kid. I hope we have in the making a late-century rediscovery of the importance of focussing our educational effort on the development of a Christian world-view so that we are serving not simply the kids, and not simply the parents, but we are serving the church of Jesus Christ in ways that are transcendent to those matters of individual service.

Now, that may seem a little bit exotic, but let me give you some propositions so that you will know where I'm coming from. I view the gospel as an intercultural reality in this world, capable of being experienced in any culture. It seems to me that one of the great contrasts between Christianity and, for example, Islam is that in order to cope with Islam as a series of religious claims, one must first embrace a great deal of the culture of the Islamic society. In other words, you cannot cleanly separate Islam from the Islamic culture. There was a period of time when many people behaved that way about Christianity. They made it seem as though you had to see Christ the way a Westerner would. You had to see Christ through the grid of Western culture. I think by now we're smart enough to know that never was necessary.

The gospel is intercultural. It is capable of being experienced in many cultures. The missionary task is international. I shift the term deliberately there. The missionary task is not uniquely American, or British, or German, or whatever. It never was. But unfortunately much of the missionary task has been interwoven with colonialism. Most of us don't like to think of missions this way, because this was never really the motive of the missionary. The missionary task is international, not colonial. That leads me to a conclusion: the whole support system for the missionary community should internationalize, not colonize.

I would argue that for missionary schools to retain a colonial posture in an internationalizing era is strictly anachronistic. In other words, it just doesn't make good sense. It is inappropriate. "But," you say, "our major purpose is to repatriate Americans into the American context." I submit to you that most Americans are growing up in contexts that are much more international than are many American communities overseas. That's something you don't want to lose sight of. I was in Chicago the other day in a Lutheran elementary school where with only sixty-eight kids, they have twenty-four national origins represented. American kids are confronting this to a greater extent than the missionary community is aware of, partly because the missionary community in the United States is largely recruited from suburban churches. The only clear-cut place of monocultural hang-out in the North American social enterprise today is in selected suburbs—not all suburbs. For example, in the Chicago area, we have some ethnic suburbs that are distinctly Slavic. The whole suburb is made up of five or six Slavic nationalities. These people hold to themselves.

But you find the Bible churches in the white Anglo-Saxon Protestant suburbs. That's where you find the missionary recruiting effort, and that's why missionaries still have this image of America as dominantly white Anglo-Saxon Protestant. This is not the case. In fact even in the United States, the Catholics are out-evangelizing the Protestants better than two to one, and we think of ourselves as being missionary minded. The new handbook on North American missionary statistics by MARC, shows that out of sixteen nations that are in the sending-of-missionaries business in the Western nations, Europe and North America, the United States is number twelve. Many of us have this fancy image of ourselves as being somewhere at the top. We rank just behind Spain.

Home, school, and community, should work hand in hand towards building the multiple identities that add up to a truly free, or liberating education. I am constantly impressed, distressed, and sometimes infuriated by the tremendous emphasis on liberal arts education in the Christian community. Liberal arts does not refer to liberal in the sense of theological tradition, but liberal in the sense of freeing, liberating. I maintain that if we can get schools and homes and communities working together overseas, they can build in young people those multiple identities that really add up to a liberal education. In other words, why don't we, for Heaven's sake, quit fretting about repatriation as our big issue? Let us work on confident personhood through the educational process. We have a truly intercultural education possibility in the overseas environment. I can get very, very eloquent about this. In fact I can get so romantic about it that people are quite sure I am unrealistic. Be that as it may, my unreality stems from a concern that much of what is currently happening would have to be called poor education.

Current Poor Education

Our schools both overseas and in the U.S. are doing a terrible job, in the sense of creating a learning impairment called ethnocentrism. If one is ethnocentric, one is thereby reduced in capability for appreciating.

Where does ethnocentrism come from? Like the Rodgers and Hammerstein song from *The King and I* says, "It has to be taught." But nobody admits teaching it. How does it get taught? It is being taught, not by direction but by default. We must deal with that.

Secondly, we must deal with the very natural outcome of fear. Anything that is different inherently inspires fear. The reason we live in a society that is so full of hostility, hate, and anger is simply because people have not had help with fear. International, intercultural education can deal with fear in a much more constructive way than is typical in American and much of Western education.

Third, superiority syndromes of various sorts. The notion, for example, that our way is the best way, is not being taught directly but informally. If there are any tensions, we attack others who are different. That kind of a posture does no particular credit to the cause of Christ.

We're talking about humanity, and we've got to get off this horse that our way is better. This is absolutely inexcusable in the name of Jesus Christ. And yet it is done.

One of the gravest tragedies is the number of children who are exposed to teachers who are in culture shock. I know of no sector of missionary society other than the school teachers (except perhaps the MDs), who are exempted from the orientation, the preparation, and the honest-to-goodness thinking through of culture that is characteristic of the more up-to-date missions today. And we turn those teachers loose on our kids!

I know of school teachers who have moved into American school situations overseas having been recruited to go to the field less than one month earlier, having arrived less than one week before the first day of classes, and being in total disarray in terms of how to get the electricity turned on in their apartment. One of the first things they talked about in school on the first day with all those kids was, "How do you ever put up with this place?"

Another thing that's learned is isolation. This can be overcome. We can help people relate. As a matter of fact, I find MKs, for the most part, a very healthy lot and quite often much less prone to isolation than Americans in general. I think we ought to capitalize on that and make it stronger yet. So much of what we do in the MK environment is not deliberate, but is allowed to accrue coincidentally with getting on with our school teaching business.

Planning for Education

When I talk about educational planning, I think in terms of three sectors of the educational process that exist in any society: formal education, non-formal education, and informal education.

Formal education is the schooling process. Usually this process of education is justified by arguing that fulfillment of•one phase makes you eligible for another phase. You ask a kid in the fifth grade why he's going to school, and he says, "How else do you get to sixth grade?" The justification for fifth grade is in terms of eligibility for sixth grade. The justification for junior high is in terms of eligibility for senior high. The justification for senior high is (and here is where the overseas schools are particularly vulnerable) largely in terms of "This is the way you get eligible to go to college." Never mind that not all go to college. Never mind that not all ought to be thinking in those terms. Nevertheless that's the way we justify it, because formal educators tend to think in terms of eligibility in the system, not in terms of the value of knowledge.

Non-formal education is much more functionally oriented. Generally it is focussed on deliberately planned events that are educative, but are not part of that larger structure that we think of as the formal school. For example, most of what we do in the church as Christian education is in fact not formal education. Stylistically it may look a lot that way. We bring kids into Sunday Schools and sit them down and put a teacher label on somebody and stand them up and make the information flow. It is a school type of activity, but the kids aren't getting anything they can carry to the educational bank and cash it in for eligibility for something else. The non-formal sector, then, is deliberate and planned, but not required in the same way that societies require their formal educative processes.

The informal sector is that which is really not planned, though it is elaborated in the process of living. Most of us have learned the single most complex electroprocessing skill rather well by about the age of four or five—first language—speaking, hearing one's own mother tongue. That's learned altogether in the informal sector. No one sets aside certain times of the day to teach kids in a non-formal way. We do that with swimming. We say, "I'm going to teach you to swim this summer." But we don't do that with language.

What can we do as schools?

Language. In the formal curriculum there is probably nothing more significant that a school can do than help kids in language. I am advocating the national language as a standard part of the curriculum. If we're really serious about internationalizing intercultural education, we certainly ought to be taking seriously the language education capabilities. Nothing grieves me more than seeing people learn a language that is not the national language while ignoring the national language. In Ecuador, Spanish can be learned much faster and more effectively if it is simply turned loose. French can be added as a third language. If there's anything research on language shows us, it's that the second language is the problem language. The third, fourth, and fifth are the easy ones. If you really want a child to learn French in a Spanish-speaking country, teach him Spanish and then teach him French.

History and geography. Americans have homogenized this to the general idea of social studies, and have lost the specifics of history and geography in the shuffle. It is a sad thing for a person to come out of a childhood in a country and not be able to tell me anything about that country except a few casual things he's picked up through a little bit of vacation travel. Something systematic in history and geography certainly is appropriate from the elementary years on.

The arts. Give them something in music, poetry, and plastic arts, even with very young children, to help them see the validity of other cultural forms.

World-view. I think an internationalized school should have a multinational faculty, preferably one that is not paid on a two-salary schedule, which tends to demean people, no matter where you do it, no matter why you do it. People are beginning to catch on to that little trick. The idea of exalting people to make them worthy to be teachers is one of the best things that a school administration can do to show that you respect people of the national culture. I can take you to some very large American schools overseas where the children only see national persons serving in menial roles—no professional roles, no roles with any particular stature or dignity. The school is not helping the children understand that there is something to be learned from a national.

Further, teachers can be helped by being trained as culture teachers. In some of our work at Michigan State, we have tried to produce a kind of culture orientation for teachers in general. It can be done, and it does pay good dividends.

In the non-formal sector there can be events that involve the community at large—sports, arts, and cultural exchange.

In the social area there ought to be, among a Christian community and within a Christian school, the deliberate seeking out of ways we can involve ourselves with the very people we claim to be involved with in the love of Jesus Christ. It is one thing to be called to be a missionary because God so loved the world. It is quite a different thing to be so isolated from those very people as a child that one does not see how to make those two ideas click. Ultimately it plays back into the child's consciousness, so that quite often by the time of adolescence, kids really begin to wonder if their parents are serious about this whole notion of the love of Jesus Christ.

These are tough matters to get at, but it's worthwhile to attack and deal with them. I am very positive about missionary kid education. But I am very distressed at some of the things I find us willing to settle for. We should have a much greater view of our potential in the service of Jesus Christ in this world.

19

Effective Educational Ministry through Cultural Diversity

David A. Wells
Wesleyan Academy, Puerto Rico

Mission and other Christian schools have unprecedented opportunity to minister to constituencies which are heterogeneous culturally and linguistically. In a number of areas around the world the missionary community has diminished, and the missionary schools are being used increasingly by nationals and other non-missionary expatriates. Other established schools are choosing to broaden their ministry to a more diverse constituency while some new schools are being developed with the express purpose of serving the national and international community as a missionary or evangelistic outreach.

The educational program in a culturally diverse situation should not seek to create an environment or culture for the children in their school, but rather assist them to adapt, adjust and become involved, and learn how to function effectively in both their home/base and national environments.

I am talking about a school that incorporates diversity in a healthy, positive and effective way. We all face this kind of diversity to some extent no matter where we grow up and no matter where we study.

Just a bit of background about my situation. Our school was designed for national students, but one of the very positive by-products of our program is the fact that we're able to effectively serve the missionary community as well.

There are a number of very significant cultural adjustments that all individuals have to make when they're in a bicultural or a multicultural community. It's not our desire to try to make everyone the same. Our desire is to maintain the positive aspects of diversity, in

138

order that we might broaden horizons and better contribute to the individual, rather than create some artificial situation for elementary and secondary study.

I'm not talking about right versus wrong. I'm talking about differences. When I walk down the hallway in my school in Guaynabo and I walk by a classroom that's taught by a teacher who came from Kansas, I have one particular cultural environment there that those students are adapting to. In the next classroom is a lady who came from Cuba about thirty-five years ago. She is very Latin, very set in her cultural ways. There's a completely different cultural environment in that classroom. One of our teachers is an immigrant from Scotland—a completely different environment.

This situation offers a richness and stimulus to our students that is difficult to duplicate in other situations. We aren't creating for them a cultural setting which will make them comfortable at all times, but we are seeking to work with them in making the adjustments to be able to live in and function in different cultural environments.

Areas of Cultural Difference

A number of areas that quickly come to the forefront as you're trying to work with individuals from different cultural backgrounds are:

Interaction. Language is vitally important. Language is generally one of the first battlefields for a North American student coming into a national school. Often young people believe that if they can resist the language, then somehow they will not have to adapt.

Nonverbal communication is very significant. If my teacher from Kansas is talking to a student and correcting that student, unless she's sensitive and aware of the cultural baggage that student brings into the classroom, she may say, "Look at me. I'm talking to you." When I correct my son I want to make sure he's looking at me, because I want to make sure that he's catching what I'm saying, and I want to see his reaction. If I force one of my Puerto Rican students to look at me, what I'm doing is forcing him to give me a message of defiance, because in the Puerto Rican culture, to look the authority in the eye is an indication of defiance.

Territoriality. Proxemics is the differences of individual personal space that we require. Many have suggested that Americans require a distance of somewhere between eighteen inches and thirty inches of personal space. "That belongs to me. You stay out of it unless we have an intimate relationship." If someone violates that space we react.

When we returned to the States for the first time after being in Puerto Rico, we quickly discovered we weren't adept at adjusting from one cultural setting to another. We acted as we had learned to act in the Puerto Rican culture and had people backing away from us. The first time I embraced and kissed one of my high school friends that I wasn't intimate with in any sense, the reaction on her face about made me turn around and leave because I was so embarrassed. I hadn't learned to live in both cultures, I had adjusted to the Puerto Rican culture but hadn't recognized that I had to be sensitive in stepping back into the U.S. culture.

Haptics is the style of touching. I'm sure if you watched Ecuadorian young people as they come to school in the morning and counted the number of times that you observe personal contact between the students and then went to a high school in the United States, Canada, or Western Europe and counted, you would find a significant difference. The embracing, the touching, some of it very overt, some of it very unconscious, is an expression of culture.

Association. The way groups and organizations are formed is significantly different depending on the culture we're working with.

Subsistence. The food that's eaten. Primarily we have two cultures represented, the North American and the Puerto Rican community. You can imagine the difficulty in trying to serve the tastes and the needs of these students in a cafeteria setting.

Sexuality. What's acceptable and what isn't acceptable in terms of roles.

Temporality. One difference that stands out the most to me as we look at the cultural aspects of our school is the difference between our Anglo monochronic culture and the Latin polychronic culture. For those of us who are Anglos, we are accustomed to dealing with one thing at a time. We function best that way.

I studied at the Interamerican University in Puerto Rico. I was the only North American in a class of Puerto Rican graduate students. There was so much circular communication taking place. There were so many things going on at the same time that I would leave the classroom dizzy. The teacher would present something and if one of my neighbors didn't get it, they wouldn't respond to the teacher. They would respond to their classmates, and you would have these little discussion groups going on until everyone was back together, and then they would jump back in with the teacher. There is a significant difference between being one-at-a-time and being able to handle this type of communication.

Do we start the Parent-Teacher Organization meeting at 7:30 when it was announced, or do we announce it for 7:30 so that we can begin at 8:00? We have to be conscious of these differences. Our elementary principal is a Puerto Rican lady. She announced that the program for kindergarten through second grade was going to start at 7:30 American time. (I try to avoid saying Puerto Rican time/American time because that can be offensive.) She started at 7:30. The kindergarten finished, sat down, and in walked some parents with their kindergarten youngsters ready to be part of the program. Their part was already finished. Decisions have to be made with culture in mind.

Learning styles. There are a number of different ways people learn effectively. Culture also affects how we learn.

Dealing with Cultural Diversity in the School

How do we make cultural diversity a positive experience without creating a third culture or fourth culture? We have to establish a philosophy and objectives. Who is it that we want to serve? What is it we're trying to accomplish? Too often our programs develop and then we go back and figure out why we're doing what we're doing.

Our school was established for the sake of serving the national community. We recognized that not only was there service to the national community, but there was also significant service to kids who were there because of their parents' assignment in Puerto Rico, whether missions, business, or government. We are seeking to serve both of those communities in what we consider to be a richer, more stimulating environment. Another focus of our program is college preparation. We're seeking to prepare students in English and Spanish to be able to function equally well in the two languages.

We need to be sure that what we say we are, is really what we are. If we say we're going to serve the national community and the mission community, and if we establish our goals, then we need to be looking for the program which will best accomplish that.

One of our greatest difficulties, especially with the diversity within the faculty and staff is that of unity. Puerto Rican teachers are on one side during lunch; the ones from the Midwest are in another part. Unity is very difficult, but how are we going to communicate to the students what we want to communicate to them, if we don't display the kind of unity that Scripture talks about between believers? It's not easy to have unity without expecting one group to conform to the other.

My premise is that it can be done, and it doesn't require that we give up our distinctives culturally in order to be united.   I feel that there's a real need, not only in our cross-cultural situations, but also in our church, mission and parachurch organizations to make sure that we're displaying to the people we serve the kind of unity that we're teaching with our words.   However, as we do that, we need to be careful to maintain the distinctives that give the richness and the health to our program in diversity.

One thing that must be established are central principles to which everyone is committed.   I'm not talking about cultural principles.   I'm talking about principles that we can all grab hold of and say, "Yes, that's why we're here.   That's what we are."

We have a broad range of cultural backgrounds in our school. But if we took away all of the Puerto Ricans and all of the Cubans and the people from Europe and left just the Americans, we would still have exactly the same problem.   Someone from New England, the teacher from Atlanta, the ones from the Midwest, and someone from California – all come from different schools.   We all have different philosophies of education; we all have different methods we feel most comfortable with.   But we have to play by the same rules.

I heard a tape a number of years ago done by Dr. Henry Brandt in which he compared an overseas school to an orchestra.   Before the conductor comes out everyone is warming up on their own instrument.   They're playing in different keys.   Everyone is doing their own thing in their own way, getting ready.   But when that conductor comes out and taps with his baton, everything quiets down.   Then he raises his arm to begin; everyone plays a different instrument, but it all fits together into a beautiful piece.

That's what I see us doing as we seek to minister in cultural diversity.   We all have our own distinctives, but they're put together in such a way that we're representing unity, purpose, and direction. Then the student is able to accept and gain the richness from each of these different areas.

Every classroom in our situation, reflects a distinct culture.   I believe that we underestimate the ability of young people to make adjustments to expectations in the classroom.   If you recall your school years, you know that within a class period you basically knew what that teacher expected, what you could get away with, what you couldn't get away with, at what point the teacher would put a brake on things. You adjusted, right? You knew the expectations of the teachers whether they stated them or not. As soon as you got back your first quiz, you knew basically what the teacher was looking for. We all adjust. When we hold students back and say, "We have to offer them a situation which will conform from one classroom to the next, that will conform to the situation that they know in their home," we're underestimating their ability to make adjustments. They are very capable. A young person can abide by the expectations and fit into the cultural environment of that Kansan's classroom, and walk next door into the classroom of the Cuban or the Puerto Rican teacher and adjust.

There are different ages at which it's more difficult for young people to make those adjustments. To bring a seventh grader into a program like this is much more difficult than putting a four or five-year old into that type of program.

Unity does not mean that everyone will think, act, and react in the same way. Spiritual unity, which we're seeking to present to our students, involves using biblical principles in dealing with obstacles and problems. It's not an easy situation. But diverse temperaments, qualities, and culturally-based characteristics of different people can be yoked in common harmony. This is the hallmark of the successful Christian institution, whether we're talking cross-cultural or not.

The three most important ingredients for a successful program are the student, the teacher, and the amount of time you give them together. We do need to be conscious of having culturally compatible materials and methods. To import textbooks on the history of Puerto Rico, or to use social studies materials that have been prepared in Mexico doesn't work. You have to be conscious of these cultural things in selection of methods and materials. There are times when you're going to have to compromise.

Language learning is vitally important. There are times when mainstreaming a young child into the Spanish phase of the program is most functional. There are other times when we have a fourth or fifth grader who comes in and is not prepared because of his own disposition or ability to be mainstreamed into a Spanish program. They may need remedial work and help and preparation to be brought up to level in the language.

We also work in English as a second language for our Puerto Rican students. It is vital in moving the Puerto Rican student from the Spanish curriculum into the English curriculum.

Lessons need to be explained in terms of the known. We need to be conscious that the student is not going to be able to fit examples and illustrations into their store of knowledge unless they have something to attach them to. It's been said that children faced with culturally incompatible material may respond to factual questions, yet fail to use higher-level skills such as making predictions or inferences from the information. You make fewer mistakes if the information is culturally compatible.

Effective learning only takes place when the teacher understands and handles the dynamics of intercultural and interpersonal relations in the classroom. This is a problem in the States. It is also a problem in our MK schools, and it's especially a problem in the type of school that's seeking to serve both communities.

The classroom must respect a student's identity and support his sense of self-worth. If the intent is to make that North American missionary kid into a Puerto Rican, then you're not going to be effective, because he is not a Puerto Rican. We have a family in our school who has sought to make their children Puerto Rican. All of them were born in Puerto Rico, but their home is North American. The parents in their halting Spanish have made the children speak Spanish in their home. If you want to meet some mixed-up kids, talk to them. They've adjusted in different ways, but they lack their own culture. Those who are respected in terms of their home base community and yet adapt to and function effectively and contribute in the other culture turn out to be very well adjusted. Students coming from this type of situation do not face significant adjustment problems as they go to the States for the first time — or as they return to the States in the case of our North American students. They haven't been catered to by an environment created for them, but rather they've learned to live in and be part of another culture.

The Student

If we can put students in a context where they can comfortably learn to live and adapt in two or more cultures, they will gain tremendous perspective. They will broaden their cultural background or cultural literacy and have greater potential in terms of their academic work and their future orientation as they enter a career.

Culture provides the schemata for making inferences. If we have a broader background, then we're better able to fit things in the right place.

One of the very difficult areas for the North American young person in this type of situation is that of being held back and not making significant relationships within the other culture. I think it's a terrible failure on our part to have a child live for eighteen years in another cultural setting and never develop close relationships in that other setting.

We need to understand that every student, whether it's the Latin student in our program or the North American student, is going to face some type of conflict. Every student as they live or work in another culture is going to face conflict. If we try to pretend that won't happen or pull back as soon as it does happen, instead of preventing the conflict or the adjustment problem, we prolong it.

The Family

Don't protect your child from differences. Don't look at differences as being wrong. When a North American parent comes into my office and says, "This teacher expects such-and-such, and that isn't right. I don't want my child in that class," instead of helping his child make the adjustment, he is trying to cut him off. "It hurts; it's hard; it's different. So forget it!" No. We need to help the students adjust.

It's often very difficult for parents to do that because especially the North American parents moving into the situation are going through adjustments themselves. They want to protect their child. They don't want him to face that hurt and pain. The home is one of the primary factors in a good adjustment. That's true of our Puerto Rican students and their adjustment in the school setting and their adjustment to North American and Cuban teachers. And it's true of the North American students.

Young people are much better equipped to make these adjustments than adults are. Kids adapt if we support and encourage them in the proper way.

We have to recognize the positive and the negative aspects of whatever educational program we're putting our children into. We need to look at the positive aspects and seek to maximize them, and we need to take the negative and seek in every way possible to minimize them. The attitude and direction taken by the adults will very often make the difference as to whether or not the young person can make the adjustment.

I came across this piece written by David Augsburger:[1]

If I Hope to Live With No Differences

When variations in thinking,
differences in feeling,
contrasts in perspective,
conflicts in behaving,
are all seen as threat,
or viewed as betrayal,
or treated as rebellion

Disagreement is seen as disrespect
differing is viewed as rejecting;
so we must claim agreement,
be adaptable and compliant,
even if we have to fake it
Since (beware)
DIFFERENCES ARE DANGEROUS
(Let's hope we can always agree.)

Let the hope die.

The natural variety of viewpoints,
diversity in preferences,
contrasts in perspectives,
uniqueness of persons,
are to be prized,
are to be enhanced,
are to be celebrated.
Variety and diversity
complete us, fulfill us.
Since (beware) —
DIVERSITY IS DESIRABLE

---

[1]*When Enough is Enough* by David Augsburger.   Copyright 1984, Regal Books, Ventura, CA 93006. Used by permission.

Conclusion

One of the severe dangers we face in our situation is related to our expectations.

So often the acquisition of right knowledge, right beliefs, and right actions, is all culturally based for us. What is the right knowledge? What are right beliefs? If we look carefully, we'll find many of our beliefs aren't really structured directly on biblical principles, but rather on a subculture we've developed for ourselves. What is the right action? It may differ with cultural settings. But I may think mine is right because that's the way it's always been for me. We need to be very careful of this.

We have the opportunity to be involved with these young people as they develop into the people that God wants them to be, not what we impose upon them.

20

Different Culture, Different Perspective, Different Curriculae, One Campus

Dennis Vogan and Rosemary Foster
Faith Academy, Manila

Vogan: Faith Academy, though it is a predominantly U.S. school, is nevertheless international. We are trying to think more international as we move ahead in different areas. We believe that in order to accommodate and provide for the needs of children coming from the United Kingdom, we need to provide a quality program. In 1981-82 we ventured into a very small, very trial-oriented program. It has not only survived, but it has done very well. We have had students take the O-level exam in seven areas, and they have done surprisingly well. The board made a recent decision to expand our present program. The British parents in OMF in Asia have unanimously agreed to bring all of their children onto the field within the next three years. That will mean that our O-level program will triple in size from eighteen students today to about fifty-five.

Americans and United Kingdom people have the same skin color, and we all speak a language called English. Yet beyond those similarities, everything else does seem to be different. We are finding that it is much easier to discuss differences with our Filipino friends because we take it for granted that there are differences. We have to qualify, quantify, define, make sure that we don't cross any cultural taboos in order to communicate with them. However, people from the United States and the U.K. leap into curricular discussions and planning, talking about educational philosophies, and we find that we have many problems. We have taken it for granted that we all share a common experience. That's not true. We have found that on occasion we have had to back a few steps away from the nitty-gritty of curriculum development or philosophy and define different things about ourselves so that we can communicate better with one another.

148

Another fact that needs to continually be repeated as we work with one another is that one culture is not better than another. Our Filipino government permit to operate, states that we are not providing a better education for expatriate students, but we are providing a different education to enable expatriate MKs to move back into their home culture. As we work together with people from different countries on our campus, we need to be very careful that we never use the term *better* or *not as sophisticated* or other terms that would give the idea that one is superior to the others. We are finding on our own campus that our U.S. curriculum is being enhanced because we are being stretched in areas that as Americans we have never considered before.

Foster: I think there has to be a willingness to understand and appreciate each other. I can't speak highly enough of the way we funny Brits have been accepted by our American colleagues at Faith Academy. I would say that is almost half the battle. When you have good relationships with people, then you can talk about your differences in educational philosophy. There are differences.

I think it would be fair to say our system (and you could probably add your Australian and New Zealand Commonwealth system) works like a pyramid. All start together, but our aim is to knock people off as they go up. It is an elitist system. In the old days in Britain, the first knocking off came at the age of eleven when you took an exam. Then you were either set for the academic course or you were a no-gooder and went to a general secondary school. They have tried to cut that out in most areas now.

I remember always being told at school that it is only the top ten percent who go to university. You cannot go to university by right, but only if chosen. The American system, as far as I can see, is much broader.

I met an American colleague from Wheaton when I was in Indonesia. We were doing language study. She said, "I don't think I could cope in your British system."

I said, "I don't think I could cope in your American one. I'm all right on one, two, or three subjects that I'm going to do on A-levels, but don't you ask me about anything else. I don't know a thing. My education and understanding are narrow."

She has a very, very broad understanding of many subjects. She would say she hadn't got the depth. That's debatable, but that's the general line.

The one time I almost came to blows with my American colleague was when we were both sitting exams for class. My exam said things like, "In three sentences explain such-and-such," and hers said, "Jerusalem is the capitol of _____." I said, "That's silly."

She said, "Of course it's not silly. That's the way we do it." It's a totally different way of testing. Ours rely on essay writing.

I was learning. I can see the Lord was preparing me years ago to come into an American system. If we can understand where we're coming from, it helps a lot.

Our grading is also different. In the American system maybe A will be 96 to 100. When I would give a test, a student would say, "Mrs. Foster, what do we have to get to make an A?"

I'd say, "I don't know what you've got to get. I must see your marks first." We work on a system where if the top mark is 85, then we will make that our A. We grade on the curve with relation to our peers. I used to get mad with my students. Now I realize they were coming from a different educational philosophy.

There is a difference too in how we agree with each other, how we work together harmoniously.

We had an in-service for teachers, and we had a visiting lecturer. She made one or two statements that some of us were not happy with. So we stood up and queried her. We later realized that we had offended her. It has since been explained to me that in American thinking, you have to agree on everything to be harmonious. When we, in a faculty meeting, query something that the high school principal says, that doesn't lessen his authority for us. But we feel that we can discuss, and there can be some give and take. He's still our principal. We are still under his authority, but we do feel that we can question and query for further amplification.

Vogan: The O-level is the ordinary level system. The equivalent to that would be grades nine and ten in the U.S. system.

The O-levels must precede the A-levels for British children if they choose to go on in their education. There are qualifying examinations that the student needs to have passed in order to move up.

If he does not pass a certain number with a certain grade, then A-levels would not be an opportunity. He could branch out into other kinds of schools.

Foster: The maximum O-levels that we can take at Faith Academy are eight — English language, English literature, maths, French, integrated science, religious education, geography, history. One of our sources of distress is that the musical kids cannot fit any kind of music into that timetable. They cannot do PE, which in a British school they could do. Our biggest problem at Faith Academy is time tabling.

We are on a daily schedule, while our average British school works on a weekly schedule which gives time for general music and general PE.

Vogan: The O-level content is different from our American content. That's something that I think we need to understand very clearly. Everything that the student learns during the course of two years of study is evaluated at the end of that two-year period, and though that student may be getting graded by quarter or by semester in our Faith Academy system, his ability to continue in education within the British system is dependent on his O-level examination score.

The structure is very rigid. The teacher does not have the opportunity to launch out into areas where she or he is able to assess where the students are faltering, or perhaps into an area where she has an interest or greater expertise. They must follow the syllabus that is given to them in order to prepare the students to sit that examination. It is very different from our American system.

We rotate on a three-year cycle revising all our American courses. We rewrite the curriculum. That is not the case in the British system. That system is dictated to the teachers, and they must follow it.

Let me go over three areas of change from the General Certificate of Education (GCE) to the General Certificate of Secondary Education.

The new General Certificate of Secondary Education (GCSE) program is to include what used to be the GCE and the British O-level program. In other words, the lower-level students and the O-level students will have one syllabus and sit one examination.

There will be standardized examinations that will be given to the students throughout the two-year course of study. Where the O-level scores have been entirely dependent on the sitting of the examination, the GCSE program is allowing about forty percent of the final score to be evaluated throughout the course of two years. They believe this will be a more honest approach to evaluating the entire population taking these courses.

I am seeing that the GCSE program is moving in the American direction in terms of allowing student participation to be a factor in evaluation. I have also seen the U.S. moving more into standardized examinations. It seems that the two different countries are moving towards one another in small areas, but I think it's significant philosophically. That's important especially as we think about overseas missionary schools. We need to do what's best for our students, and the way we do that is by understanding better what each system is made up of.

Foster: The American biology teacher will know just as much, I would think, as our O-level biology teacher. It is a question of technique, of how we handle our exams. I would be very happy for a U.S. teacher to teach O-levels, but I would want them to go into a British school for a year to see how we do it.

It would seem that it is easier for us as British people to teach in the U.S. curriculum, provided we don't make the sort of mistakes that I made when I first started.

We have had students who have straddled both the U.S. and O-level programs. Maybe they have taken four O-levels and then they have done woodwork and music from the U.S. system, which is fine at the moment. However, as an O-level department we are thinking about going onto a different schedule from the rest of the school. We would go onto a weekly schedule, which would immediately cut out these kids who are trying to straddle both systems.

Have you ever done any of the correspondence courses? This is how we started because we didn't have enough teachers to do all the O-levels the students wanted.

Foster: For O-level, no. We have had Australians doing correspondence. That is very interesting. It depends on your student. In fact we have one student whose parents are taking her home now to Australia because it hasn't worked. We had another student who went straight into university in New Zealand.

They are a very socializing bunch, and I just can't see sticking some of our kids in the library for seven periods a day.

Vogan: The largest issue we have confronting us now is our time tabling. We know that there are many models in the U.S. system. There are some that appear very much like the British time tabling. We have not yet decided how we re going to do this, but we do believe it is possible. We want to take the risks. We want to venture out so that we can do what we need to do in order to allow the entire system to function profitably for everyone.

We've just run an experiment. We've put two of our normal Australian kids into O-levels without any special preparation. They took O-levels at the middle of grade 11. We had our top student and one of our middle students. The top student came out top. Significantly the only one he missed out on was religious education. That was purely on technique of answering questions. The other one did about midway without any preparation.

Any American kids could do the English test because of the great stress there is on language and grammar in the American system. Religious education goes by topics, and we have got our religious education in the whole school based round at least three of the topics. A kid must do religious education in grades 8, 9, and 10, and in different semesters we will do different O-level topics.

Why can't the Americans sit in on the O-level classes?

Foster: Not only our educational philosophy, but our educational approach is so different.   There is so much stress on essay writing in our O-levels, and there is less stress on creative writing in the American educational system.   Although we say we start our O-level course in ninth grade, we have had to pull our children into a British Commonwealth stream in seventh grade.

We tried an experiment this year.   We were short of teachers, so our Northern Ireland English teacher who is married to an American said, "I would love to teach an eighth grade mixed class of U.S. and British kids."   The U.S. kids rebelled.   "Why do we have to do all this writing?"

She helped some of them to appreciate it.   She understood she was introducing something totally new to them.

21

How to Deal with Socioeconomic Differences in an MK School

Ron Whippe
Headmaster, Ben Lippen School

Last summer a student told me, "I almost decided not to come back to school this year."

"Why?"

"Two reasons. One is the history course I have to take. It's a tough course. I'm not sure I can handle it. I'm a little scared of the teacher. Number two is that all the kids are going to be talking about their new wardrobes for the first six weeks of school. I'm not going to have a new wardrobe, and I'm not sure I can handle that."

I was chatting with an MK from Mexico. She has been with us four years—very secure, solid type of girl. She said, "You know, Mr. Whippe, the other day I decided to wear a pair of earrings that I got just on a lark. I hardly ever wear them, but kids talked to me that day that had never passed the time of day with me before. It's really interesting to me how those earrings made a difference in terms of kids talking to me."

I noticed in the last few years we had more girls who got formals and more guys who got tuxes and flowers to go to our Christmas program. The amount of money being spent was going up. This year I legislated with the dean's approval that tuxes were not appropriate. We decided to let them get the flowers. It's one of the niceties that goes with all that. We got some feedback on that. Some of the guys were looking forward to getting tuxes, and some of the girls had been saying to the guys, "You're going to look sharp in a tux."

Four years ago we had a boy from Uganda on campus. All he carried was a knapsack over his back with all of his possessions in it. What do you do with that?

Those issues are also the issues that an MK coming from overseas is going to face in college. They find an increase in materialism.

Discussion

What are some of the problems that MKs face as far as socioeconomic differences in school?

- *Amount of spending money available, either earned or given to them.*
- *Standards of dress.*
- *Ostracism of MKs if they are in wealthy international schools.*

What is being done in our schools to help our students deal with the differences between MKs and business and diplomatic corps kids?

- *Getting involved the students in sports and music, where you are judged by ability rather than material possessions.*
- *Stressing neatness and not overdressing in the dress code.*
- *Communicating the school's philosophy at the beginning, especially to non-mission families.*

Ben Lippen School

Ben Lippen students in grade 10-12 were surveyed concerning socioeconomic issues. When asked if the issue of having or not having material possessions was difficult for them, 60 percent indicated it was somewhat difficult, while 22 percent said it was, and 19 percent said it wasn't. They felt most pressure regarding clothes.

Sixty percent of the students received an allowance, with an average allowance of $45 a month.   Forty percent received no allowance.

Areas of concern

As you increase your rate schedule, what bearing does that have on the composition of the student body? Do you price yourself out of the market? Our market is those in the Christian service community, and yet at the same time we have to make ends meet.

What kind of image are we projecting through required school functions? We can plan a bunch of activities without recognizing that it's going to cost money. Who is going to pay that? What do we say by our dress requirement?   We require our guys to wear ties to classes. Most of our guys coming to us have never worn a tie. That costs extra money. What are we doing? There is a balance between teaching proper dress and economics.

In no way am I trying to say that we need to get to a one-class society. That is unrealistic, and I don't think it is biblical. I think we need to teach biblical principles about possessions and people. The key is what goes on in a person's heart. We need to be teaching that to the parents, the faculty, and the students in chapel, in classes, in counseling, but especially by the modelling of our lives. Am I willing to accept a person, not by what he wears but by the type of person he is? The Bible does not call for a one-class society. There will always be differences. The key is to teach students to accept and respect differences. Their self-worth and value as a person is the key.

Possible aids to coping with socioeconomic differences

- One answer would be uniforms. I personally have problems with uniforms. I think it takes away from the individualism of the youngsters.

- Faculty to encourage right attitudes. We're developing a course in peer counseling, and we're hoping to use that.

- Faculty and administration to be sensitive to the matter of expense, to look for creative ways to keep expenses at a minimum. Just this year we took a Thanksgiving holiday for the first time. We took the whole weekend off. We hadn't done it before because we have kids coming from all over the world. Where are they going to go? What are they going to do? We ended up with about 25 kids left on campus out of 190. We worked hard to make that a good weekend. One of the things that I cautioned the social committee about was not to plan activities that would cost those kids extra money, because those were the ones that couldn't afford it. Those kids that could afford it had their parents fly them back to Florida or Michigan or wherever it was.

- Establish special accounts to help those students with financial needs. I don't know how feasible that is in your school situation. We have a fund at school that we call the Hendersonville Fund. Several years ago a number of churches from a nearby community called Hendersonville gathered together to contribute to a fund to be used for missionary kids or kids who needed clothing or bus fare. I guess over the last twenty-five or thirty years, that group of churches has brought in close to $50,000.

- Another way is through scholarships. We have alumni scholarships. That's more for tuition.
- It is important to teach the principle that it is better to give than to receive. Our strongest student organization on campus is Student Foreign Missions Fellowship. Every year they come up with two or three projects which they challenge the students to contribute to. It's exciting. Some projects have been a hospital in Haiti, a gift to Dalat school, providing some of our own students with money to join Teen Missions for the summer.

  One of the things I sometimes see in MKs and TCKs, is the attitude "You owe it to me." We have to combat that.
- Be sensitive when assigning roommates.

Conclusions

This is just a start. We're doing a lot of thinking in this area, trusting God to give us wisdom to know how to help our students deal with value systems at this time in their lives.

I hope this has stimulated you to do some more thinking in this area.

Part IV

MISSION BOARD INVOLVEMENT IN MK CARE

22

Mission Board Involvement

Bob Blaschke, SIM International
Fredrica Schlorff, AIM
Lillian Davis, North Africa Mission

Bob Blaschke: What a mission does depends largely on their view of the responsibility that the mission has to their MKs; their organizational and financial structure; their family policies; their MK educational policies; and the mission's view of the place that MKs have in the total mission strategy for reaching people for Jesus Christ.

The more I am into MK ministries, the more I realize the strategic place that MK ministries have in the total outreach of any mission. For instance, it can determine where and how you station your missionaries. MKs have a vital part in the total evangelism of the world, and the more stress and importance any mission puts on this, the more provision they are going to make for their MKs.

Fredrica Schlorff: Our ministry to MKs began about three years ago when I was asked to take on a ministry of preparing a confidential prayer sheet which would be sent out to all our prayer constituency. For some time before that I had been noticing that very little was ever said about the MKs, so I made out a questionnaire for them and included a question concerning their prayer requests. Their answers were very interesting. This one reinforced why I felt we had to do something about our MKs:

> When I moved to the States, I left behind my friends, school, city, country, way of life, and equally important, but more subtle, frames of meaning and behavior in my life. The only continuity in my life at this point was the presence of my family, who stayed in the States for one year before returning to [their country].
>
> I have now spent as many years of my life in _____ as I have in the States. I do not consider myself a successful transplant, even though I have a successful and challenging career,

161

and a wonderful growing marriage of eight years. In order to cope with my loss of identity sixteen years previous, I have emotionally compartmentalized my life into two parts with a sort of lobotomy of my feelings and attachments prior to my uprooting from _____. I harbor a great anger and resentment towards my parents and the mission for having provided me with no support system or ways to integrate these experiences in my life.

This was the beginning of our MK ministry. Our mission had been giving financial help to MKs. MKs were receiving an allotment while in college, one round trip back to the field while in college, and medical, dental, and eye exam expenses, plus glasses or contacts, while on support system. In 1983 we began to send greeting cards to our MKs for birthdays, graduation, marriage, and births. This ministry usually begins when a student leaves home for boarding school. We had one get-together in January '85. We send out an "MK Newsletter" twice a year and send care packages for Valentine's Day to college students. They receive mission publications plus "Prayer Target" and field "Fellowship of Prayer." We send a booklet to high school grads entitled "Especially for MKs ... Going to College" and "Alone at Home" to parents. We encourage MKs to go to a re-entry seminar, with the cost paid by the mission. Several numbers are given to them that they are able to call collect when there is an emergency.

I want to develop a much wider program to help the MKs by getting books for them. I want to do something with the younger families who have little children. I want to help prepare them for what their children will face, so they can help their MK children realize the feelings they may have are normal, and so that there can be communication.

Lillian Davis: I am the secretary for the AIM furlough services. I have a particular ministry with MKs that are in colleges and universities. Since AIM realizes it bears the responsibility of its missionaries, we feel we are accountable to our MKs into the young adult years.

My contact with these MKs start when they are high school seniors at the Rift Valley Academy. My intent is to be like a bridge over which they can find support as they pass from there to here in the various areas of their lives. Upon graduation from the school, where most have spent eight to ten years of their lives, they scatter to many parts of the world, back to the home lands of their parents. They enter into the stream of education and work, sometimes feeling like strangers. I receive letters from all over the world telling of their struggles as they try to understand themselves, the people around them, and the culture of the new places, and to know the reality of the living Lord.

One part of my ministry with MKs is having them in my home, an open home, a place where they can come to talk, to have a cup of chia or tea, to stay overnight or longer according to their need. I try to provide a place that they can call home. Every year in October we have an MK week-end reunion. This is not just AIMers. I have helped organize and attended reunions in a number of different states. It is encouraging to see the alumni planning their own class reunions today, or just having general get-togethers.

What do we do on these week-ends? Mostly I try to be a good listener as we spend time discussing the MKs' transitions into U.S. life and culture. They speak of loneliness, the sense of not belonging, the sense that no one understands. I listen with interest, sympathy, empathy, and acceptance as they share intimate concerns—hearing their reactions and conflicts, sharing their joys and sorrows, understanding their desire to be accepted and loved.

They come with their fiancees and spouses. We've had one spouse who has come for four years. He says he would not miss the week-end experience because he keeps learning more about his wife.

They share and learn from each other. There are times of Bible study and prayer, fun times of volleyball, going for a hike through the mountains, having a goat roast reminiscent of African days.

Why do we have these reunions? Because they are people in need; because of their parents who are in Christian ministry; because of the potential of their lives for meeting the needs of the world in which we live.

The RVA Alumni coordinators help me to produce a yearly alumni letter, and every two years, an address directory. We send alumni information which we hope will be informative and helpful. Keeping in personal contact with AIM's college and career young people means a lot of letter writing, a birthday card to each one, a letter a day to some one of the MKs, and answering when they write. I find this ministry one that I term a ministry of encouragement.

Blaschke: SIM has a quarterly news sheet that goes out called *SIM Roots*. It is completely edited and compiled by MKs. The mission prints and distributes it. And this goes out to a mailing list of fifteen hundred MKs around the world through the home offices.

After graduation the RVA staff divides up the names of the graduates, and in the coming fall, they send personal letters to each of their graduates.

OMS has home and information centers on several college campuses, throughout the country. They are used for recruiting, for information, and MK care.

The Southern Baptists' biggest program for MKs is the five week orientation with their parents, prefield. After the end of the first term, all missionaries are required to come back for a debriefing session, bringing their children.

Blaschke: That is a furlough orientation just for first-term missionaries. They need to be away from the veteran missionaries when they spill their guts. The veteran missionaries come back with the option of bringing their children or not, but the first termers come back as a family.

Davis: I keep looking for and praying for different ways and means to help our MKs and our families. For wedding gifts, we're now giving guest books. They really like having the guest books. We've been sending Christmas packages to the first-year students in college. We send them so they arrive during exam week. We are also sending sophomores a monetary check at Christmas time, and of course they are very pleased with that.

This year I've been invited by the Rift Valley Academy administration to go out for two weeks to work with the juniors and seniors regarding re-entry to the States. I'm a little nervous, but I know the Lord is going to help me.

A lot of times we'll work with our college students the first or second year but the most crucial year is actually their senior year, when they're ready to leave college and don't know where to go. I'd like to see follow-up through the senior year and even after the years of college.

When our family went back on furlough for one year, we had a goal of having all of the MKs into our home one night per month. We're still hearing of the benefits. Early on it was just the MKs themselves, and we ministered to them and encouraged them. Then I asked these MKs to bring in some promising missionaries, and it turned out to be a very profitable recruiting tool.

I'm with the World Mission Division of the Church of Nazarene and serve as missionary pastor. We have an MKs' Aunt and Uncle Club. Through our missions magazine, we let this be known. People close to the colleges will write and say they would like to help in a program like that.

23

Prefield Preparation of MKs

Rhoda Lindman, Alliance Academy
Pat Mortenson and Ruth Rowen, Missionary Internship,

Rhoda Lindman: Prefield orientation is as necessary for children as it is for adults. At the present time I see problems because many mission boards and MK schools know very little about the children in the family. How does the child feel about the move to the mission field? About himself? About learning a new language? What are his fears? How is his health? What are his strengths and weaknesses? Will he be able to adjust to the new situation?

If we knew as much about the children who come on the mission field as we know about the adults, we could help prevent many problems that arise. This information could be discovered through an orientation program in which the child is observed, counseled, and helped to understand his own role as a missionary kid and a child of God serving God overseas.

Those on the field would benefit from that orientation for children in several ways. The MK school would receive children who are more confident, more relaxed, more ready and willing to begin their school work. The total family would be better prepared to begin the work that God has given them to do if the children were happy. In turn, this would benefit the mission board and the nationals, because the adults could better get to the business that they are in the foreign land to do.

Pat Mortenson: At Missionary Internship, we've always had a child-care program for infants and preschool children. Then one summer we had a group of middle-aged adults at our orientation program. Almost all said, "Our children need this as much as we do. We wish they were here going through the same types of experiences."

Our prefield training program is transcultural. We have people going into all types of ministries in only one training program,

165

because there are issues involved in moving cross-culturally that fit everyone. Our goal is for them to accept personal responsibility for learning, adapting, and moving into a new culture. We seek to give them some skills, tools, and principles that enable them to take charge of their own learning experience and build relationships in a foreign setting. As we had programs for the children, we began to realize they could be taught some of the same skills and perceptions.

Ruth Rowen has been involved in the development of our prefield orientation for MKs ages seven through sixteen.

Ruth Rowen: The question I was confronted with when asked to take these kids was, "How can you help prepare children to go to the field?" I have since asked many people that, and they all respond with a blank look. I haven't been able to get much help, but by raising kids and working with kids for years and years, I seem to have come to an understanding of what kids' needs are.

Premises regarding prefield training of children

1. Children are people; therefore, their basic human needs are no different from adults'. The only difference I find in children's needs and adults' is the sex drive. The needs may exist in different degrees and manifest themselves differently, but the same basic human needs are there.

2. If a child has a positive self-concept, he can move anywhere in the world and get along. That is a pretty strong statement, but I truly believe it. The more I read, the more this has been confirmed. I think a child can reach his full potential and be all he wants to be if he has learned to accept himself and live with himself. *The Stressproof Child*'s message and theme is that the child who is able to handle stress best is the child who really feels good about who he or she is. I think we know that even as adults. Feeling that you are a worthwhile, valuable person gives you confidence to go through traumatic events. That is a premise I work on.

3. The family a child grows up in is more important than the country. Kids everywhere have the same sorts of problems, but the difference I see is the family they are raised in. Carol Herman has done some research trying to find out what helps a child to adjust. She studied MKs and only came up with one factor common to those who made a good adjustment. That was that the mom and dad expressed love between them. There again, it's the family unit. You can look at our

experiences and the people we know, and you can see how important the family unit is.

4. Effective prefield training for the first-time MK is a strong preventive measure. I think if prefield kids can get off to a good start, and they have some tools they can work with, they will be spared a lot of difficulty. I realize that my influence in three or five weeks is going to be very small, but it is a start.

5. One of the greatest needs is giving parents ongoing support and help for their kids. I see kids expressing themselves and learning while they are with me, but I know as soon as they get back in their family, they are going to resort to undesirable behavior. We've got to give parents the tools to help the family unit.

6. All MKs have the same basic needs whether they go abroad or move only a short distance. I give them all the same helps.

The Program at Missionary Internship

About 75 percent of our time is academic; about 25 percent is games and swimming. Even then, the kids are learning to relate to one another.

Developing interpersonal skills

We teach them how to introduce themselves, how to approach a stranger in their Sunday School class. We do some role playing. I have two go up front and I set up a situation. They're at a party at Sunday School or school, and a stranger comes in. They usually just stare at each other or make some smart remark like, "Who's that kid?" You teach them what to say, "My name's Ruth. What's your name?" or "Where are you from? Are you staying here, or are you on vacation?" Give them some simple sentences and ideas of what to talk about to help somebody feel at home. We teach them appropriate words to say. We also teach them the nonverbals: the eye contact, the smiling. One whole week is spent on what we call "building community." They are taught to care about one another, to share, to support, to give, to make friends, to work together, encourage, forgive, give of themselves, and to get along. Those are our goals for that one week.

Activities to develop interpersonal skills

We have Bible studies about Jesus and how he related to people, especially Peter, James, and John. We look at other people who had close friends — how they related, how they trusted, and how they forgave one another. We have a thorough inductive study on the book of Acts, which is missions and people related.

I show films from the public library on making friends and how to build trust. We play a lot of noncompetitive participation games.

We have an exercise called "Broken Squares," a nonverbal simulation on communication which helps kids realize they are communicating by nonverbals.

They write a paper entitled "Why Missions?" The parents of these kids say, "Gee, I never thought about helping my child understand why we are going to the mission field." Of course this is the first question kids ask, "Why are we going?" Parents say, "The Lord called us," which is a little abstract and not too helpful to children. So, I have the children write this paper. I give them thirty or forty verses from Scripture to look up so they can get ideas. They read and interpret them according to their level of understanding. I have written an exercise for the family to work on together. They can discuss together why they are going to the mission field and what it means to be called. That's something a family can share, but it is also something I have the children share in class.

I take Bill Gothard's *Pineapple Story* and at intervals I ask questions, "How would you react here? What would you say? What would be a better way to answer this person?" You can take any story that a kid would relate to and stop after a couple paragraphs or a page and ask, "Now how would you answer this?" or "What would have been a better way?" or "What would you have appreciated somebody doing or saying?" That's a way to get kids to think about other people and their feelings.

We have short skits on making friends which we do in small groups. I have several situations they role-play.

We do a study on the book of Philemon. They write out answers as if they were Philemon.

We have a caring and sharing hour at the end of each day. I think of something for them to share, like "Share with the whole group something that you've done for someone today, maybe in your family, maybe for your little sister or brother, maybe for someone in the group." I try to get them to think about helping other people and sharing with others. "Tell something that you really like about the person on your right." This is hard sometimes when brothers are sitting next to each other. It's sad, but it's true. They can't think of anything they like about their brother. But it's good for them to start thinking positive things about the next person. I have a list of about twenty-five questions like that.

We have secret pals for the three or five weeks, which gets them thinking about what they can give to somebody else. Sometimes they don't get anything from their pal, but they give, and that's good.

I have a lot of written exercises: building friendships, building trust, "For my friend I would ... "

I have an exercise on the Golden Rule. I have them write down about twenty answers to the question, "What would you like others to do for you?" Then I tell them, "That's what you should be doing for other people." It gets them thinking about others and gives them ideas.

We do the Trust Walk, and we have a debriefing on that.

We have a prayer request list for each child each day. They share requests for themselves.

I have a friendship evangelism study, teaching them what it means to make a friend in the light of eventually sharing the gospel with them on their level.

Developing a positive self-concept

I think kids need affirmation that they are worthwhile, valuable people, not because they are MKs, but because they are created by God. I think they need this from their grandparents, their Sunday School teacher, and their neighbor, and from me. I always try to emphasize that they are really valuable people. I try to help them feel they are worth something.

I have a book on human uniqueness that talks about them being created uniquely. We memorize Psalm 139, which is all about how God sees man and watches over him. This is something they can take with them to support them forever. I get films on self-awareness and self-acceptance from the library. I get films on how people are different yet alike. I have a lot of exercises that help them to look at themselves, their own personalities, their own tastes, their own schools, their own churches, their own homes, how they're all unique, but in God's sight they are all important and none is better than another.

I have exercises on how to handle stress and conflict. We discuss what to do when you have a problem: kick the wall? scream? slam the door? kick the dog? We go through this as a group. Then they work out one of their own personal problems to get in the habit of thinking about stressful situations rationally. "What are my options? What are the consequences? I make my choice and live with that, or if it doesn't work, I choose another." After we did this exercise one time, a parent told me his kids were fighting that night, so he made them sit down and work out their whole problem and solve it. They were very pleased. I would love to see the whole family learn this process.

There is an exercise I have on feelings: how to be sensitive to other people's feelings; how to understand your own feelings; how to express and interpret them appropriately.

I have an exercise called "Who's Normal Around Here?" Its purpose is to show that we're all normal, but we do things differently. There's one on values and rating yourself.

We have a Bible study called "Who I Am." It deals with us as creations of God, as Americans, as MKs, as Christians, and as guests in a new country. We look at how those identities affect us when we move to another country.

We list forty or fifty interpersonal qualities like being flexible, being patient, being sensitive. Then the older children read four case studies dealing with college kids who moved into a new culture and had some conflict with the family they were living with.

Developing awareness of their new country

Fear of the unknown causes stress in children. The more we can acquaint them with what their new country is going to be like, the less fear and stress they will experience. In order to do this, we have them make a notebook. We go to the library a couple of days. They look at books on their country, and they write a two- to four-page report. They draw a flag of their country, and they learn what the symbols mean. When they go to their country, there's the flag they drew. It won't be strange to them. They draw a map of where they are going to be living. They make a notebook with all kinds of things regarding their country.

We take some trips. One is down to Eastern Market in Detroit. It's an open-air market very similar to what many of them will be shopping in but have never seen before. It's a good experience.

We go to Greek Town, which is an ethnic community, and buy foreign food.

We go to the airport. Many of the kids have never been to a big airport or flown before. The parents never thought to take them to an airport. It's overwhelming when they see those huge planes for the first time. We get a tour of the airport.

We go to a place called Talley Hall that has foreign foods. We buy Chinese egg rolls. I cut one into twelve pieces, and most of them can't even get that down. If they're going to Africa, they wonder why they have to eat egg rolls. I tell them their taste buds have to get used to different kinds of foods.

We go to my home one day and make a foreign meal. This is a winner, because when they cook it, it is the best food they have ever eaten. They have eaten some real slop through the years. I have a wild menu. Some comes from Africa, some from China, some from Jamaica. They love it because they have cooked it, but if their moms made it, they'd never touch it. Parents could do that at home; they could make food with their kids and learn to enjoy foreign foods. You would be surprised how many of these kids have never eaten any foreign food. I thought all American families had gone to Chinese restaurants, but it's not true. They haven't.

I have a newspaper article, "Shopping Can Be Fun and Tricky in African Markets." It's a great article on bargaining, which is entirely new to the kids. They've never shopped that way before. After reading the article, I usually give them the opportunity to role play. A buyer and a seller will come up front, and I'll give them my diamond or watch or something. One will buy and one will sell. I make them follow the ground rules that the buyer has top dollar and the seller has bottom dollar. I make them write it down so they won't change in the buying process. They love it.

I have an article from Zimbabwe entitled "The Healer Examines the Patient's Spirit". They learn all about a healer and what his purposes are.

We see films from the public library on every country that the children are going to. They may not see their specific town, but usually the country.

We have MKs who are home on furlough come speak to the group whenever possible. I try to make sure they have positive feelings about their own experiences beforehand. I give them a list of about twenty questions ahead of time, so they know what we're interested in and are ready with answers. The kids have really appreciated hearing from other kids who have had good experiences.

I write to the embassy or consulate of the country they are going to and get all sorts of brochures, booklets, pictures, and posters to put in their workbook.

I have a set of key questions that deal with situations they are sure to confront. For example, to a blond girl going to Africa I say, "You can be sure they are going to touch your hair. How are you going to react: jump back? push them away?" We discuss these questions so they're ready.

We do observation when we walk through Greek Town and when we walk through Eastern Market. I use a series of pictures of Penang with the kids so they can begin to learn to observe and inquire.

We went to a beautiful Catholic church, Saint Mary's, in Greek Town. Two girls observed, but they didn't inquire. They walked up to the very front where only the priest goes. The nun caught them just in time. She almost panicked. They let us roam all around the church, but we didn't know we couldn't be up by the altar. It was an excellent lesson on observing and inquiring before doing something that will offend people.

I have a series of pictures that I mount. "What do you think the people are doing? How are they feeling? Would you like to do that?"

I have another series of pictures on comparisons and contrasts. In our country, we do so many ridiculous things, but they don't seem that way to us; the Easter bunny looks very healthy and normal and good to us, but the dragon in China looks ridiculous. We try to compare symbols we have here to symbols they have in other countries.

I have about four pages of different customs that we talk about: the way you shake hands in some places, the way you don't cross your legs in some places, the way you compliment, the way you should smile. (In one country, if your teeth are much prettier than the person you are talking to, you don't smile and show your teeth because that would make them feel bad.) It's a great time for sharing and unloading their feelings, and their questions.

We talk about MKs having a closeness which begins in our prefield training. When these kids come from all parts of the States, they each feel like they are the only child in the whole world who is being taken out of their home and their school and their community. But when they get there they find fifteen kids who share these feelings. It is so supportive. Instantly it does something for them. The kids under twelve who don't want to go to the field are usually changed by the end of the week. It doesn't happen that way with kids that are thirteen and older. But the younger ones change when they make new friends who are excited about going.

We discuss the concept of TCK and the paper "I Am Green" with the older kids.

We deal with lifestyle adjustments. The kids actually draw pictures of their favorite activity in this country, like going to McDonald's or playing baseball. Then we look at where they're going. If they won't be able to do that activity in their new country, we blank it out so they can see it is going to be something in the past. We fill it in with something new that they can look forward to, and they draw a picture of that activity. Maybe they won't have baseball, but they'll have soccer in their country. They draw a picture of soccer. They make the mental transition from things they can no longer do, to things they can anticipate doing.

Frequently children hear such things as: "Those people are dirty; those people are lazy; those people don't appreciate us." I have a whole list of these things. We talk about them in our group. When kids encounter these, mentally they should be raising a red flag that these are not the right attitudes to have about the people they are going to be ministering to. It is an excellent exercise, and one that I would be thrilled to see a whole family unit become familiar with. If I said, "Those people are stupid," my kids would not hesitate to say, "Mom, that's not the right way to look at them," or "You really shouldn't be saying that." We all let these things slip out, but if your whole family worked together on this and could remind one another, how beautiful it would be.

Training the Family as a Unit

At Missionary Internship we have started to do some things as a family unit. I feel this is the direction we have to go if we are going to help MKs. The kids need the ongoing support and help that parents are able to give. However, I'm sorry to say, many of the parents need to be taught how to help and support their kids.

Mortenson: We would like to encourage mission boards in the screening process to look at the family as a whole. One mission board wants to make it a policy to see how the family functions in their own home setting, not just at the site of the mission headquarters. What we're seeking to do at MI is to integrate the adult and the children's program at every possible juncture. Then we'd really like to see some more on-field family enrichment. Families go through so many phases and transitions. It's not a static lifestyle by any means.

Discussion

What about taking adolescents to the field?

Rowen: In my experience, it has been the boys from thirteen to sixteen who don't want to go. I've not yet had a girl in that age group who didn't want to go, but I have had a lot of boys. The sad thing is at M.I., it's almost too late for these families to change, because most of them have sold their homes. They're all packed. They're on their way. But we do confront the parents. I have an interview with the parents and ask them if they have any concerns about their kids, and then I share my concerns about their children. It's very difficult to do. I try to be very sensitive, and yet to alert them that there will be problems.

They say that the Lord has called them, and what can I say? "The Lord's will." That ends it. Sometimes I wonder if we're not fulfilling our responsibilities in meeting our kids' needs. Is it the Lord's will? That's what I try to let them ponder as they go. They go taking their chances that the kids will change their minds. But I don't think they do.

I was fifteen when my parents decided to go to the mission field. I did not want to go at all. My parents said, "Son, if you don't want to go, we will not go."

I said, "Well, if you feel that strongly about it, I am willing to go, but I want you to know that I don't want to go."

My first year here in Ecuador was miserable. I hated it. That was mostly because I had decided in advance that I was going to hate it. The first year was pretty miserable, but the last two were fabulous. There IS a difference between not wanting to go and not being willing to go.

What happens when you have fifteen kids at ten different age levels?

Rowen: I have rewritten many of my exercises on two levels. Sometimes I bring in a second person to lead discussions in one group. It is true that they are at different levels and have different outlooks on life. The night they come, they look around for someone their age. If there's nobody their age, they want to go home. I try to help them to understand, "Look, this is one of the adjustments to differences. They may not be your age, but you need to learn to adjust to these other kids who may be only a year younger." It's a learning process. By the end of three weeks, the older ones do come around and say, "I see that I really had to learn." We've had a mixture of backgrounds, lifestyles, and some doctrines. They have to learn in this group that they're all one and all working together. If they can come there, make friends, and adjust, they can do it on the field.

24

Prefield Orientation of MK Teachers
and Boarding Home Parents

Pat Mortenson, Missionary Internship
Phil Renicks, ACSI

Phil Renicks: Some mission organizations have taken on the responsibility of providing a full program of orientation for their missionaries.   Others have left that responsibility up to paramission organizations.

We're going to present an alternative that we have designed specifically for the MK school teacher and the MK boarding home parent who do not have mission programs.   My feeling is that the success of the teacher or the boarding parent going to the MK school is directly related to the kind of preparation he gets.   That preparation needs to begin well before he ever gets to the mission field.   In fact, the orientation process should begin when the application form for candidacy status with the mission is filled out.

I believe the focus of the orientation program should be on preparing that teacher or that boarding home parent in such a way as to increase the chance that his life and his ministry are enriched through the cross-cultural setting.   We have a very definite responsibility and stewardship before the Lord for the lives of those people that we guide into areas of ministry.   In sending them out to places to teach or to be boarding parents, we're the ones that bear the responsibility, to some degree, for their failure.   I have seen some people who have been put into a no-win situation.   They have been, in a sense, programmed for failure.

In order to make their time successful, three groups of individuals have to take responsibility—the MK teacher or the MK boarding parent, the mission sending agency, and the MK school.

176

I believe that for orientation to be effective, it must done in two parts—prefield orientation and orientation on the field. If we just give them the prefield orientation or if we don't give them the prefield and try to do all of the orientation on the field, we may succeed to some degree, but I don't think we're going to be totally successful.

Observations on Orientation

The mission organization that has a well-organized orientation program is the exception rather than the rule. Most mission personnel policies related to the recruitment, selection, and orientation of teachers, administrators, and boarding home parents are poorly defined or nonexistent. The recruitment, selection, and orientation of personnel for MK schools is left too much to chance, often resulting in poorly selected, poorly qualified staff or no staff at all to fill vacancies in key positions at the start of the school year.

As a result of the upcoming teacher shortage in the United States, there are going to be fewer teachers available. Unless we have those who are willing to commit themselves, and unless we do a proper job of orienting them, then we're not going to have the people that we need.

Predeparture orientation and on-site induction of MK school personnel appear to be low priorities of mission sending agencies. Most personnel proceed to their place of ministry with little or no preparation beyond their professional training.

Often the amount of time given to the orientation of short-term people is reduced. I guess we feel that the investment is not worth it. How much preparation and training should they get? Shouldn't we be preparing them to do the best they can do in the time they're able to spend with us? If we did a better job of orienting and training our short-term people, would they become long-term?

Lack of orientation probably contributes to the high turnover rate among personnel in MK schools. Predeparture expectations are often vastly different from the actual reality of the assignment. I know teachers who left their home country thinking that they were going to teach one grade and found themselves doing something completely different when they got on the field. The whole matter of expectations versus reality is a very critical issue.

I feel that we should base orientation on the premise that the individual teacher or boarding home parent should be given every opportunity to maximize his or her potential as an individual, as a professional educator or caregiver, and as a missionary. The person must be pointed in a productive and liberating direction. It's not really a question of giving them more information. The major concern is to enable the individual to creatively cope with the new situation.

Prefield Orientation Program

Pat Mortenson: This is an overview of our three-week program for the orientation of MK teachers, administrators, and boarding home parents.

Weeks One and Two

First of all we form a community, perhaps a simulation of the community that they will be in overseas. In that community, they learn from one another through activities, projects, and field trips. We hope that it is a very safe environment in which to fail and to accept where they are in order to move on to another level of adjustment or adaptation. We help them to be in charge of their own personal growth and development.

MK personnel have all sorts of levels of adaptation. It's very important for them to feel at home in the host culture, to understand and learn the cultural uniqueness of that group. There is also the expatriate community and the missionary subculture. There are the MKs themselves and their parents. If they get involved and adapt in only one group, the adjustment won't be complete.

As they approach the new situation, they have a choice of attitudes. They can start out with suspicion, fear, and prejudice. Or they can start out with openness, acceptance, and trust. It helps a great deal to realize that feelings of frustration, confusion, tension, and embarrassment are normal.

Very often as we look back on our own adjustments, we can see those negative coping strategies of blaming, criticizing, rationalizing, or withdrawing to an extreme degree. Negative coping strategies result in alienation and isolation.

How much better if they can employ skills and attitudes that allow them to observe, to listen, to inquire, and to keep interacting even when it's really tough, in order to achieve rapport and understanding. It is a lifetime process. How much more productive it is to be able to assertively take the responsibility for getting involved in all these levels.

Week Three

Renicks: In the third week, we have an introduction and a general orientation to the nature of the MK school.

Oftentimes, folks who have worked in church settings or in a Christian school or even in a public school come into the MK school not expecting any differences. When they get into the missionary subculture, they find that there are differences. They find that the missionary is not that perfect individual they had conjured up in their minds. There are some areas of the missions community subculture that we have kind of glossed over and haven't looked at critically enough in terms of new people coming into the MK school setting. What is the level of trust that the parents out there have for a new teacher? And what kind of pressures do they bring to bear on a new teacher?

We also believe that it's important for that boarding home parent or that MK school teacher to have a biblical basis for ministry before they ever leave their home culture. We hope that we can help them refine what they already believe.

Discussion

If you were given the responsibility of developing your own pre-field orientation program at this point in time after having been on the field, what are some things that you would include?

Language learning. I've seen so many people come to our school in Bolivia not knowing the language and immediately it is a barrier. It continues to be a barrier. I've seen too many people go home in defeat because they don't know the language.

People need to be orientated to the mission subculture. Make people aware of the multicultural situation with the kids and with the staff members.

We would have greatly appreciated being put in contact with a person who had been there recently and knew exactly what it was like.

Mortenson: Teach them what kind of questions to ask.

I feel that the most valuable part of my orientation was being able to quiz kids that live here.

I believe that there are a number of schools that are in the process now of developing video cassettes of their school. I think it's important for people to be able to see the place that they are considering as ministry.

One thing we did to help orientate ourselves was to talk on the telephone with people who had been there. We found out exactly what was there and what wasn't there, then we packed accordingly.

I think it's very helpful to sit down and just think through all the kinds of things that you might have questions about, and not feel that it's silly to ask them.

Dr. Ted Ward trains us how to handle being exposed to a brand new situation by making comparisons. What is different from what I'm used to? Try to think through why it is different. You train yourself to think, and it minimizes culture shock. You discipline your mind; you avoid anxiety; you try to control yourself. Some of our teachers felt they were abnormal because they never knew they were going to go through such a thing. Yet culture shock is basically normal. The one book that I would suggest is Dr. Ted Ward's book titled 'Living Overseas.'

Renicks: Our mission organizations have got to get serious about orientation, and in getting serious about orientation have got to start working a full year in advance of sending people out.

Oftentimes personnel do not arrive on the field until forty-eight hours before time to actually begin their responsibilities. I personally have seen teachers arrive the day school started, or after school started. That's a very, very frustrating kind of experience for a person coming in. It doesn't give them the opportunity to settle, adjust, adapt, or to work through an on-site orientation program. That's tragic. We've got to do our best to avoid those kinds of situations.

I'd be glad to send you a complete on-field orientation package which I've put together.

25

The Home School Movement

Paul Nelson
Superintendent, Wycliffe Children's Education

Rather than giving any kind of a history of the home school movement, I would like to give it a characterization. People in the home school movement are distinguished from people who happen to be teaching their children at home by a difference in motivation. Those who have chosen to be involved in the home school movement usually have done it for a particular reason which tends to be more negative than affirmative, at least initially. The negative reason has to do with dissatisfaction with whatever educational option their children have available to them.

In some cases they have felt very strongly that the public school environment is not healthy for their children. Another reason for a large group of people is that they feel formal schooling begins too early. Their perspective is, "Delay formal schooling, and in doing that you make it more practical for your child to cope with formal education as he matures."

A third reason the home school movement has gained a great deal of credibility is for a theological reason. There are people who believe that this is God's design for the family, and if you abdicate the responsibility of teaching your own children, God will hold you accountable. There is such an absoluteness about that theology that we have to factor that into the home school movement and its impact on missions.

A lot of folks come to Wycliffe who see missions as a good way to carry out what they consider to be their mandate in the family — that is to home school their children. They see the mission field as a place where nobody is going to sue them and nobody is going to have any other influences on their family. The fact that they are more

181

broadly involved in a ministry is almost incidental to that desire. You recognize the inherent problems in that approach.

I put together a policy statement for Wycliffe Bible Translators which is now used with all of our candidates.[1] I recommend it to you not as an absolute statement of what every mission ought to be doing, but as a guideline. The majority of the people who read this can conclude, "Missions are still an option for our family. We view this as a viable way we can carry out our ministry." Others say, "That's not for me. I really feel more strongly committed to home schooling than that, and if that's the mission's position, we don't fit."

I believe that if you draw that kind of dichotomy, kindly, ahead of time with your candidates, it saves the folks on the field an awful lot of grief about false assumptions that have been made.

Impact on Missions

I'd like to look at the home school movement and its impact on missions. Young couples are making specific demands on missions concerning their desires to home school their children. It's been part of the theology they have grown up with in some cases. It is almost a theological mandate. "If I compromise on this, I compromise on my faith." That's part of the issue.

The second problem is that mission personnel people are reacting to these demands with some very judgmental responses. The dialogue is cut off. They say, "That couple would never fit into the missions context. They're inflexible. They have no room to take leadership." But it isn't necessarily the young candidates' fault.

Here's where I believe part of the problem comes from. Influential Christian leaders are teaching parents that it is their responsibility to home school in the U.S. as well as on the field. I'm not sure how to deal with this. I've had a lot of correspondence with Raymond Moore; I've corresponded with Jim Dobson. I've worked with other home school advocates and tried to help them understand that it is not that the missions community is opposed to home schooling or that we're enemies of the family and don't want to accomplish all the things that are claimed for accomplishment by the home school movement. The issue is, how does it fit in our context? There is a big difference between home schooling in Dallas and the support system that goes along with that, and teaching your own children in a

[1]Editor's note: This has been published in *Evangelical Missions Quarterly* 24, (April 1988): 126-29.

village in Papua New Guinea. Most of the people I've mentioned are completely ignoring the fact that our context, our ministry, our demands, and our pressures are different, and because of those differences we have to approach things differently.

Here's another part of the problem as well. If folks who have come from a home school movement get to the field, sometimes we have the campaign continuing. "If you're really a Christian, you're going to be teaching your kids at home. That's part of God's responsibility for you." If that person is teaching their kids at home, and you're sending yours to boarding school, there is a conflict. It's not just, "If that's right for you, fine, but I'll do this because it's right for me." There is an evangelistic spirit that says, "I'm going to have to change you in order for you to be able to be what God wants you to be. The problem with you is you are ignorant of God's teaching in this area." We have an evangelistic campaign going on for home schooling that somehow is a carry-over from the support group in their community. This judgmental issue can be very divisive on the field.

Part of the interesting phenomenon of the home school movement is that parents who are doing it form support groups. They have newsletters; they plan field trips together. In our part of Dallas, a lot of families get together and say, "You teach reading and I'll teach math," and all of a sudden you don't have a home school any more. You have a cooperative school that meets in your basement. But the support group doesn't exist on the field. That's part of the problem. When they get to the field, they don't understand why they are out of sync with what is going on. They feel the problem is a spiritual one and not a pragmatic one that they're dealing with.

It's obvious that not all mission settings lend themselves well to home schooling. If you are working and living on a fairly large mission center with a school there, there is a price to be paid if you choose to isolate yourself and not send your children to that school. That price can negate the effectiveness of your ministry. We have had families who have left the center because home schooling really did not fit in that context.

There are settings where the demands made on both parents make it impossible for the parents to devote much time to teaching their children.

The mission setting has to be evaluated in the assignment of a family who is talking about home schooling. Whether they are evangelistic for it or whether they are just practitioners, the setting is a very critical element.

Role Conflicts for the Mother

Another problem in the mission context (and I focus on the wife here, because no matter how philosophical we would like to be about it being a shared responsibility, teaching generally falls to the wife) is that the wife is frequently limited in her involvement in the ministry when she is responsible for teaching their children. That becomes an issue where there are a limited number of visas available for a country or there are significant staff shortages. We in the missions community rely on the involvement of every family member in some settings. If the expectation is that most wives work part time or full time, and one family chooses not to follow that pattern, the pressure that is placed on that family can cause some real heartache.

In the translation process with Wycliffe, for example, many times a husband and wife have prepared as a couple to work on a language project. We have a lot of wives who are better linguists than their husbands. Many of them are better scholars and can do a better job in the translation process. Yet saying, "Home schooling is most important for us," can prevent that team effort in some cases.

Part of the dilemma for missions is that we need people who are willing to alter their lifestyle to home teach their children when necessary. We have a lot of settings in Wycliffe where there is no other alternative. Families need to be willing to change priorities for varying lengths of time.

But we don't want people who *only* want to home school their children. That's an interesting dilemma, and I'm not sure how to resolve it. I think it has a lot to do with the flexibility with which the people approach home schooling.

Not all mothers or children can separate the role of a teacher from the role of a mother. That's not an easy thing to do. These support groups that send out newsletters telling you how wonderful it is all the time, revelling in the joy of learning together, are not truthful. Anybody who has spent any time in the classroom knows that's not the way it is every day. Nobody is "on" every day. Nobody is that joyful and excited to get at it every morning. Those family conflicts can completely destroy a ministry. I've seen it happen.

I had a father come into my office a short time ago. They were going back to the field. He said, "I need to get some materials for our kids. What would you recommend? My wife is going to teach the kids."

I asked a few questions like, "What have you been using?" and within about thirty seconds I knew he didn't have a clue. He wasn't involved.

He said, "I better have my wife come in and talk to you about it."

Later that afternoon she came in and talked to me. Within a minute, literally, she was in tears. She said, "I can't do this. We did it for awhile until our furlough. The kids have been in school while we've been here. The closer I get to going back, and as I start looking at materials that I need, the more I know I can't go back and teach our two kids."

I brought the dad back in and we did a little regrouping in a hurry. They delayed going back.

We need to recognize that the conflict between the family members can be compounded by the teaching process. The teaching process can be the trigger that makes family life really difficult.

Not all mothers and children can cope with the intense relationship of daily one-on-one teaching. If you're in a classroom you can drift off. If your mother is sitting right there watching you, and she's a little antsy because there are other things she has to get done, you both had better be at that task, and you'd better be at it without any kind of distraction. There are times when the kid spilled the milk in the morning, and he had other problems that didn't get things started off right. Now he doesn't even know two plus two. There's an intermixing of relationships that makes learning very difficult. Not all families can handle it well. Any of you who have done it know it's not an easy relationship. It's not an easy relationship with somebody else's children, let alone with your own.

Other Limitations

In missions other educational options are frequently ignored in the defense of home schooling. Parents are not out there looking for alternatives. To admit that there might be a better way of doing things is to sort of go back on what they have learned over the years in the home schooling support group. "It ought to be a good experience. This is a fulfillment of God's purpose for your life. Why should you be looking for anything else?" So they do not explore other options. They bang their heads against this one until it tends to get to be an impossible situation, and then it's almost unsalvageable in cases.

We're not talking about people who teach their own children out of necessity. We are talking about people with a different level of motivation who become a part of the home school movement. However, some of those factors still exist even when parents choose to teach their own children because of pragmatic reasons.

There is limited outside help requested or welcomed in many home schooling families. That's part of the theology of the whole thing. "We do it ourselves. We get the information. We do the exploration." If anybody wants to make an evaluation of how that educational program is progressing, the response is, "Wait a minute. This is my job. I don't need you sticking your nose in it."

One of my colleagues at New Tribes has been using the term "academic abuse." I believe that is a legitimate term to be used in some families. I've been in some settings where the kids who were supposedly being home schooled picked me up at the airport. They were around all the time. They did all kinds of errands around the city, but they never once took any interest in the fact that we were there to talk about education, about how they were doing with their correspondence courses. It's a legitimate outcome of the fact that you can get involved in too many activities and education can take a very low priority. That's not normally the case, but it is a legitimate concern, especially at the secondary level where kids want to be much more self-directed.

Anybody who has been on correspondence for any length of time has gotten behind. I don't think there's anybody who has done it perfectly. The kids who do well at it shouldn't be there. They need a lot more peer interaction than they're getting. The ones who are bouncing off the wall probably need that kind of discipline, but it never works out that way.

Curriculum

That brings us to another element of the home school movement—materials and curriculum. Most correspondence courses that are available to families are built around textbooks that are designed to be used in a group-paced environment. They are not designed to be the total instructional package. The essence of the correspondence materials is to tell students which pages to do by which date, and which other activities might be done along with that. It's not really designed to provide the additional tutorial elements that are not included in the textbook. No reputable textbook company would claim that their textbook is all the curriculum you need. (Notice I said "reputable.")

The problem that we get into is that a parent in the role of a teacher is really required to do the same things that a classroom teacher would do. That is, look at that material, determine what else needs to be done, what pre-instruction needs to go into that, what kind of modification needs to be developed if that is not really appropriate for your child because of his learning style. We're asking the parent to do that, in many cases without ever having had any kind of frame of reference to work from. They don't have an education degree. Or in some cases when they do, they still don't have adequate resources. They don't have a resource library to work from. They just have that textbook and this sheet of assignments that need to be done.

Home schooling is made significantly more problematic because of the curriculum materials that are provided for the families. The mothers get frustrated. The kids get frustrated. They would do anything to avoid jumping back into that correspondence course, partly because the material is inappropriate.

I believe sincerely that there is a place for parents who teach their own children in the missions context. I believe it can be a successful experience. And I believe it can work for a relatively long period of time if the assignments are appropriate for that context, if the expectations are realistic, and if there is an opportunity to have a consulting teacher with whom to work.

The Field Education System is not the answer to everyone's problem, but it is conceptually different from most other approaches to home schooling. It tends to be much more activities based and is built around an instructional theme. All of the instructional activities that grow out of a particular theme, whether it is language arts or reading or science, are designed to be used in the environment where the family is living as opposed to an environment that exists someplace else. You don't need to spend a lot of time studying about the causes of smog in Atlanta when you're living in a village in West Africa. You discuss and explore reasons why the environment people live in is impacting the people who live there. It's logical to design an educational program that allows families to use the environment in which they live instead of studying about a system that only exists in our textbook.

Most materials are designed with the assumption that there is a whole ethos that supports that system. For example, all of the story problems for math, all of the stories in the reading books, and all of the examples in the social sciences are based on the assumption that the kids who use those books see those things being put into practice in other places.

To illustrate local government, a textbook may talk about a mayor and a city council. The local government in which most of our families are functioning is totally different. The issue is not to discuss the mayoral system and the city manager system. The issue is, how do people organize themselves to get things done?

Role of the Professional Teacher

The assumption that we make in the Field Education System is that teacher consultants can provide some of the expertise that parents don't have. I sincerely believe that the teaching profession has something to offer in the instructional process. If I didn't believe it, I couldn't with integrity accept a paycheck for doing what I believed any parent could do without ever going to school. I think it is legitimate to involve a professional teacher in diagnosing the specific needs of children and prescribing appropriate instructional activities. I believe that involves a set of learned skills that most parents don't automatically have, regardless of their desire to do a good job with their children and the conscientious work that they do with them.

To me the best approach we can have is one that combines the skills of the professional teacher with the nurturing, care, and commitment of parents who are willing to work with their child. They are not a threat to one another. In reality it's a partnership. That partnership can make for a good instructional environment. I believe whatever models we use for home schooling, the partnership of the professional with the parent can make it a successful experience. A rejection of that partnership can make it a struggle to the point of failure.

The Field Education System that I have referred to is only one model. There are a variety of other models. There are cooperative schools where parents get together and teach courses periodically. There are cooperative efforts with a teacher consultant working out of an Educational Resource Center. There are other home school models that use various correspondence programs and modifications of those programs. All of those things can work for varying lengths of time, depending on the temperament of the mother, the temperament of the child, and a variety of other factors, but they should always be looked at as short-term solutions to a long-term educational problem.

The missionary task is longer than the elementary school years for your children. The tasks that we have before us require language learning, enculturation, and a credibility that needs to be built. This requires longer than just a few years to develop. I believe that we need to work very carefully to build longevity into our educational programs so we can presume the family will be there long enough to complete the ministry to which God has called them.

I believe that it's naive to send a family out with only the option of teaching their own children. We all know stories of somebody who has been able to do that successfully, and their kids graduated summa cum laude from Harvard, or something, but that's the exception and not the rule. We have to be realistic about the rule that it is a short-term solution, and not a long-term approach to keeping a family on the field.

Integration into the Classroom

Then the last thing. At some point teachers are usually given the responsibility of integrating a child into the classroom and providing remediation. Depending how long it has taken to get to that point, that teacher is asked to pick up an awful lot of responsibility. There are some kids who honestly do not have basic reading skills, not because their mother wasn't loving or wasn't conscientious, but because that child did not learn the way that textbook said he ought to learn.

To function as though there is no next step to a traditional school is to be extremely naive and to do a disservice to that family and to the child. There has to be an agreement that education can take place in a variety of structures and a variety of forms, and there has to be a willingness to be flexible, to work cooperatively between our traditional schools on the field and our nontraditional environments which allow families to remain together.

Bottom line among all these reasons for looking at the home school movement as negative or supporting and embracing it as a positive thing, is that for some young children, being together with their families is a reasonable trade-off to whatever advantages they would gain in another environment. It's not that one's better, or one's worse. It's an issue of trade-off. It needs to be the best possible alternative that could be developed for that child.

26

Implications for a Model of MK Ministry

William Viser
Foreign Mission Board, Southern Baptist Convention, Brazil

I am going to share what I feel is an intensely practical approach to MK ministry. I will divide these suggestions into three time elements: stateside preparation, field ministry, and re-entry.

Stateside Preparation

I believe that some problems appearing on the field can be traced back to the parents' perspective of the child's role in missions. Some say, "We have to make home the priority," and others say, "No, the work has got to be the priority." There's room for disagreement, but I don't think any of us would question the fundamental value of the MK within the ministry of the missionary family.

We are aware of the technique for preparing a young child for the arrival of a new brother or sister. The mother and the father carefully explain, even with the use of dolls, the mother's need to go to the hospital, when she will return, etc., because they do not want the event to traumatize the child. Can a move from one's native culture to a foreign culture be dealt with any less carefully?

I believe the parents' attitude toward the move is quickly perceived by the child. When one is reluctant, anxious, or worried, the child quickly picks up on those feelings. The parents' perspective towards the field itself should be one of harmony and anticipation. I also strongly believe that children should have a place in the preparation for the journey. Such ideas as making a scrapbook of the new country, visiting the library to read up on the home to be, visiting with missionaries (not necessarily of your own denomination) from that country and making them welcome in your home, as well as asking them to talk with your children can go a long way in easing tensions and anxieties that might carry over into the new field. Even trying new recipes from that land can be turned into a fun evening. Enough lead time to adequately prepare one's children as well as one's self for the move shouldn't be an ideal. It is a necessity.

The preparation itself should be as joyful as possible. No one approaches their stateside departure overjoyed. There are natural emotions when leaving loved ones and one's homeland that ought to be expressed by parents and children alike. Nonetheless, there is a deep, abiding sense of God's presence in this process and a profound sense of joy and excitement as you see the completion of this stage of God's will for your life. Our children should be allowed to feel this and sense it as much as possible. This should be a priority in this preparational stage.

I feel our churches might need a little education in assisting the missionary with his departure. Many colleagues have testified to the hectic pace of trying to get ready to depart. Perhaps the church members feel they are intruding on the missionary's privacy if they get involved in the move. Those who have been there know what a welcome relief it has been to have someone take care of your children when packing, clearing out, running one of hundreds of errands.

A word should also be said here relative to age. At least one denomination will not appoint missionaries with children who will reach thirteen years of age during the calendar year of appointment.

In a classic work on the effects of children and an overseas commitment, Dr. Sidney Werkman addresses the dilemma of uprooting the adolescent when he writes, "Experts unanimously offer the same answer to this dilemma. They suggest not to take teenagers out of high school and move them overseas, unless no alternative exists. The social network of an American high school is a rigid one, hard to leave and very difficult to reenter."

In addition, let me quote from a letter from psychiatrist Henry Holland who is accustomed to working with missionaries and their children in the appointment process.

> I believe that the Foreign Mission Board of Southern Baptist Convention has found that more problems exist for adolescents going to the mission field than for any other group. Adolescence is a difficult period in the stages of development in any family constellation or culture. Peer group identity during adolescence is extremely important, and to translocate adolescents from one culture to another during this period of development is naturally quite stressful. Ego development involving sexual identification, the development of meaningful interpersonal relationships, the development of abstract thinking and

the formulation of new ideas, and the dependency-independency struggle are all considered in assessing adolescents in candidate families. In a healthy adolescent I would look for evidence of a positive peer group involvement, meaningful interpersonal relationship with both sexes, goal directed behavior, and at least reasonable or healthy control over sexual drives and aggressiveness. I would hope that the adolescent is neither an extreme introvert or overly rebellious toward authority. I would also want to be sure that one of the children, particularly in adolescence, is not triangled into some type of tension that exist between the parents. Frequently an adolescent with problems is focused on as a problem in a family when the real problem may exist between the parents.

I believe we would all agree that the children definitely enter into the preparation in a significant manner.

Field Ministry

I am using the term field ministry to describe the time span spent on that foreign field. It is here where problems may become more apparent and affect the MK in various manners.

One of these may be through the father. Raymond Chester discovered in a missionary survey that husbands show a marked increase in stress with five children (one hundred couples were randomly chosen with 90 percent having two or more children). Being the father of two very active children I can certainly understand this! Chester concludes that as children are introduced into missionary family life, stress increases, especially for the husband.

The MK is affected not only through stress on the father but also by the father's work load itself. There are not enough hands to do all the work that must be done on the mission field, and the longer one serves, the more he sees to be done. In addition, the demands made upon him increase from nationals and/or from his own colleagues. Add in a strong level of motivation, a gradual diminishing of physical energy as the years take their toll, plus the discovery that some personal dreams will not be realized, and one can quickly see what this can do to the father. Freudenberger has been cited as saying that "as people grow older and see more of their dreams fade, they become increasingly susceptible to burn-out. They are what I would refer to as the Interface Generation, those who like Janus, the Roman god of beginnings and endings, look ever forward and back." He adds significantly, "the segment of the population I am likening to him are those who straddle two cultures."

I am concerned with how the MK is affected by pressures upon the mother as well. In 1978 while completing my doctoral dissertation, I surveyed 578 Southern Baptist MKs throughout the United States. I would like to isolate one of the three most frequently mentioned sources of problems listed by the MK. This may generate a bit of controversy. It was "absence of mother."

In a general sense, I believe the MK expects that the father will assume a larger share of the mission workload. I'm not trying to be chauvinistic, and I'm certainly not trying to excuse the father because of his work load. While it holds true that both the husband and wife are appointed as missionaries, the idea seems to prevail with many missionary wives that they, too, must assume a heavy load alongside of their spouse. While this idea might be feasible in later years when the children are older and less dependent, it quite often prevails at a time when the dependency needs are strongest. Let me illustrate with two testimonies from an article by Webb and Kelly. A missionary wife expressed it as follows: "In my first years as a mother on the mission field, I didn't know whether I should be a mother or a missionary. I felt an obligation to be out with the people. I thought being a mother and a missionary were two different things. I didn't realize until my children were gone that they could be one and the same." The second mother shared her feelings as follows: "Now that my children are grown, I realize even more clearly that these children are our first responsibility. My children now in their maturity have expressed to us that there were times when they were younger that they felt somewhat neglected because we were so busy doing 'God's work.'"

Whenever I inquire of the missionary mother as to where this "sense of obligation" comes from, she invariably responds, "Those back home expect it of me." There are many other causes as well—a demanding husband, a need for self-gratification, or even an escape from one's own family responsibilities. Nonetheless, I encounter the first mentioned more than any other.

There are those in the church who possibly demand a heavy load for the missionary mother, but they are the exception rather than the rule.

I believe the only way we will be able to minister to the missionary mother is first, through counseling, verifying not only her understanding of her responsibilities and role, but also verifying that the husband is supportive of her. Secondly, orientation of the sending churches would be helpful. This could be accomplished through articles in mission magazines and through testimonies and could even be incorporated into a "sending service" with the missionary family.

We need to remember that the well-adjusted MK within a healthy family is a source of deep satisfaction to the parents and is certainly a positive influence on their work. It makes for a very healthy climate for that MK to grow spiritually and emotionally. It also influences, more than we can know, the mission work itself.

The bottom line to me is that if you have a distressed MK, it is going to be just about impossible to have a happy ministry on the field. More likely than not, it will end in resignation. I believe it is important that in all of this, we do not forget the MK and his own perceptions.

How does the MK perceive his parents' (both father and mother) attitude toward their work? In my dissertation survey, I asked each MK to prioritize his three most common problems. Significantly enough, the statement "I resent my parents' work" did not appear in the top three. As a matter of fact, only five out of 234 indicated this as a problem. However, it can become a problem when the MK perceives a consistent negative attitude on the part of one or both toward their work.

Theodore Hsieh in his survey of seventy-eight MKs attending four different Christian institutions carried the thought further when he wrote, "The missionary child's perception of his father's satisfaction with his routine and daily activities related significantly to the MK's decision in choosing a missionary career."

How is the MK actually involved in the work of his parents? One of the most exciting things for my children is to give Brazilians evangelistic tracts. They understand why they are doing that, and they are excited and feel a part of the work. I don't think we have an excuse to say "My children are too young to be involved."

All MKs are involved to some extent. An MK from Jordan shared it beautifully with me as follows: "I love the work my Mom and Dad do because (1) it is God's will for their lives and (2) it's what they're happy doing—what they want to do. I was never old enough to really be a part of Mom and Dad's actual work, but in retrospect, I feel like I had an influence and played a part whether I knew it or not."

Certainly MKs are continually reminded of their involvement by having to respond to that often-asked question, "Why are you here?" Wise parents take the time to explain clearly why they are there and what they do in their work.

MKs will likely have problems if they do not understand what their parents do and why the family is living in a foreign land. They will have problems if they perceive a difference in the glorious terms their parents use to describe their work and the not-so-glorious terms they use within the home.

Gleason (1973) in his comparative work with American adolescents from overseas military, federal civilian, missionary, business, and foundation scholar homes found that the adolescent from a missionary home evidenced more components of world-mindedness (the expression or manifestation of open-mindedness toward different concepts of national identity and cross-cultural values), than did any of the other classifications. I would say involvement and world-mindedness go hand in hand.

A mission board staff member who regularly interviews large numbers of prospective candidates shared with me that one of the three most often asked questions is, "What about raising a family overseas?" Part of the raising will involve the educational process.

My worldwide survey in 1978 asked the question, "As a result of the educational method used with your child/children, do you feel that they are as well-educated as their peers in the U.S.?" The response was overwhelmingly positive, regardless of the method used. The MKs themselves felt that their educational background prepared them well for college.

In my research, I found that the MKs surveyed did not feel that their method of education cost them overall in their ability to relate to their peers in college. To be certain, there are adjustments to be made by MKs who have spent the majority of their life in another culture. However, the majority of MKs handle and resolve these differences very well. To place the blame for adjustment difficulties solely upon the educational process would be most unfair.

Implications for MK ministry

1. We could provide more resources to help prepare the missionary father and mother for their parental roles and the demands these roles place upon them.

   This should be an integral part of the preparation and counseling prior to departure for the field. Every missionary personality is different, just as different fields will exert different kinds of pressures. We need to consider these personalities and pressures as much as possible and the type of schooling called for before sending a family out.

2. The missionary mother needs to feel secure in her own role.

3. Parents should look for ways to naturally involve their children in their work and explain to the children the nature of their work.

4. Mission boards would do well to plan regular family conferences enabling missionaries to come together both to learn and to benefit from qualified speakers.

5. We would do well to create a model that would detect MK problems early on, so that they might be treated at the beginning rather than much later when the problem is more severe.

6. A network of resource persons on the foreign mission field, capable and well-trained, could be dispersed to key points throughout the world and be utilized in a preventive sense as well as in times of conflict.

7. Our churches stateside could do more to keep in contact with MKs while on the field, and MK parents could do more to enhance this contact by attempting to furlough at the same place, and as much as possible in the same church.

Re-entry

When I use the term re-entry here, I am using it to mean the transition from the foreign culture into the U.S. culture for an unspecified length of time.

Factors in furlough adjustment

I have found that the positiveness or negativeness of the furlough experience for the MK will depend on the following factors:
1. Age of the MK
2. How his parents have or have not prepared him
3. His overseas experience
4. The personality of the MK
5. The church environment—more specifically the pastor and/or staff member with whom the MK will relate
6. The attitude of his or her peer group both at school and church

Ten MK myths

I have made a list of what I call ten MK myths (1986). I feel more MKs would have an easier time with their relationships if more people were aware of these common misconceptions.

1. MKs feel they have "given up much" because their parents are missionaries.

2. The MK family "has it all together." Missionary families are subject to challenges and stresses like every other American family. Just because they are missionaries does not mean that they do not face difficult circumstances or that everything is always "on an even keel."

3. MKs consider the U.S. "home" and cannot wait for furloughs to come. I believe one would be closer to the truth if it was said that many MKs are counting the days until they can leave the U.S. and return to the country of their parents' work.

4. MKs return to the U.S. and just "slip right into place." Many missionaries, for various reasons, do not furlough in the same place twice. When I surveyed my South Brazil colleagues I found them split evenly down the middle—half did and half did not furlough in the same place. However, it is significant to note that of the half who did, the feeling was unanimous that it was a positive factor in the adjustment of the child.

   One MK said, "I wish my family's home leaves or furloughs could have been in one place in the U.S. We went back three times and lived in three different places. I can't really say or feel I'm from anywhere in the States."

5. MKs love to be the center of attention.

   MKs must be treated just as individuals. They should be given the opportunity to tactfully accept or decline offers to speak to groups. Not all MKs will react alike.

6. All MKs are alike.

   Some have a great deal of trouble with this concept. I have had more than one MK share that they felt others regard them as an MK first and a person second.

7. MKs are "Super Christians."

   MKs have shared with me their frustration at being labeled "super humans," wanting instead to be treated like everyone else. "We have needs too," some have shared.

8. MKs are Bible scholars.

   Difficulties in mastering a language can render worship in the church as a somewhat difficult experience week after week. The lack of a highly developed educational program and youth ministry can be negative factors.

An MK from Africa shared with me that "We went over and over the same things. I know well the stories of Jesus but who were Balaam and Barak?" Her conclusion, rightly so, was that MKs are not always knowledgeable about the Bible.

9. MKs want "special privileges."

This would only serve to further isolate and separate him from those with whom he wants to be regarded as equal.

10. MKs are different.

One MK from Rio de Janeiro, Brazil said, "They view me as coming from a disadvantaged corner of the world. How could I tell them that the city of Rio de Janeiro, a metropolis of 6.5 million people and a major cultural and economic center of the Western Hemisphere, is an area superior to many places in the U.S.? It's frustrating for people to think you're from the jungle when you're from a larger urban area than most of them live in."

An MK from Africa affirms this in saying, "Most people think my parents live in a little grass hut without running water and go around stalking the bush country looking for people to convert."

MKs are not problem kids, though the problem MK does attract considerable attention. Research by Dr. Ruth Hill Useem and a number of scholars at Michigan State University led them to the conclusion that third-culture kids have fewer psychiatric problems than any young people from similar backgrounds in the U.S.

I came to the same conclusion while researching my doctoral dissertation and using the Minnesota Multiphasic Personality Inventory. MK norms revealed great stability in comparison to the national college norms.

Characteristics of the MK

We have looked at MK myths in an attempt to better understand the implications. Let's consider the MK personality itself by means of these generalizations:

1. MKs are more intimately related to and dependent upon the family than would be true in the United States.

2. MKs appear more sophisticated in relations with adults, but may be relatively inexperienced and insecure in peer group relations, particularly with members of the opposite sex.

3. MKs do not make friends easily, but do depend on one or two very close friends.

4. MKs are self-directed, self-disciplined, subdued on the surface, but likely to think deeply and seriously about personal and community concerns.

5. MKs are good observers.

6. MKs are gaining in measured intellectual performance at the same time that general test scores in the U.S. are going down.

7. MKs do a great deal of reading, frequently of adult materials, and are likely to enjoy writing more than the peers in the U.S. Their often long letters constitute an example of a nearly extinct skill among their contemporaries at home.

8. MKs are more likely to be accomplished to some degree in the field of music.

9. MKs are more conservative in values than their peers in the U.S.

10. MKs take academic work seriously and are frequently over-achievers.

Implications

As we consider the MK and his re-entry process and the implications for a model of ministry, I would like to mention the three most common problems cited by college-age MKs surveyed in 1978: first, longing for their foreign roots, second, culture shock, and third, no sense of loyalty or commitment to the local church.

1. There is not a lot that can be done to ease the longing for that country in which they grew up. Time and stateside adjustment usually help.

2. Culture shock will depend to a great deal on where the MK is living in the world and the kind of situation in which he is living. Is he in a metropolis under heavy Western influence or is he living in a very primitive isolated situation?

   Periodic MK re-entry retreats on the foreign field with an "off to college" theme or other themes could be helpful.

3. Regular contact with the youth group from a stateside church could be very helpful, remembering the MK's birthday and special events.

4. Church or family "adoptions" can help create a sense of family for the MK separated from his own.

5. College MK organizations can and do fill many a need for MKs especially when sponsored by someone knowledgeable about MKs and MK needs.

6. The parents' arrangement of furlough to coincide with their son or daughter's freshman year can be of great value to the MK.

7. A network of counselors could be established throughout the U.S. to help MKs when needed.

Conclusion

The MK has a unique heritage. Living and growing up in two cultures is not an easy matter, but there are so many blessings that go with it. It is an opportunity unparalleled.

Lorraine Kress, in her fine article "Child of Two Worlds: The Third Culture Child," says it well when she writes:

> Yes, there are missionary children who look back at their overseas experience and resent it. Some blame every unhappiness on their abnormal childhood, saying they were denied normal friendships, their fathers were too busy for them, they were sacrificed to the missionary cause. Certainly some can make those claims with an element of truth. But I feel that the true root of those difficulties lies not in the overseas experience, but in the life of the family as it was lived overseas. In many cases, the same family would have equal difficulties had they stayed in Podunk Corner, USA.

> For many missionary children, the memories are happy, response is positive, and life-style is well-adjusted. They are the truly rich ones—not because of some romanticized misconception of how wonderful it is to experience another culture, but because in reality they have developed strong and healthy personalities.

References

Bridges, Erich. "Missionary Resignations Down But Reasons Still Complex." *Baptist Press* (February 26, 1982).

Freudenberger, H.J. (1980) *Burn Out: How to Beat the High Cost of Success.* New York: Bantam Books, 11-112.

Gleason, Thomas P. (1973) "The Overseas-Experienced American Adolescent and Patterns of World-Mindedness." *Adolescents* 8, p. 486.

Holland to Viser. October 12, 1981.

Hsieh, Theodore. (1976) "Missionary Family Behavior, Dissonance and Children's Career Decision." *Journal of Psychology and Christianity*, Vol 2, No. 4, pp. 11-13.

Lindquist, Stanley E. (April 1983) "Use of Psychological Tests in Missionary Candidate Assessment." *Evangelical Missions Quarterly*, pp. 78-83.

McKay, Marie (November 1974) "God Bless the Missionaries." *Royal Service*, p.9

Sanford, David. (1986). "Marriage; A Strong Foundation." Paper presented to Wycliffe Workshop, Dallas, Texas.

Viser, William C. (1978). "A Psychological Profile of Missionary Children in College and the Relationship of Intense Group Therapy to Weekly Group Therapy in the Treatment of Problems as Reflected by the Minnesota Multiphasic Personality Inventory." Unpublished Doctoral Dissertation, Southwestern Baptist Theological Seminary, Ft. Worth, Texas.

Viser, William C. (1986) *It's O.K. to be an MK*. Nashville, Broadman Press.

Webb, Leland and Dora Kelly. (1974, November) "Finding Her Role." *The Commission*, p.5.

Werkman, Sidney. (1977) *Bringing up Children Overseas: A Guide for Families*. New York: Basic Books, Inc., p.5.

27

Recruiting and Screening Quality Teachers for MK Educational Programs

James Smotherman
Wycliffe Children's Education

A Model for Recruitment

I would like to present a model for recruiting and choosing the people that should be in your school programs. This is a U.S. model that we are using in our Wycliffe headquarters in Huntington Beach, California. We are moving in three areas of recruiting.

1. Making our membership aware. If we can make our membership aware of our needs, without any expense the word can be spread through members' prayer letters. If you have a hundred people in your mission, and each of those has at least a hundred constituents, you can quickly get information into ten thousand homes and to some churches.

2. Relating to churches. Encourage your home agencies to make your needs known to churches.

3. Making use of publications, films, and all those things that give visibility to our mission. Work with your agency to make sure their publicity materials include the support person, including the MK teacher.

During the last two years we've gathered some information from 137 of our teachers that went out. Fifty-two percent of those came into our organization primarily because they met and interacted with a Wycliffe person. Thirty-five percent began to move towards missions through the emphasis of the church—a missionary committee, a conference, a pastor who was missionary minded. Twenty-seven percent saw something in a publication, a book, a magazine, a mailing; twelve percent on film and radio; eight percent in Urbana; and four through Intercristo.

Follow-up

Once you have an inquirer, follow-up is absolutely essential. Encourage the prospect. Find out that prospect's real intent. It will save a lot of time and save the field personnel from heartbreak. We have young people who are interested in missions, but that is not their focus.

Let them know from time to time that you're interested. Have a tickle system that goes after them. "Hi, how are you doing?"

Help them find God's will

It is not my role to recruit teachers. It is my role to help people who are trained in education to find God's will. The burden of filling the need for a hundred teachers in Wycliffe around the world is God's business.

I never push for a teacher. I never put guilt feelings on them about the need. I simply say, "Would you like to get involved in the great commission with your talents? I'll give you all the information I can. If you don't fit, I'll tell you as soon as I can. I want you to find God's will, and if that's with another mission, I will take you there. I will do anything I can to help you find God's will for you life."

You know what happens when you work that way? You get them. But what happens if you begin to put the pressure on? They retreat. It's not only a spiritual way to deal with people, it is also good management. We're all in this together. I'm telling you the secrets of my trade. We have a job to do. Your MKs are no less important to me than Wycliffe's. We need to help each other.

Give a clear statement of:

1. Qualifications needed.   Don't keep any person guessing. Some qualifications can always bend if necessary, so deal with that individual as a human being. You might find somebody that doesn't quite match up to every qualification, but who may be the finest teacher you can find.

2. Mission entrance. I've asked some teachers about their mission's policies, and they don't know.

3. Career paths possible. A teacher coming into your organization, may say, "What happens in ten years? What are my options beyond teaching for two years?" Let them know what options are available.

4. Job description and expectation. This may be the toughest.

An administrator says, "Send me somebody who can do core 9 through 12."

I say, "What subject?"

"Specifically math, but if they can't teach math, I would still be interested in them."

And I'm supposed to go out and recruit this person!

Give your home office all the information possible. Most of you would like to say, "Send us a flexible educator with ability to teach K through 12 who can speak three languages." Any excellent teacher in the home country is secure in a certain area, but the minute you start moving out of that area, you've brought in a variety of insecurities that may keep that person from going to the field.

5. Prefield training. We need to give our people more prefield training. It is my impression that the average teacher in a mission context will either make it or not make it depending on his ability to function in the mission subculture as opposed to whether he can or cannot function in the larger host culture. We must clearly let that teacher who's coming into our mission know the subculture, and predict if that person will be successful there.

When I know there's a teacher candidate in Minnesota, I find a veteran who is on furlough in the same area to interview that teacher. That missionary may not know a thing about teaching, but if he reads people well, I simply say, "Have an hour with the prospect. Tell me, will he fit into Wycliffe?"

A teacher can be successful at one school and not be successful in another school in the same district. It has to do with who the administrator is. What's the climate there? For example, some of your schools, because of the nature of your mission policy and your doctrinal stance, are very conservative in behavior and dress. At some schools a beard would be prohibited. Don't send a free thinker into that setting. You have a clash already. Send the person to the right place, and make sure they can fit into the missionary subculture.

Interviewing the Supervisor of a Potential Teacher

This is designed to share how we go about gathering data in the United States. This would have to be modified for England or Australia to make it as culturally relevant as possible.

I suggest collecting information by telephone, particularly because of some of the new laws in recent years that have opened files. I find that I get more information from what's not written than from what is written in today's world. A telephone conversation is very safe. You can get candid information from a telephone conversation, but you cannot get candid information on paper unless you read between the lines and make some guesses.

Ask the person you call, "Do you have twenty minutes?" If there's somebody sitting in the office, you won't get a good interview. Just say, "I sense that you're hurried; could I call you back? When?"

If we do not get enough information talking to the current supervisor, we go after a chairman of the department or a colleague in a school where they taught two years ago until we find somebody who can answer our questions. If we explain that we're going to send a teacher to the most primitive areas on earth, and we need to be really sure who that individual is, they are usually so helpful. "Oh, really? Why are they going there?"

"Got a minute?"

If that person is comfortable with the whole concept of Christian missions, they may say, "This person will fit. They are really exemplary. They need to be in your kind of organization because they could be more fulfilled."

Sometimes they say, "I've got two years left. Could you use me in a couple of years?" I can't tell you the number of administrators that are believers and are excited about what they hear.

The telephone procedure, I admit, is an art. If you have listening skills, you can become a great telephone interviewer. Every hesitation of the voice you register, "Aha, what's the hesitation?" You don't call them on it right then, but maybe later you go back and say, "Before, when we were talking about sarcasm, you paused. Why?" You catch them off guard, and there comes the real truth. You can get that data by telephone.

You can't read eyebrows; you can't read nonverbal clues at all, so whenever possible go visit them personally. If possible go see them teach. That's the ideal. I'm suggesting another possibility when you can't. You can still use some of the same questions.

Background on school or program where prospect has taught

First we gather information about the school setting that the person is in. We find out what the school was like and how many were on the faculty. We find out what the community was like: inner city, urban, or rural; the ethnic distribution; the percentage of professional to blue collar people in the community; and so forth.

That helps you interpret who that teacher is and what the principal or headmaster is going to say to you about that teacher. It also helps the field person interpret the papers you send him.

Information on the interviewee

When you gather all this data, you must evaluate the evaluator. If that data is going to be any good, you've got to know what that person is really saying to you.

- How long have you known the person being evaluated?
- Under what circumstances have you known the prospect?

You should also attempt to discern whether the interviewee is sympathetic towards Christianity.

Discipline or student management

- What methods are used in classroom management?
- Is there any evidence of problems in controlling behavior of students?
- Is sarcasm used as a form of discipline?
- Is the prospect willing to ask for help if needed?

Rapport with children

- Do the children enjoy the prospect as a teacher?   As a person?
- Does the prospect like students and expect them to reciprocate?
- Does the prospect command respect?
- Does the prospect spend time with students after school hours?

Rapport with parents

It's absolutely crucial to know about rapport with parents. Unfortunately, you're not going to get a lot of information, because most teachers live in another community.

> Most administrators say, "They do well."
> "Give me an instance."
> "Well, no one has ever said anything negative."

That's all you get. You really don't know how well they do with parents.

Try these questions:

- Do parents ever ask for their children to be placed in his/her class?

- Can you share some examples of him/her interacting with parents?
- What have the parents shared with you about him/her as a teacher?

Teaching characteristics

Does he/she:

- Enjoy teaching?
- Appear to have a deep underlying belief that all students can grow and attain spiritual, social and emotional maturity?
- Use new ideas and techniques?
- Ever share with you the joy of some student catching on (learning)?
- Do most of the talking?
- Listen to children as well as teach them?
- Employ anything other than straight lecture as a teaching technique?
- Individualize instruction? How?
- Provide extra help for students outside class time?
- Become involved in helping or participating in extracurricular activities?
- Integrate biblical information and principles into instruction?
- Have a teacher-centered or student-centered classroom?
- Appear to be more on the traditional side, or contemporary?

Is he/she:

- Knowledgeable in subject areas?
- Able to stimulate students to think and learn?
- Creative in working with students?

Planning

- Is the class planning meaningful and related to children's needs?
- Do children's needs come first, or teaching structure?
- Are goals established and pursued?
- How does this prospect make decisions? Is he decisive? Does he waver after a decision is made? Is he wishy-washy?
- Are facts and an understanding of the situation obtained regarding a problem before deciding or acting on the situation?

- Does the prospect persevere through difficulties more than the average person? Follow through on things?

Dealing with authority

- When talking with you, does the prospect also have the capacity to listen to you?
- Is the prospect open to your evaluations and suggestions?
- Is the prospect willing to disagree openly with you, or does he keep his views inside?
- Do you feel the prospect is assertive enough? Too assertive?
- Does the prospect ever question your leadership? How?

I am never contented unless I can get a "for instance" from that person I'm interviewing.

> They say, "Well, they do well," or "No problems."
> I say, "Give me an example."
> "Well, you caught me ... "
> So I name a few. "Have you ever changed grade levels on them weeks before school started? Have you ever canceled an assembly? How did they respond?"
> "Come to think of it, they were pretty hostile."
> "Have you ever had a confrontation? Tell me about that. How did they respond?"

You'll get a pretty clear picture if you go after the information.

Peers

- How does the prospect get along with fellow faculty members?
- Do you see the prospect as a leader or a follower?

Tolerance

- How tolerant is the prospect of the opinions of others?
- Does the prospect push religious doctrine or beliefs in an unpleasant way?
- How tolerant of other cultures and racial backgrounds is the prospect?
- How tolerant of children's different behaviors?

Other personality traits

Is he/she:

- Always right? Is it difficult for this person to admit mistakes?
- Aggressive or mousy?

- Responsible, finishes jobs?
- Moody?

How does the prospect respond to change?

- Day-to-day change?
- Long-term change (change roles, assignments, etc.)?
- Ambiguity—black/white/gray areas?

Overall

- Does this person have sufficient self-confidence as a teacher? As a person? Is the self-esteem high/low?

    Get evidence of self-confidence. We have a lot of people in Christian circles who are self-effacing. That is different than being inadequate. They may have to learn to be more realistic and not down themselves all the time. But a person may be self-effacing, and still have a pretty good self-image.

- Is the prospect on the growing edge in his walk with the Lord?
- What evidence of spiritual maturity have you observed?

    A good teacher came to Faith, but was absolutely bombed because she was a fairly recent believer. She knew quite a bit of Bible, but she was out there teaching some kids who knew the Scriptures, cognitively, better than she did. That began to intimidate her until she began to have some real problems.

    How will their self-confidence hold up in the subculture to which they're going? Do they have any Bible background? Are they free thinkers enough to say, "I don't have to have chapter and verse. I know my basic convictions, and I'm a learner"? I would rather take a teacher on the cutting edge of his faith, a learner and a pilgrim, than I would a cognitive person who has all the answers.

- What is the prospect's strongest area?
- If you were ranking this teacher on a scale of 1-5, with 5 being the highest, what ranking would you assign?
- If you were solely responsible for hiring teaching personnel, would you re-employ this teacher for the above-mentioned teaching positions?

Growth

- In what two areas does this prospect need to grow?

They usually say, "I don't know," but when we ask them to rank the teacher on a scale of one to five, five being excellent, seldom will the teacher get a five.

We ask the same question of the individuals themselves.

Godliness

I look for godliness. This is not trite stuff. I'm looking for authenticity in a teacher. I don't care if they know where Ezekiel is or not. Are they authentic? Are they growing? Will they model that before kids? Will they be able to ask, "Would you help me find Ezekiel? I know it's in the Old Testament, but I can't find it right now." When I get a teacher like that, everything else being equal, I say, "Let's go for that."

Short-term versus the career teacher

The stats show that many short-term people are coming to the field as teachers. Some of those short-term people go back to their home country energized. They impact others who will then go out. But when it comes to teaching and the continuity of a program, many of us struggle with the problems caused by staffing our schools with short-term teachers. How can we utilize the short-termer, but at the same time, how can we go about getting the career teacher?

The problem is prefield training. "How long will it take me to get there?" The short-term option works because it moves people out there now. If you take two years to get them there, basically there would be no reason for short-term people.

Dave Pollock says, "Let's shore up the prefield. Whether they stay a long time or short time is not the issue. Whether they are prepared to be there is really the issue." We could give them greater prefield help, minus the local language. That would be one way to get people out there for a couple of years, and help them fit in better.

If I have a school that's largely career people, a short-termer can fit in very well without much prefield orientation. They are going to be taken in like family. But if the school is already half short-termers, we have more of a problem.

Ninety percent of the people we deal with check "short-term." We get three to four hundred intensely interested prospects. Some of those go through our Quest program, get turned on, and make a decision for the long haul because they have more information. If your agency sends you good, well-selected, short-term people, I think it is your responsibility to turn them into career people.

As people coming back to the States come through my office for a debriefing, I ask the, "How did you do?"

They often say, "I don't know."

An American after six weeks on the field needs to know how he's doing.

A colleague in Papua New Guinea says, "If the headmaster never comes into your room and never talks to you about your teaching, you're doing well." We have to know the culture they come from in order to nurture them.

28

Upgrading Faculty in MK Schools

David Lotz
MK Coordinating Committee, New Tribes Mission

A few years back, it was almost an anathema to talk about going out to the field and not going into tribal evangelism. Working in a school was a second-class type of job. Now our mission has totally swung around and we're actively encouraging people to think about a boarding school ministry.

When I first went to our school in Bolivia, I thought my contribution to the missionary effort was giving the MKs an education comparable to what they'd get in their homelands. I would relieve the missionaries from that responsibility and the tremendous amount of time it would consume, so that they could be free to carry out their tribal ministries.

Preparing MKs for Ministry

I wasn't there very long, before I realized, "Hey, this is a much bigger thing than that. These MKs have tremendous potential. These MKs are our future missionaries, and I'd better be preparing them well." My whole concept of my own ministry changed. I believe mission boards and all those having to do with MKs have finally recognized MK's potential.

When I first went to the school in Bolivia, I was on the field committee. Issues concerning the school were always at the bottom of the agenda. No one even wanted to talk about the school, because everything else was more important. That is changing. We are seeing more and more the importance of planning for the future. Planning needs to go way beyond thinking in terms of how many MKs we are going to have in our school over the next five to ten years; how many teachers we are going to need; how much money we're going to

212

need.   We need to think in terms of our potential, our MKs, and begin to prepare them for ministry.   If we're thinking only in terms of giving them an education equivalent to that of their home country, we're missing out.   I believe it only starts there.   It must go much further than that.

Our traditional MK school has been Little America, and I suppose if the British set up their school, it would be Little England. That has been the traditional way of doing things, and it has had it's point.   We are talking about roots.   Roots need to go down.   Our kids need to have some kind of roots in their parents' culture, but I believe we've gone so far in that direction that we've lost out on a whole lot of other things.

We may do a little bit of evangelizing in the immediate area. We may play soccer against some of the local teams.   But our MK's are growing up with the idea that cross-cultural ministry really isn't very important.   If we have personnel in our schools who are committed to winning souls, who know the language, who can reach out, who are concerned for the people in their community, our MKs will catch that.   If we don't have personnel with that kind of commitment, they won't catch it.   If we're going to prepare our MKs for a future cross-cultural ministry, let's give them some experience in that.   Let's plan for it.

It is not enough to take people that are trained for the teaching profession in one country and transpose them into a cross-cultural situation.   We cannot expect them to do the kind of a job that we want to do with our MKs.   We want people that are trained to teach in a classroom.   We also want people that can minister in a cross-cultural situation as role models for our MKs.

By the way, when I talk about school personnel, I'm not talking just about the certified teachers.   I believe that everybody in our MK school is a teacher.   I know MKs that have been more influenced by members of our staff that were not teachers than they were by teachers.   We better have our full complement of staff trained in this way. Too many of our schools have people that don't even know the trade language.   Sometimes we haven't been able to find teachers, so we use people that should never even be in a school in the first place. But if our goal is to produce MKs that are able to do cross-cultural evangelism in the next generation, we've got to change our thinking about our whole staff.

Upgrading Faculty

In order to upgrade faculty, we need to be clear as to what we want in a faculty, how to choose them and prepare them for a very special job.

Identifying and Describing Personnel Needs

We already know that a majority of MKs choose cross-cultural careers, mostly in Christian service. Since this is true, their MK educational experience ought to include many things that are beyond the usual, standard educational process—a strong evangelism program, courses in world missions, emphasis on cross-cultural contacts, and language learning. These programs and others need to be developed and emphasized.

Precise goals and guidelines should be worked out within each mission board and then standards can be set for choosing and training personnel.

Job descriptions

Once goals are established, job descriptions can be developed. With job descriptions, the process of searching for candidates can begin. The value of a job description is threefold:

1. It helps the mission board focus on the qualities and skills of sought-for personnel.
2 It becomes a guideline for subsequent prefield training;
3. It gives the prospective candidates an idea of what they're getting into.

Once goals are clear and standards are set for desired personnel, the mission board should develop a recruiting and screening program.

Specialized Prefield Training

Most times, we will not find people that exactly meet our criteria, and that's where the special training comes in. Using the goals and job descriptions, specialized training can be provided. I want to mention a few things that I think should be included in such courses.

Adapting and improvising. Most MK schools are limited in resources, materials, and funding. Teachers need to learn how to get along with minimum materials and equipment, and to be resourceful and creative.

Bridging cultural gaps. Teachers and other school personnel are likely to encounter children of several nationalities with their various cultural differences. In addition , there will be the national culture to cope with. Our teachers should be role models in establishing cross-cultural contacts with nationals. This involves learning the trade language and having motivation and skills for witnessing.

The MK culture. MKs have a special culture of their own, and school personnel should have considerable knowledge of how MKs think and act, of MKs' academic potential, of MKs' future ministry, and of parental goals for MKs.

Cross-cultural experience. Cross-cultural knowledge may not be enough. Each candidate should have some first-hand experience in a cross-cultural setting. This could involve some short-term overseas projects or it could be an assignment in a city ghetto.

Witnessing skills. All candidates should have some training and experience in witnessing. This is not limited to door-to-door witnessing, but could involve campus ministry, jail ministry, or a ministry in homes for the aged. It should include at least some cross-cultural experiences, even if a translator is required. This is an extremely important skill to develop so that school personnel will be able to teach and demonstrate by example this skill to our MKs.

No mention has been made of college degrees. Most of us would probably agree that a degree is relatively meaningless in itself; the learning involved in earning a degree, however, is important. Whether the training I'm speaking about is tied in to college courses, credits, and degrees is irrelevant to me. Concentrate on the development of knowledge and skills that will get the job done. The training must be pertinent to our goals. That is the issue.

Who will be responsible for developing this kind of training? While the prime responsibility remains with the mission board, certainly some parts of the training program can be delegated. Colleges, churches, and other agencies can provide expert, specialized help, with the mission board providing input. There should be a good deal of open and frank dialogue between mission boards, colleges, and churches.

In-Service Training

In-service training has been around for a long time and the usual programs associated with the term are still needed. Seminars on the field have had excellent results.

Mission boards can send out professional teams to upgrade a field program. In NTM right now, we are developing a program of this kind where a team of well-trained professionals will visit three or four of our schools to provide expert help. We hope this will become a standard program.

In addition, the mission board should be encouraging personnel who are expert in certain areas to share their expertise with the rest of the staff. Some of our most rewarding professional experiences were in sessions of this sort where we openly discussed grading systems, graduation requirements, discipline in the classroom, etc.

Wouldn't it be great to have missionary schools in a given area meet together in a joint seminar? Such an occasion would provide an ideal forum for discussions on many issues that could benefit each school and mission board involved. Who will pioneer this?

Of course, all in-service training should be in line with previously developed goals.

Continuing Evaluation

Along with the commitment for progress in these areas is the need to constantly evaluate both program and personnel.

There should be continuing evaluation of the curriculum, and extracurricular activities. In effect, the whole program of the school should be evaluated with regard to the MK — his lifestyle, strengths, weaknesses, and above all, his potential — and with regard to the goals previously established.

Not only should the program be continuously evaluated; so should every staff member. Does a staff member have good rapport with the students? Does he understand the MKs? Is he meeting their needs? Is he contributing in their spiritual growth? Does he challenge them? Does he take a lead in cross-cultural contacts? Is he a good example? All of these matters should be evaluated at regular intervals — by interviews, by check-lists, or by other means.

Evaluating the program and the personnel will lead to more changes, changes that will lead to further improvement. Perhaps some goals might have to be modified or new ones added, but evaluation must take place on a regular basis if progress is to continue.

The MK is truly a very special person. His unique experiences have prepared him well for whatever lies ahead, but especially for cross-cultural ministries. It behooves us to capitalize on this potential, and take more concrete steps to train him specifically for a future ministry. To do this requires that we improve our programs. Even though our schools have done a good job (witness the many second- and third-generation missionaries), we can have an even higher percentage of MKs go into global ministries and we can prepare them better for those ministries. To do this well requires a good deal of planning and effort and probably more funds. It also means greater cooperation within the mission community as well as with colleges, churches, and other supporting agencies. There needs to be sharing of ideas, working together, interdependence, and, perhaps, delegation of responsibilities.

The potential is too great to ignore. The next surge of missionary endeavor, I believe, will be led by a host of MKs, cross-cultural missionaries trained from the cradle up for the last great thrust in reaching this world for Christ. Let us not fail them!

29

Caring for "Down Under" MKs

Roger Dyer
Overseas Missionary Fellowship

I see a desperate need to assist mission administrators throughout the world to be aware of and responsive to strategies that will
care for MKs from Australia and New Zealand.[1] There's conclusive
evidence that kids' education is a major factor in missionary families
returning home from the field, particularly for secondary education.

"Education is the formal, intentional process of learning or the
acquiring of knowledge and subject mastery. Its basic functions are
related to the transmitting of culture." So there's an interrelation
between education and culture that I don't think we can separate.

Cultural Differences between the U.S. and Australia

One of the first steps in caring for down under MKs, particularly with respect to education on the field, is the recognition and
acknowledgement that there are cultural differences. If we see all
Western educational systems to be the same, I think we're dealing
with a counterfeit notion. All Western cultures are not the same. In
theory I'm saying that education for Australians is best handled by
Australians and by New Zealanders for New Zealanders. However,
that may not be possible.

Let's be more specific about educational differences. On most
fields missionaries from the U.S. or in some situations the U.K. pre-
dominate. Most MK schools have a U.S. ethos and most of them

---

[1]Editor's note: See also Manila ICMK Compendium, "Providing An
Adequate Education For Children of Non-American Parents on the Field,"
pp. 360-365.

have U.S. accreditation. In my knowledge, none have their own predominant New Zealand or Australian bias.

In some cases there's far less writing in the English courses. Generally the system of marking is different. The students receive more marks for less work than we are used to in Australia. Most students can obtain A's or B's if they hand in their required assignments and submit extra work for extra credit.

We were in Faith Academy from 1981 to 1984. Our daughter Sarah was really upset when she came back, because at Faith she managed straight A's, but when she came back home, she didn't get that. That was a terrible shock to her. She really struggled. She lacked some background.

Report methods are quite different in design, purpose, and content. What's a transcript to an Australian?

I could say something about accents, too. During their time at Faith they were forever being ribbed about their accent. Guess what happened when they returned home? After three years at Faith our kids obviously had an American accent. The first thing somebody asked my son was what U.S. state he was born in.

It's difficult at times to convince folk that the two educational systems are different, not one right and the other wrong, or one better than the other.

Let's explore the educational differences from yet another direction. At the school where I taught we had an American exchange student. Initially she came to Australia because she had heard so little about it. This is somewhat different from the constant exposure that we in Australia have to the U.S. through television, world news, etc. She did make special comment that a large number of Americans think Australians speak another language. She then went on to say that there are many words that have different meanings.

"Twelfth grade in the U.S. would be a breeze compared to grade twelve in Australia. When we reach university the hard work begins."

She said she will be able to count the subjects she studied in Australia for credit when she returns at home but warned her fellow Australian students that the same is not the case when an Australian student studies in the U.S. It would be necessary for them to repeat a year spent in the States.

Prefield Concerns

When travelling to and from the field, timing of departure and arrival are of paramount importance as it relates to children's education. There is no tidy answer to this dilemma. But we need a consciousness of the problem to be addressed both by parents and by mission personnel. The school year of most mission schools in the northern hemisphere just does not fit the Australian schedule.

Information from skilled educators is generally available, both within and outside the sending mission and local church. Ask for it, and having gained it, use it. It should not just be short term, but may need to involve a four-year contingency plan.

Counseling of students in relation to courses will be different on the field from that which they would receive in the home country of Australia or New Zealand. The correctness of such advice, I would question.

Concerns on the Field

The use of correspondence courses results in many traumas which need to be considered. In one case I know of, it hasn't been successful. In another case it has been successful. A New Zealand lad went through Faith without any problems at all, and seemed to have his foot in both worlds, both the U.S. situation and the New Zealand situation. He now has finished his first year at University in Dunedin in New Zealand. It appears that his parents had thought his education program out quite well. He is successful. However he did have some traumas early when he got back from the field.

The last principal at Faith worked very closely with us for one family and asked whether we would get the curriculum from Australia. The teacher was very helpful. In small ways things were done to prepare this second grader to return home to Australia. It didn't cost any money. It didn't cost any traumas. It was just something the teacher was conscious of, and it balanced out very well. That's possible anywhere in the world. It's just being aware of the differences and trying to balance them out. You're never going to have a perfect situation.

The academic challenges of year eleven and twelve become a cause of tension and friction as the differences between the two systems reach their widest point.

Examinations in the Australian context are not just a test of intelligence or general aptitude within subject areas. They are the specific fulfillment of a carefully stated and studied curriculum which may vary somewhat in content from state to state in Australia. They are the ultimate culmination of a year of intense and rigorous study. Well-qualified teachers from Australia or New Zealand are needed for this to be successful.

Caring for MKs

Learning

This is a letter from a lass that came back to Australia:

> I would like to ask for your help in writing me a reference. As you know, I have recently returned to Australia. I am currently trying to look for work to do until February, when I hope to enter university here in Sydney. Unfortunately, finding work has proved to be rather difficult. If either of you could write me a reference, there seems to be no one else in Australia who I know well enough to write me one. It would make my job-finding task a little easier. Your help in this matter would be greatly appreciated.

That's nothing great, but it certainly was something significant. There are lots of things that we can do and that we can encourage others to do to make a transition from the field to home much easier.

Certainly the hassle of finding a suitable school when somebody returns home to Australia is a challenge. I suppose it's a challenge wherever you come from. In most cases MKs have been in a Christian environment. Most state schools in Australia are humanistic in their philosophy. There is no doubt that folk at home who have a genuine knowledge and understanding of education need to allow God to use them. If they don't have any such knowledge, it's important that they just keep praying. An excellent example of help we received on returning home from the field was of our mission representative who acted as a go-between for setting up an appointment at a school our kids eventually attended. That was very simple, but we really appreciated it.

We have a church in Melbourne that accepted our kids' schooling as a prayer target. We certainly saw answers to that while on the field and at home. MKs experience intense culture shock when they return home. Often local culture of the host country has rubbed off.

> Our eldest boy came into a real problem with the principal because as the principal walked past him and said, "Good morning," Tim responded in a typical Filipino fashion. He simply raised his eyebrows.

This happened about six times until the principal actually contacted us and said, "You will have to do something about your son. He does not respond when I say, 'Good morning' to him."

We then mentioned to him that there was nothing really unusual about him. He just was responding as he had for so long.

Leisure

Most MK parents want their kids to go to university, but it's not unheard of for an Australian or a New Zealander to actually leave school at sixteen and go into the work force. Thus there's a need for an understanding of unions, wages, conditions of work, and actual job opportunities. Just learning to fill out forms would be helpful. Lots of people in an MK school overseas do not understand that.

Conclusion

This succession of words is of little value unless it's applied and acted on, by missionary parents, by mission organizations, and by the local sending churches. It's not enough just to acknowledge the problem. That's what I think we have been doing for too long. I think action is needed.

It's not sufficient to say that the mission has a policy. It must be actively engaged in pursuing a practical, supportive, and educationally adequate program. Accommodating Australians and New Zealanders into another system is a beginning, but more careful consideration for these young people must be given before parents will feel confident regarding the suitability of those curricula and will be persuaded to remain for longer periods.

Part V

ISSUES FOR MK SCHOOL
ADMINISTRATORS

30

Marketing Principles and the MK School

William Rice
Dept. of Management and Marketing, California State University, Fresno

Marketing is what we do in life. Most of you are already very adept at being marketers. You have learned how to market yourself to be acceptable to society. You've learned how to use certain jargon and certain mannerisms.

An MK school has to do the same thing but on a much broader scale. I want to give you a brief overview of marketing theory that I think is applicable to an MK school.

The Eight P's

Precepts

Those are the things that we have to understand as given. Sailing in a ship, I can not control the wind, the waves, or the temperature, but I have to maneuver through the weather in order to accomplish some task. An MK school has to understand political and social constraints. I believe that today there has been a drastic change in the consumer attitude towards missionary schools and how they fulfill needs.

We're talking about MK schools and an image—how people perceive you, what you do, how you do it, where you do it, and the output of what you're doing. You need to understand something about marketing and how to market what you believe in. What people perceive of you is reality, not what reality is in fact. If people perceive that a person with long hair and a beard is a freak, they will relate to him as a freak. If somebody who has on a business suit is perceived as conservative, people will view that person as conservative. The person may be a flaming liberal. It makes no difference

225

what that person is; it's how people perceive him. How people who want to send their kids to a missionary school perceive what the school is, or how people who want to sponsor a missionary school perceive that school is, is far more important than how that school perceives itself.

Most products fail, not because of what they are able to do, but because of how people perceive them. I believe today there's a misunderstanding of what goes on in missionary schools. Even seasoned missionaries may have an idea that this is supposed to be a surrogate parent experience. I think each school has to understand what they are trying to sell.

People

Marketing has to have people. In the Christian realm ninety percent of what we accomplish is done by volunteers. In an MK school you have to have volunteers who are actively involved and committed. If you do not get volunteers turned on, they will not participate.

Part of the missionary effort depends on ten thousand volunteers and is affected by the lowest motivational factor. If just one person is not exuberant about what you're doing, the school will begin to dwindle in total energy. Paul said to the Corinthians, "I'm coming to you to find out, not whether you know the Word, but whether you have the power, the energy, the anointing of God to communicate to those people around you."

As an educator, I'm not interested in whether a teacher has all the knowledge. I'm interested in whether or not he is turned on about teaching and turned on about turning minds on. In marketing, people are our most important ingredient, if not our only ingredient.

Product or Service

What are we really selling? Is an MK school selling education? Are they selling a total life-extension experience? Are they selling the ability to be a surrogate parent?

What is your mission statement? If an MK school does not have a mission statement, they'd better sit down and come up with one, because that's how you will be evaluated. It's amazing to me that a one-sentence mission statement can permeate every area of what you do. The mission statement of a company like Chrysler is to produce the best automobile in the world. Everything else is backed up by that statement.

Place

Where does this take place? We're finding out in America that the traditional halls of learning are obsolete. If an MK school feels that the classroom is the only place learning goes on, they have lost the impetus of marketing themselves. Non-Christian entities will offer a unique learning experience, and people will begin to say, "I can get more education out of a non-Christian environment." Sophisticated young missionaries under forty are saying, "The education of our kids is crucial." Talk to some of the people in their late twenties and early thirties who are going to the field and ask them what their motivation is concerning their kids. It's very different from ten or fifteen years ago.

Marketing or showing what you're offering in the educational experience called the missionary school is crucial.

Promotion

How do we inform people of what we're doing? I have found that missionaries do not go around blowing their own horns. They're not people who stand on rooftops and say, "We have this to offer." They quietly go about doing what they are doing. A lot of administrators in MK schools have this mentality. The promotion materials that I see do not clearly enunciate the benefits of the school. They enunciate the features.

Price

Kaiser said, "I'd rather receive 1 percent of 100 men's efforts than 100 percent of my effort." I think that the missionary school has to understand that it's better to have a hundred supporters that are enthusiastic about you than to have one administrator who is burning himself out trying to do everything. Missionary groups need to understand how they can get sponsorship.

In the United States, there are perhaps eighty Christian colleges with business programs. They have professors that are waiting for you to call up and ask, "Can you design a marketing program for our MK school?" I look for projects every single year to challenge my students. "Market this situation. Come up with advertising. How do you reach them? Where do you reach people?"

At a hundred hours per student per semester you're talking about two thousand free hours of creative energy to help market yourself. The students would gain; you would gain; it would be an optimization process.

Policy

How do you go about establishing policy? Do you have a steering committee? Do you have a long-term strategic planning committee? How do you go about making decisions? Do you gather marketing research? Do you ask people what they think?

One of the schools I did research for was interested in knowing, "How do people perceive us?"

I asked, "How do you think they perceive you?"

They listed all the things they felt people should think about them. I went out and asked about sixty-five people what they thought of the school. For example, in out-of-classroom education, people rated them extremely low, while the school thought they were doing a great job.

If a company perceives their product is great, they advertise accordingly. "Burroughs Computer Company is number one." Everybody else may think, "No, Burroughs isn't number one. IBM is number one." If there's an incongruity between how you market yourself and how you are perceived by the consumers, they'll just say, "That's unacceptable." They will wipe you out. How you are perceived, how you make strategies, where you want to go—that's policy.

Propagation

How do we go about growing? Growth can be brought about by linking to other organizations, by co-sponsorships with other organizations that need MK schools' extended educational material or need counseling services. I think we have to understand that in the kingdom of God we're all servants. Sometimes we do not share in the body of Christ as liberally as we should. We have a tendency to want to develop our particular ministry in our particular direction rather than sharing information.

Benefits versus Features

Let's talk about benefits versus features. Suppose I want to sell you a house and say, "This house has 212 Kerostan carpeting, a fireplace, sound-absorbent plaster walls, two-hour-burn ceilings, and genuine eight-by-twelve plate glass windows that are dual pane, with dual glazing. The sidewalks are all crushed brick to keep skidding down. Are you interested in buying it?"

"Oh, I don't know. It sounds OK."

The next salesman walks in with the same couple and says, "This house can be your home. This is where your kids can have plenty of room to grow up. They can have plenty of space to play. Take your shoes off and feel how the carpet massages your feet. In fact in winter you could sleep on this carpeting in front of a crackling fire in the fireplace. Through that plate glass window you can see the seasons unfold before you. You can hang your most precious paintings on that sound absorbent wall. Are you interested?" All of a sudden, we're talking about benefits versus features.

If I only sell features, I don't turn on what's inside. When you came to Christ, what sold you—features or benefits? Features are Jesus died on the cross; he gave his blood; we have access to the holy place. Benefits—I'm free. I'm no longer condemned to hell. I can now have fellowship with the living God. Which got below the threshold of your need structure and was a "hot button"?

Brochures for MK schools usually list features. "We offer twenty-five courses. All our teachers have M.A.'s. We have a library of forty thousand books."

"We offer individualized instruction. We offer career counseling." Those are things that allow you to become a better person. Those are benefits. Those are hot buttons, and everybody has a hot button.

I have what I call the Big Five to help you analyze your MK school and present your package of services in a way that will hit hot buttons.

The Big Five

1. The SOS Model—Situation, Objective, Strategy

Where are we? Where do we want to go? How do we want to get there? That's the foundation for almost all the strategic planning of major corporations.

I'll give you an example out of Scripture. The situation was that Peter owed a poll tax which he did not have. The objective was to pay the tax. Jesus' strategy was a very creative one. The Lord said to Peter, "Go down to the river and throw in a fish hook. When you catch a fish, open its mouth, and you'll find a gold coin. Pay for both of us."

We have a situation where a need had arisen. The objective was to come up with the money to meet the need. The solution in this situation was to go fishing. The SOS model is nothing more than a template for thinking.

2. The PSA Model – Problem, Solution, Action

This model can work for the highest levels of business strategy to the lowest levels of personal need.

"Ready, fire, aim." Ninety percent of the time we take action without knowing what the problem is.

There are a lot of problems that exist in MK schools. If you can identify the solution, then it's easy for me to come up with the actions that you need to take in order to eliminate the problem.

It's the same thing in marketing. For example, if you tell me your school is not getting enough exposure (identify the problem) and you say you need to reach x number of missionaries (identify the solution), I can come up with the action very easily – mailing programs or whatever.

Remember the centurion who came to Jesus and said his son was sick? He said, "Master, you don't have to come. All you have to do is speak the word and he'll be healed."

Jesus said, "I haven't seen greater faith in all Israel than this man has. So be it." And sure enough, when Jesus spoke that word, at that hour the son got well.

Jesus was creative. He realized that he was teaching many lessons there. He was not only healing a son. He was teaching about faith. He was teaching about the relationship between authority and obedience. He was teaching a multilevel series of lessons.

An MK school has to understand that when they do things, it's multilevel.

3. FANAF – Find A Need And Fill It

There are three modes to marketing – proactive, passive, and reactive. Passive means we let things go on the way they are. "This is the way we've always done it." Reactive means that we see what other groups are doing and do what they are doing. And I can tell you that unless the Holy Spirit is orchestrating how things are done, you may end up doing things that are beneficial but that do not solve problems.

Proactive means that I am actively going after some vision, some goal, some solution. One need right now is to prepare kids how to think. Missionary parents have a need to know that their kids are being prepared to become productive people.

Be sure that the dollars you spend in an MK school have a maximum amount of impact on the student. Some of the MK schools are still using books from back in the forties. They're archaic. I point this out to the schools and they say, "Well it's the only thing we can afford." That, to me, is ludicrous. What we're saying is that we can not afford to give our students the best.

The way I read Scripture, God always gave his kids the best. I find that God wants to bless us. He says, "We have not, because we ask not."

Jesus found a need and filled it when he fed the five thousand. We have a situation where the people had need of physical food. Jesus had need of expounding his Father's kingdom. He met both needs when he multiplied the five loaves and two fishes.

4. USP — Unique Selling Position

Every Christian is called of God to be a unique part of the body of Christ. As Paul said, "Not all of us are fingers; not all of us are eyeballs; but we all have a part in how the body of Christ functions."

When I get cut, somehow the rest of my body knows. "Hey, all you white corpuscles get down here to this little finger because we need to be sure bacteria doesn't get in the body." If I happen to be hungry, the body tell the eyes, "You guys look out for something palatable to slip down to the digestive system."

What an MK school's function is and how it performs that function in the body of Christ need to be better defined and enunciated more clearly to the rest of the body. That is your unique selling position. You are providing something unique to the body of Christ.

What is that? Sit down with the teachers, the administrators, and the board of directors. Find out what you can do and what resources you have. Make a very realistic evaluation of what your unique selling position is.

All of us have a tendency to think more highly of ourselves than we ought. The missionary school is no exception. We want to become all things to all men. And as a marketer, I can tell you when you become all things to all people, all of a sudden you do nothing well. Unique Selling Positions says that you figure out those things that you can do well, and you put your resources behind them.

5. AIDA — Awareness, Interest, Desire, and Action

Jesus was at the well, and he sent the apostles off to get some food. Along comes this lady who draws some water. Jesus says to her, "Draw me some water." She's now aware that he's standing there at the well.

He says, "I could give you living water." Her interest is aroused.

She says, "What do you mean you're going to give me living water? You don't have anything to draw with."

Jesus says that those who drink the water he gives will never thirst.

Now, not only does she have interest, she has a desire for what this man is selling.

She takes action. She runs back to her village, and many come to believe because of this woman's total conviction that they ought to listen to this man who is a prophet of God.

Jesus didn't immediately say, "Hey, go get the people in your village, and I'll tell them how they can be saved." No, he went through the entire AIDA process step by step to ensure that she was locked in, that she did not falter.

So often we get caught up in thinking, "OK, if you don't want to be saved, tough luck. We'll go on to the next person." We're not interested in the process of bringing somebody along. We don't take this awareness, interest, desire, action approach to sell what we have to sell.

Today, as Christians we need to become proactive, not reactive. We need to become market driven, as Jesus was market driven.

The missionary schools have great potential in the world. They are in a fixed location. They are seen. They are evaluated on the world standard. The world is judging that MK school based on its educational excellence. It is being judged on a world standard, but it is doing a spiritual activity.

The missionary families are saying, "Are you fulfilling the spiritual needs of my kids?" The world is saying, "Are you fulfilling the educational need?" I believe unless we become proactive, creative, led by the Holy Spirit, marketers of a better way of finding needs and filling them, of a better way of solving problems, of better benefits in the world's eyes, we will begin to lose the impact of our Christian witness.

31

ACSI Services to MK Schools

Phil Renicks
Missions Director, Association of Christian Schools International

The Association of Christians Schools International began its ministry as an association under that name in 1978. Missions was at the focus of ACSI from the very time of its conception.

Recruiting Teachers

One of the needs that was expressed by many of the administrators from MK schools was for someone to help them in the area of recruiting teachers. I'd like to mention some of the ways that we've been working at that.

Approximately twenty-five thousand teachers attend the twenty-one ACSI teacher conventions held throughout the United States each year. We're touching base with all of those people in an attempt to sensitize them to the opportunities there are in missionary teaching.

Most of the people that we talk to have very little idea of what it is to teach in a school for missionary children. Some of them are not even aware that schools for missionary children or boarding schools exist.

I don't think our churches are doing a very good job of stimulating people toward missionary service, especially in the area of caring for the missionary child in school. I'm not sure we in the MK schools, when we do our deputation work, are doing all that good a job either. In my own particular mission, the two-year service/three-month furlough schedule (not the extended full-year furlough) has cut back the number of MK school teachers who are able to be on furlough ministering in churches to make people aware.

We are just beginning to help people understand that there is a missions ministry opportunity in MK schools. We teach a seminar at each one of the ACSI conventions, and we set up an ACSI missions booth. We invite any of the MK schools who can send representatives to do so. That gives that school a personal contact with people who are expressing interest in teaching.

I try to get a letter out to our MK schools much in advance of the beginning of the school year saying, "Get your teacher needs to us as quickly as you can, so when we start the ACSI conventions the last week of September, we have those needs on the table." For the convention this year we sent out a yellow book, Overseas Schools, which listed teacher needs. We found that many were asking for copies of that information.

Many teachers were asking, "What are the qualifications?" "What kind of a preparation do I need to teach in an MK school?" I knew there were some general qualifications that everybody expected and that each individual mission had their own specific requirements, but I couldn't find anything written down or in print. So I started asking a lot of questions and came up with what I believe is a good listing of general characteristics and general qualifications. That, along with some strong statements about the matter of commitment, is being used as a recruiting tool.

We have made up a preliminary application sheet that collects biographical data, professional data, and data about their church background and asks what their interest is in teaching overseas. We computerize all of that and get it out to our ACSI member schools and say, "These are people who have indicated an interest. We haven't screened them. You need to screen them and see whether they are the kind of people that would fit in your association." Last year approximately ninety-two people sent in those preliminary applications. Ten of those people actually are on the mission field today in MK schools.

For the 1987-88 school year, we have approximately five hundred open positions. We're looking at ways that we might be able to broaden our base in terms of being able to make contact with teachers.

I'm concerned that we're not getting more teachers from Christian schools in the United States. The majority are coming from the public school system. Some of our administrators struggle with the fact that some of the people they are getting have no background in Bible or in any kind of a Christian philosophy of education which would enable them to integrate the Bible with curriculum materials. We've got to stimulate those people who are in Christian schools to consider missions.

There is an organization that has contact with Christian teachers in secular schools throughout the United States. They have been very gracious to us and have said, "We will advertise in our magazines for you. We will give you space to put in an article. We'll list all your teacher needs if that's what you would like for us to do."

I will be at the missions conference at the Dallas Theological Seminary, also the missionary conference at Prairie Bible Institute in Canada this coming spring. I hope to attend other large mission conferences where we would contact experienced teachers.

I'm beginning to get more and more invitations from our Christian colleges saying, "Come and do a seminar for our kids on teaching in the MK school," or "Come speak in chapel and tell the kids what ACSI is doing."

Close to four thousand Christian school administrators who are members of ACSI in the United States received a letter from me telling them of the critical need for teachers in MK schools overseas. I asked them (1) if they would present that need to their faculty as a prayer request; (2) if there were any of their faculty members who had ever sensed the call of God toward missions, if they would sit down and have a personal conversation with those teachers and encourage them to consider such a ministry; and 3) what better missions project could they have than to send us one of their teachers?

In addition, I wrote an open letter to teachers that I asked the administrator to post on the teachers' lounge bulletin board along with a list of all the needs in the MK schools. That brought us a great deal of response.

I have another mailing that will be going out in January. It's a matter of making people aware and helping them to see that there's a need. I believe as we keep this constantly before people in our Christian schools, we'll begin to see some response.

I firmly believe that someone going overseas needs to sense the direction of God in their lives for that kind of ministry. But I'm also convinced that probably eighty percent of that direction is exposure to the need. Until we expose people to the need, God doesn't have an open channel to really work in their lives.

Some Christian college professors who are committed to missions are beginning to ask their students, "Have you considered the MK school as an alternative as far as teaching is concerned?" Those are the people we'll be looking at five, six, or eight years down the road. That's a long-range kind of a plan, but nevertheless it needs to be instituted.

Overseas In-Servicing

Another area that we have been trying to help with is overseas in-servicing for teachers. ACSI has sent resource people to the Missionary Kids Overseas Schools group that meets every year in one of the different locations throughout Asia. We will go to individual school locations if there is a request.

This past summer two of us went to the Black Forest Academy in Germany where all of the schools from Europe came together for the first-ever European Conference of Christian Schools. Not only did we have people from the MK schools, but we also had people from European national Christian schools. It was so neat to see our MK school people and those national people sit down and say, "We need to join hands in a partnership." "How can we as an MK school help you to get your ministry started? How can we help you extend your ministry? We want to stand beside you and be a resource to you in whatever way we can."

A number of our schools are talking about becoming accredited. ACSI has an accrediting program for Christian schools that is on par with most of the regional accrediting associations in the United States. The difference is that it takes into consideration the teacher's biblical training and Christian philosophy which the other accrediting associations leave out. The first question that usually comes from the MK schools is, "If we use your instrument, how do we in-service our teachers who do not have those backgrounds, and how do we meet the standard?" We've been very flexible with that, but say, "You develop a plan to outline how you're going to meet those needs, and we will help you with that in any way we can." For example, Gene Garrick is going to be doing in-service for the teachers at Black Forest Academy in Christian Philosophy of Education. He's also going to be helping at two of our schools in Africa that have asked for someone to come and do that.

Other Services

ACSI has set up a transcript depository. For our ACSI member schools there is absolutely no charge whatsoever. You just need to send us your transcripts and then let your graduates know that if they want a transcript, it can be sent from our headquarters office in Whittier, California.

We have been attempting to publish the ACSI World Report each quarter. We have tried every angle that we know to cut cost on postage, but there's just no way to do that. We would be glad to accept any donations for postage, because it's one of our tremendous expenses.

We are in the process right now of setting up about five school-to-school partnerships with Christian schools in the U.S. and MK schools overseas. It's exciting to see the kinds of things that can come out of those relationships. We are not just linking schools, we are linking people. That is teacher to teacher, administrator to administrator, kids to kids.

We have been looking at expanding services to the ACSI member schools in the area of materials for computer instruction in the classroom through a group called the Minnesota Educational Computer Consortium, MECC. MECC provides some software to you each year plus the opportunity to buy other software at reduced cost. It's all very well field-tested, and it's material that has been extremely helpful to a number of the schools.

We are in the process of setting up a video tape library for teacher in-servicing. We are going to be putting together a whole series of video tapes on the Christian philosophy of education that can be used overseas, that will meet the requirements of ACSI for teacher certification and also for accreditation for your school.

We can't begin to carry out the plans that we have for the MK schools with just the membership fees that we get from MK schools. What we get in from membership is probably about 15 percent of our total budget. The rest of that budget is raised by faith pledges and offerings at ACSI conventions. That involvement is building a worldwide family of Christian schools.

I guess if we're limited by anything right now, we're limited by resources. It truly is a missions endeavor. Teachers are giving; students are giving. I got a check just recently for a thousand dollars from a student council group who said, "We want to be a part of it."

In the Northeast Region of ACSI, they have a student leadership workshop every year with from five to seven hundred kids. Last year they called me and said, "We want to present some kind of a missions challenge to our kids. Do you have any suggestions?"

I said, "Well, tell me some of the topics that you're going to cover in your leadership workshop."

They went down through quite a list, and I said, "Well, why don't you challenge the kids to give toward providing cassette tapes of some of those sessions for the overseas schools, because they're always looking for material in student leadership."

So, they provided me with twenty-six sets of twenty-eight tapes each. Every time I go on a trip, I pack the whole bottom of my suitcase full of cassette tapes, and I'm getting them out to the schools.

Then they said, "Now what are we going to do for our missions project this year?"

I said, "One of the things that I'd like to see is for you to invite some national student leaders from overseas to come to your workshop and begin to establish a relationship that way."

"How can we do that?   Could we pay for their way to come?"

"If that's what you want to do, that would be very nice."

"We'll make it a two year project, and we're going to aim for next year."

This year they received over $900 in offerings from these kids that's being held in a nest egg for next year. The student leaders all went back to their various schools, and they are doing fund raising projects to raise the rest of the money to bring a student, or if they get enough, two students, to the United States to participate in their student leadership workshop. So, it is building a family, and we're excited about the opportunities there are.

At Grace College and Seminary in Winona Lake, Indiana, each year in the summer they have a week-long institute for Christian school teachers and a week-long institute for Christian school administrators. Our ACSI mission budget sets aside money every year for scholarships, and Grace College and Seminary matches that amount. Last year we sponsored six teachers or administrators who could pay their transportation, but didn't have the money to pay for the cost of meals, lodging, and the seminar. If you have someone that's going to be in the States, and your school can't afford to have them come, let us know. We'll put their name on the list and do the very best that we can to provide some scholarship money for them. That's another way we're trying to help our overseas schools.

32

ACSI School-to-School Program

Phil Renicks and Will Rich
Association of Christian Schools International

[There was no tape of this session, but the following explains the rationale for the program. Further information can be obtained from Dr. Rich by writing him at the address in the Appendix.]

Many Christian schools are interested in having a relationship with another school that would be mutually beneficial. Often schools for missionary children feel this need for involvement with another school because of their relative isolation from other compatible educational institutions. Staff members do not have easy access to resources such as publishing companies and equipment suppliers. They often feel the need for contact with other professional educators to keep abreast of what is happening in education. Many desire a group of interested people who will pray for them in specific ways.

Christian schools in the United States and other sending countries seek a school-to-school relationship because they want to know more about the mission field through personal contact. Staff, students, and parents can become involved in missionary projects through this channel.

ACSI is interested in assisting schools which wish to enter into a school-to-school relationship with an overseas school. Assistance will be given in matching schools, facilitating their contact and interaction, establishing the relationship, and providing some degree of assistance and supervision in the program. These services will be provided without regard to ACSI membership.

33

Accreditation and the MK School

Lyle Siverson
Former Executive Director, Western Association of Schools and Colleges

If your school is not involved in the accreditation process, I'd like to encourage you to give it serious consideration.

There are six regional accreditation associations in the United States. We have never had a national system of accreditation, but in the twentieth century the schools themselves wanted something that was not state-centered in setting up standards and criteria for schools, both private and public. Membership in the association is voluntary, but most good schools become involved. There are six independent, loosely affiliated associations. All six regions meet together once or twice a year. There are differences among those six associations, but there is much more in common. The differences are minor and procedural.

My experience is primarily with the Western Association. Western covers California and Hawaii, the Territories of Guam and Samoa, and the independent and church-related schools in the Pacific area as far as Burma.

The Southern Association covers about twelve Southern states, and overseas schools in Latin America and the Caribbean. The Middle States Association covers about six of the Middle States and overseas schools in Africa and the Middle East, and as far as India. New England accredits the New England States and European schools. North Central accredits Department of Defense schools all over the world. Northwest isn't involved with overseas schools.

All six regional associations are recognized by the U.S. Department of Education, but regional accreditation is nongovernmental. All six regions prize and preserve their independence from any governmental control in order to protect the program and the schools that are being served.

They work with both public and private schools with both church-related schools and independent schools. In Western, for example, we accredit the Seventh Day Adventist schools, the Catholic schools, the Christian schools, the independent schools, and all the public schools that choose to be accredited.

As a young superintendent in 1958, I brought in the accreditation process for the high school in our district. That board, staff, and community looked at itself through the self-study process. "What is it we're trying to do? How well are we doing it? How could we do the job better?" Then outside teams representing the college community, other schools, faculty, and administration looked at the self-study and made recommendations. The team evaluation had great value, but it was secondary to the self-study. Usually people feel that it's the self-study that has the most meaning and benefit to the school.

I became a believer in accreditation because of the program that was developed from the self-study and visiting team. Our board, faculty, and community were able to make progress and changes that were fantastic.

I became so sold on the accreditation process that I said, "I want to be on a visitation committee every year."

As a result of working on teams and chairing, I was appointed to the Commission in 1970 by the California Superintendent's Association. In 1975 I became the Executive Director and worked with the program in California, Hawaii, Samoa, Guam, and East Asia.

There are thirty-six East Asian and Pacific Rim schools that are now accredited by WASC. Ten of those classify themselves as MK schools. I sent a questionnaire to those schools and asked four simple questions of current and previous administrators. They are listed below with some of the responses.

1. What are the benefits that you felt your school received from accreditation?

All ten schools reported that they saw improvements in personnel practices, curriculum, and instruction. All except one or two indicated improvement in organization and communication between departments or levels. Half of the schools noted improvements in purposes and goals, facilities, evaluation, and long-range planning. Other areas cited were improved community and student involvement.

2. What problems arose?

They agreed that conducting the self-study is a lot of work and that some extra help is needed, but that the results were worth it.

3. Would you recommend it for other MK schools?

There was a unanimous "yes" to this question. The responses were emphatic and overwhelmingly positive. Many benefits were cited. Most often mentioned were: lending credibility to the school, helping the school improve, helping the students, bringing objectivity, and promoting ongoing evaluation and follow-up.

The accreditation process is a way to keep you honest with yourself. In the WASC process you're never evaluated on anything that you don't really want to be evaluated on. You state what your school is, and that's what the study deals with.

It gets the total staff involved. It helps you to see your problems and to get those dealt with by the next time you go through this process.

Morrison has been accredited since 1977. Our school is three hundred percent better than it was then, because we have dealt with real problems and have come up with real solutions.

You have to have a fairly stable administration for at least a couple of years to go through the accreditation process. Administrative turnover held up Dalat for a couple of years. Until we got some stability we weren't able to actually enter into the accreditation process.

Accreditation was and continues to be a very good means to address issues that are sometimes difficult to address within the community. The school had been making recommendations for awhile, but the mission headquarters wasn't listening. The accreditation commission got their attention, and we've seen some changes.

When you have to fill out demographic data, look at your goals, and evaluate where you are going with those goals, it really helps, not just on an administrative level, but on the level of the individual teachers.

I know of a case where a student was refused admission to Duke University because his school was not accredited. Also, college students have problems transferring credits from a school that is not accredited to schools that are accredited. These problems are avoided with accreditation.

Hokkaido International School has about thirty students. When they came into the program, the administrator was only there for two years. She was an experienced administrator from the States. She said, "I'm just finding out what the score is and I'm leaving. I'm going to be replaced by a young man whom I have not met. We're not even going to have a chance to see each other. If I had had one of these self-studies and a visiting committee report sitting on the desk when I came, what a great thing it would have been!" She got the process started.

Is thirty students as small as you go?

Shanghai is a fine school with only about twelve or fourteen students. The turnover is tremendous. But that school now has a document on how those who were there before saw the problems, and what they were doing about them. As part of the program you establish a follow-up committee, and every year you look at how you are doing in terms of the recommendations. It's more work proportionately for a small school, but the benefits are, I think, even greater.

For a school to be eligible for candidacy there are several criteria. One is that the school must have been fully operative for two years. Part of the definition of "fully operative" is that it must be operating all grades that it intends to operate.

With WASC, candidacy is granted for three years. You are expected to apply for full accreditation or do your self-study the third year. If you feel ready, you could do it the second year. If you feel you need to take more time, you can apply for an extension. You could get one three-year extension.

4. What suggestions would you give to improve the process?

In WASC, we developed a specific overseas schools self-evaluation instrument. MK schools are well represented in that self-study format even though it's not specifically for MK schools.

Teachers feel that the level of professionalism at Alliance Academy increased as we went from a non-accredited school to an accredited school back in the mid-sixties. It has continued to clarify needs that we have in our school. It also gives us a means to compare ourselves to a standard of a large group of schools in the States. We have a much better idea of where we fit in educationally. We also had good interaction with other schools, both by being evaluated by the members of the team from the local committee and by being part of teams that evaluate other schools. We've learned from other schools as well. We're totally sold on it. The level of interaction among our faculty members during the

*accreditation process helped each of us to grow profession-
ally, as well.*

*Amazon Valley Academy is in candidate status now for
accreditation with the Southern Association. What motivated
us was the self-study. We thought we'd take a good look at
our school.*

*Five years ago my daughter wanted to go to Wheaton
College and wanted to get a guaranteed student loan. She
applied to a bank in Pennsylvania to underwrite the loan,
but they wouldn't recognize a diploma from Amazon Valley
Academy until it was sent to an accreditation office in the
state capitol. I understand that if you are accredited, this is
not a problem.*

*We understand that teachers returning from an accred-
ited overseas school are on a par salary-wise and experience-
wise with any public school district. They can't say, "You
taught in a bamboo hut for some years and that doesn't
count."*

*We're entering the age of a teacher shortage, and that's going
to affect your getting teachers in the MK schools. A lot of
teachers who might consider teaching in an MK school are
going to have debts. Some of those debts will be waived if
they teach in accredited schools. If you're accredited, then
they can come to your schools and teach. If not, then
they're going to have to stay in the States and teach. The
same thing is true with placing student teachers. We can't
send you a student teacher unless you're accredited.*

Problems?

*One of our problems was to get our non-U.S. staff interested
in the process. It is not normal in this culture to come up
with recommendations for your own improvement. "It's my
boss's job to find where I'm supposed to improve." Materials
that would explain to non-U.S. educators the value of
accreditation might help.*

*A visiting committee always has to find something wrong. In
our case, many times they recommended things they should
never have recommended. They recommended specific curricula to a specific teacher. They recommended things that
were very picky, well beyond the scope of what they should*

have been involved with.   To the teachers that was very confusing.

We suggest something between 30 and 45 recommendations, but I saw one with 144 recommendations.   Picky, picky, picky.   That's what that report was.   It happens.

I've been involved in five different accreditations.   One con is that all the accreditation committees that have ever been in a school where I have been, very seldom talked to a teacher. They always talked to the administrator.

We have a specific request that every teacher be contacted at least once.   That has always been a must.   I won't say it happens in every visit, because we're dealing with human beings.

The recommendations are non-binding, but a lot of us in the trenches teaching were not aware that they were non-binding. It wasn't until our mid-term evaluation that a totally different team came down and said, "Oh no, all the things that the last committee did are non-binding.   You didn't have to do them.   Just discuss them."

In our process what is required is a response that lets us know it has been considered.   One response which may be very good is, "We rejected it because ... "

The accreditation committee should have credible people on the commission.   One commission that came to our high school had a high school senior girl on it.

I think we're the only region that uses students on committees. High school students may be on visiting committees if the school requests it.   In California these students are nominated by the California Association of Student Councils.   It has been one of the most successful innovations we have ever used.   The feedback on committees is just tops.   We get an evaluation from the schools, and 97 to 98 percent of them rate the individual committee members and the teams from excellent to good.

Unless it is a specific requirement for accreditation, you are not required to follow recommendations.

The Southern Association recently put together a handbook for Latin American schools that should be ready in a year and available by writing them.

How have others chosen who constitutes the School and Community Committee?

We ask the school to define its own community. A school near Santa Barbara defines its community as international. They draw their students from all over the United States and many foreign countries. They don't talk about their community in terms of that geographical area.

In Ukarumpa the school is run by SIL. Sixty-five percent of the youngsters are SIL, but our school board includes SIL people and members of the local community. One or two of them are not even Christians but represent the local community.

Western Association developed a joint accreditation program with ACSI in California several years before I retired. No overseas schools have taken advantage of it, but it's available to them.

The first school for missionaries' children that was accredited through ACSI received dual accreditation with the Middle States Accrediting Association. That school is in Dakar, Senegal, West Africa. We are currently working with the Southern Association as well for dual accreditation.

My recommendation to every new school is that they look at the criteria they are going to have to meet for accreditation, and then set things up according to the evaluative criteria.

Why don't schools seek accreditation?

I happen to be a Lutheran and I find a very strong feeling among them that we're a governmental body. They steer far away from anything that represents the government. I'm not able to reach them on that point.

The evaluative criteria from ACSI looks at the whole matter of biblical training of the teacher and also the Christian philosophy of education for that teacher.

The WASC program evaluates the school on the basis of its own goals, purposes, and objectives. That's the number one step. If a school fails to even get candidacy, nine times out of ten it is because they have not defined their mission and purpose. That's why it fits in so well with the MK schools.

Bob Christian of Hong Kong International School said, "We found this group was more critical of our religious education program than any other aspect of our school, and helped us do a better job with that. And we were originally more fearful of that because we thought that would be an area they would be suspicious of."

What is involved in a visit from a visiting committee?

For the first visit Southern will send out a full committee from the United States from the Latin American committee. They make a tour of South America, and they'll schedule a visit to your school in that tour. You have opportunity to invite other school administrators or teachers from your area to be a part of that accreditation team.

A year ago I wrote to Southern Association and they sent Dr. Brown, who is headmaster at Rio School to visit and determine our candidacy. He made a three-day tour of our school. He looked at our material. We received candidate status in August. In October we worked out a timetable. This year we established our School and Community Committee. We're hoping that they have some kind of report by May. Then we'd like to establish the Goals and Philosophy Committee to work through next year. In the meantime all our staff is working on updating and clarifying our curriculum guide according to a format we've established. We hope to have this completed by the end of next year and then do our self-study the following year. In the fall of '89, two years from our initial start, we're hoping to have the visiting committee come down.

One of the things you will have to have is your philosophy and objectives for the school. That should be used in almost all the other committees when they do their reports. It takes a good year to put together that self-study. And if you don't schedule it and keep it on schedule, you'll have trouble completing it in a year, probably.

The committee wants current information. You need to hold off on collecting the data.

What is the criteria for evaluation?

Each region is different. WASC gives general guidelines concerning (1) philosophy, goals, and objectives; (2) organization; (3) student personnel services; (4) curricular program; (5) co-curricular program; (6) staff; (7) school plant and physical facilities; and (8) finances.

Those general criteria fit in with the ACSI instrument. We'll set up a joint committee with them. We've not done this with an overseas school because there's not been a request for it. The mechanics are there to set it up.

The standards of the Southern Association are more specific, but you still go through the same kind of self-study process.

We didn't have to pay for the person to come from the continental U.S. That was included in the fees. We did have to help pay for local regional people to come in. Another great cost was the duplicating of our self-study.

Some of the people on the visiting teams are going to do more than one visitation and costs are shared. It's a good idea to make sure that representatives from MK schools are on those visiting teams. If there is a question as to whether your goals are appropriate, you've got somebody there who can take your case.

Do all teachers have to be certified?

Southern Association has alternative standards for overseas schools which make allowances if a teacher has a degree in the subject area or if your shop teacher is a professional carpenter.

In WASC, they look at each case and if you can justify that that person is capable of fulfilling that position you're not going to get static on it.

34

The Future of the Boarding School

David Brooks
Principal, Morrison Academy, Taiwan

The issue of boarding schools is not a new one as far as mission school education is concerned. We've had boarding schools around for a hundred years at least. As a matter of fact, for many people missionary kid education has almost been synonymous with the boarding school experience. As time has gone by, that's perhaps not as true as it used to be. But it is still true for a substantial number of the young people that we classify as MKs, children of missionaries serving the Lord overseas apart from their home country.

Let's refer to a few people who've talked about the issue of MK education and the boarding school.

"We believe that God has called us to tribal work, but we will not send our children away to one of those missionary schools. It's wrong to give our children to some stranger to rear." An increasing number of prospective missionaries and missionaries on the field are making this statement. Is it really wrong, or sin, as some have said, to send MKs away to be educated by "strangers" in a missions school?

This is the introduction to an article by Ray Chester, "MK Education: The Controversy Grows," written back in 1983. His question is valid today. Is it really wrong or sin to send kids away to a missionary boarding school?

This next one comes from Dennis Hollinger. It was written as a paper for the Christian and Missionary Alliance as they as a mission tried to deal with the issue of boarding schools and the place of missionary kid education. He says:

The major question confronting us at the moment is whether the boarding school situation functioning as a surrogate parent, an extended family, can adequately perform the family's task? This is not primarily a theological question, as long as the

249

parents and school intend to make the situation an extension of family covenant. It is rather a practical question: Can and does the boarding school with its necessary institutional framework, provide the personalized holistic nurturance which God desires for children?

Another one is the paper that was written by Dan Harrison called "Causes and Effects of Changing Attitudes Towards Boarding Schools." [Manila ICMK Compendium, pp. 302-310]

Frankly home schooling is a force to be reckoned with, not only in the United States and Canada, but in the mission field context as well. Many people have perceived home schooling as a threat to boarding schools and to the established way—the right way, as we would consider it of educating kids in a missionary school. I'm not sure that's the way it should be, but I think it's the way it is often considered.

Some states in the United States the issue of a parent's right to educate their kids at home has been tested in court, and in many of the cases the parents have been found to have to have that right to do it.

The concept of home schooling is an emerging concept and will have to be considered carefully and perhaps adopted in some cases in the mission field setting in the coming years.

Positive Aspects of Boarding School

What are some of the positive things that kids have gotten out of boarding schools?

Milton and Pat Brown, from Christian and Missionary Alliance, said that of 150 kids they've had under their care, they know at least 144 of those kids are walking with the Lord. That's a source of a satisfaction and brings great glory to the Lord.

I think it's safe to say that the great majority of kids have very good spiritual development and emotional well-being. They have an above average social skill.

Their academic achievement is good. If you look at the philosophy of many of our MK schools, up at the top of the list is that we will provide the kids with an education that will allow them to enter the best colleges and universities in their home country. I think the mission boarding schools have been successful in meeting our goals.

In most cases there is a generally successful transition to college and life in their home countries.

The Exceptions

The fact of the matter is that most kids who have gone through the boarding school experience have had a good experience. But there are notable exceptions. And every notable exception is a real person, and if that person was experiencing difficulty, their family was experiencing difficulty as well. And if their family was experiencing difficulty and trying to serve the Lord as missionaries, their mission and ministry probably wasn't as effective as it could have been either.

And beyond that, just think of that in terms of the personal pain and hurt and disillusionment and frustration and everything else that the devil brings into our lives as we relate to our kids. It's an important topic we're talking about here, and so I don't think we're dealing with one were we can easily brush the exceptions aside. We have to always keep those kids there in mind.

Basic Givens

1. The boarding school is an MK education model that has worked for many years for the majority of the people who've gone through the experience. That doesn't mean it's been the only way to do it, but it's worked for many people.

2. There's a growing division within the mission community as to the appropriateness and effectiveness of the boarding school. I think anything that tends to divide us is a potentially dangerous issue. That doesn't mean it's an issue that doesn't need to be talked about, but things that divide are things we have to be careful with.

3. As God asks people to serve him, he provides the means to accomplish whatever he's asked them to do. And that includes providing for the education of their kids. It can be carried too far, and it can be ignored, but the fact of the matter is, if the Lord calls us, he's going to provide for us.

4. There are many opinions on this particular topic, and there's very little research to support any of those opinions. There's an institutional as well as a parental role in making educational decisions, because the parents are missionaries who represent organizations, and those organizations are institutions that have purposes and goals that they wish to accomplish. If anything impinges upon the way those goals are carried out, then the mission is going to be involved in that process. That's sometimes ignored. Somehow the issue of how

kids should be educated is considered the parents' problem or the school's problem, but it is the mission's problem as well. As a matter of fact, in terms of setting policy it may be even more important.

Discussion

Who decides if kids are to attend boarding school?

I don't think anybody could say, "The mission made me do it, and I didn't have any choice in the world." They can always find a different mission.

As the body of Christ we have to lean perhaps a little more in the direction of mercy. Many mission boards lose the opportunity to recruit many fine families because the mission board is not flexible at all in the way they want to approach a particular problem.

I think it depends a lot upon the board and their attitude towards the way in which you want to raise your children. Our mission board encourages us to use MK schools, but they tell us, "Whatever you think is better you do." So even where our board has our own school, we have kids that home school up through junior high, kids that begin boarding in first grade, and MKs who have never attended our school at all. They've gone to national schools right on up through high school.

I think that sometimes our mission offices at home are more flexible than the missionaries on the field who have always sent their children to boarding school. For instance, our mission office has a policy of allowing people a choice. Our field, until a couple of years ago, had our missionary kids school as the only alternative.

There's a certain threat for all of us who've been there awhile. "Maybe I did the wrong thing in sending my kids there twenty years ago."

Young parents coming out need that flexibility of making the choice, and it takes a whole missionary community to allow them that flexibility. I think a lot has to be done in getting this word around for all of us who are from the old guard.

In our situation, when we allowed home schooling we went from school that had fifty-five students to one that last year had only twelve. How many students are you still going to have a school for?

Our mission has always had the option that the parents could keep their children home and teach them. We're starting at our school to question this option because of some of the situations we're seeing. Our mission works with primitive tribal people. For several of our families who teach their children at home, we're seeing these children becoming more native than anything else. Even outsiders are noticing.

    I think that we need to put pressure on the parents and have them send their children out if the child's education or social life is suffering, or if the work is suffering.

I think it's hard to argue against the right of the parents to decide about the education of their children, but I think it is the right of the mission to decide whether or not that family should be on the mission field. If, for example, there's a family with four children and they have to be home schooled, what in the world are they going to do besides home schooling their children? The mission may well say, "Well, why don't you stay in Michigan and get a job and raise your kids?"

Mission boards need to decide what options they will allow that are consistent with their ability to finance those options and their stated goals in a particular country. Parents need to be aware of the options that are available. Not every parent should be making the same decision about how to educate their children. It's quite possible for three out of four kids to thrive in a boarding situation and for one not to. One of the difficulties that parents and mission boards face is to know what the non-financial cost of any kind of education are.

    Parents need to get advice from mission boards, and they also need to get advice from schools, because we've got some kids in boarding school that ought not to be there.

One of the great needs in missions today is more responsibility on the part of the mission board to inform new parents of the consequences of options with the children. The tendency of the child to become tribalized ought to be mentioned to young parents.

In the school settings that I've been in, I've done more counseling with parents than I have with the students. Couples say in their interview, "Yes, we'd send our kids away to boarding school." But eight years later when that first grader gets ready to leave, suddenly it's a very traumatic situation. They're wondering, "Are we going to live through this? Are we doing the right thing?" We give a lot of counseling. Some don't do it. We lose them off the field. Some come through it.

There are some feelings on the field between the old guard and the young guard about "You're not as spiritual because you're not willing to do it." They're working with a whole different set of information about the family.

In Manila MKs gave testimonies about national schools and home schooling. We know boarding school don't work for every child. But I'm sure national schools don't work for every child. And home schools don't work for every child. And I'm not sure I'm hearing about that.

Often those in mission boards in the States as well as the parents are influenced by certain missiological trends such as bonding with the nationals, or educational philosophies such as home schools. Many of those philosophies, both missiological and educational, were formed within a different context. Those in the field itself, who have considered those philosophies and ideas within the context of the culture can often make the best recommendations.

We've had recently a new couple come to Guatemala. They wanted to bond with the culture, and they wanted their kids to go to bilingual schools. A friend counseled them, telling them they weren't going to receive the education that their children needed. They came very idealistically, "We're going to do it, and you traditionalists get ready to change." They had new information and were more enlightened than we were. After two months they took their kids out of the national bilingual school, and there was no room in the missionary school. It was a very traumatic experience for them. They came to realize that they needed more help than they were receiving.

Research:

The Christian and Missionary Alliance is going to do a longitudinal study comparing the boarding student and peers back in the United States. They will address how MKs are doing as adults.

Mona Dunkle is finishing a doctoral dissertation at Michigan State that compares boarding school kids to home school to international schools. We keep taking about MKs as a group, but how they're educated does have significance.

Prefield orientation for parents regarding boarding

How can prospective missionary parents be helped to understand the realities of the boarding home experience before they arrive on the field.

SIM has a four-week candidate orientation and include a lot of that. We have panels of people who have home schooled, people who have done boarding school, and MKs themselves, trying to give these parents a lot of perspectives.

That ought to be an important part of everybody's preparation for going to the field. Some things you can never face until you live them, but you can anticipate the fact that you may have to face them.

Optimum age for beginning boarding

Is there an optimum age at which students should begin to board? One study indicates that the younger you start kids in boarding school, the better off they will be in terms of their boarding school experience. Other studies might not support that.

That's looking at it from the kid's point of view, but parents have a view on this as well.

As a dorm father, I would rather not see first graders come to the dorm, because they're a whole lot more work. The hours you put into them are multiplied with their youngness.

Most of the kids that go to boarding school are flexible. The parents' perception of the boarding school has a whole lot to do with how the kids get along there.

From the parents' point of view, the later they have to send their kids off to boarding school, the better for them.

As more and more parents come to Pakistan, I've been amazed at how many parents have decided that it's the best choice for their child to go boarding school. And that is a sacrifice. In a Muslim country they saw the options and said, "I see that this is the best for my child." And then that small child is free. Sometimes until you see that situation it's very hard to make those decisions.

Studies show the MK's self-esteem is higher the earlier you start boarding school, but the best time is when the parents and child are positive that it's best.

For elementary children, the children do fine, but the parents struggle. The switch comes in junior high and high school. Kids who haven't had boarding experience until junior high or high school find it much more difficult to adjust. They struggle with fitting into the clique.

In adolescent psychiatry, we look at twelve years old as a time when kids are still very dependent on their parents. At thirteen or fourteen they start becoming much more involved in their peer group, and they must have a gang to hang out with at school. At that time when peers become so important, if they haven't been to boarding school yet, that might be the time to bring them out of the jungle, because they need to be where there are peers that they can relate to. The transition later will be much tougher.

That is such a tough time for kids in terms of trying to figure out who they are anyway that the change may produce stress.

Morrison has taken a position, probably because of the geography of Taiwan, that we try to keep kids home with their parents through the eighth grade. We are able to do that with very few exceptions because we have started branch schools. Taiwan is a small urban society. Locating schools in strategic cities can allow virtually every kid to live at home. I'm not sure we took that first of all on a philosophical base.

Are we working on the assumption that our child's formal education is priority over all of his social, spiritual, and familial development? From a Western point of view, formal education is where we're willing to make sacrifices.

Implications

Mission boards need to:

- Consider policies.
- Prepare of people better.
- Take a hard look at clarity of goals as related to the role of the family in mission work.

Parents need to:

- Deal with fear of boarding school.
- Have an attitude of keeping options open.
- Gain more practical knowledge.
- Commit to have their children educated on the mission field.

Boarding schools need to:

- Be more accommodating to people who are looking for other options.
- Look at their policies.
- Consider what should be the role of the boarding school in this change process.

All should be committed to research.

35

Resident Schools as the Helping Hub for Alternative Education

Don Boesel
Overseas Crusades

My proposal is to have the resident school be the education center for the total field or area. This would help us as educators to look at ourselves as servants to the missionary community. We could set up an Extension Division within our present resident school area, put an administrator in charge of it, and give status to this department so it receives equal time and staff.

At Faith Academy for many years we did not have someone in the Boarding Department who had equal status with the principals of the schools. There was always the feeling, "Hey, we are second-class citizens." When we installed a boarding administrator at the same level as a principal, some of our problems of bickering and feelings of insecurity vanished. That is why I feel some administrative allowance for an Extension Department is important.

Alternatives in Education Options

Home schooling or correspondence. At times we may come across as hostile to the family choosing correspondence because we think we have a better option. But we know that parents need to have a choice. I believe if we ask these parents what we can do to help them, it is going to help our PR. We probably will have their children in our schools later on anyway, but they will come with a more positive attitude if we tried to help by counseling and assisting them.

At Faith we did some achievement testing for some of these people so they would know how their kids were fitting in with norms from the States or at Faith Academy. Sometimes the teachers would help the parents with ideas on how to teach or allow them access to library facilities.

Itinerant teachers. Another alternative is the traveling teacher. The teacher visits different places where there may be one or two students, sees how they are doing, makes assignments to be worked on, and goes on to the next area. A little different system is used by Wycliffe. Under their Field Education System [see vol. 1, pp. 229-269] the teacher sets up the assignments, and the parents assist and see that the child gets the job done. Then a few weeks out of every quarter, the children and the parents who are doing the teaching come in to a base where the teacher can work with them.

If this base were at the resident school, the children would have an opportunity for socialization with the resident students, and the parents too would be able to have interaction at the school. Maybe some of the fears of "sending my children away to this unknown place" would melt away. This interaction could be very helpful to the school for a future time.

The satellite school program. The idea is to set up a school where the hub school provides teachers and a curriculum for a number of students in an outlying area [see Manila ICMK Compendium, pp 311-317]. The advantage of a satellite situation is that you have control over what is being taught while delaying the need for a student to leave home.

The community or cooperative school. This system could be quite similar to the satellite school except that the parents would not use your curriculum. The parents would work together in educating their children on a correspondence basis. "You teach my fifth grader; I'll teach your third grader because I also have a third grader."

If there is a cooperative school within the realm from which the resident school would be drawing boarding students, offer assistance to the parents in testing, counseling, and acquiring materials.

Local schools. You could offer services to parents sending their children to local schools. "Hey, would you like to know how your kids are doing? We can give you some achievement tests."

> There is a family using a Chinese school in the Philippines. They were talking about starting a satellite school, but I said, "How do you know that the system you are using now is not working?"
>
> They said, "Well, we do not think they are up in their achievement."

I said, "Well, we will give you some tests and help you know if that is true." We gave them a test, and the kids were basically doing OK. We averted the need for another satellite school.

Advantages to the Resident School

1. You would be providing quality, balanced education for a greater number of students representing a broader segment of the missionary community. If your goal is to educate missionary children, this would give you a platform to do more of that.

2. The positive, helping contacts from the school might encourage parents to place their children in the boarding situation a little earlier because you were willing to help them out.

3. The use of the testing and counseling services of the school would help detect learning problems earlier and hopefully help the family work through most of them.

4. There would be better use of your testing and counseling services and the library. You would have more people using them, which would be better stewardship of those resources.

Problems for the Resident School

Funding the program is a challenge. Obviously, those that are using the services should pay for those services. Parents that are sending their children to the school should not subsidize this other program. You need to clearly show that these other parents are paying for what you are doing to assist them, just like the parents who are using your day school and boarding school are paying for the cost of that school.

The other problem is getting **staff**. It is not easy to get qualified teachers, but I think some veteran teachers who are getting older and find it a little hard to control a large group of students in a classroom all day would fit into this situation. Classroom control would not be a problem, since it would be more setting up materials and working with each child individually.

I do not believe this program should be implemented on the high school level. I think by that time students need social interaction. My goal would be to get them into boarding school by middle school.

Set up and organize a program to make the resident school a helping hub, the center of the education of MKs within the area. Not only can it be helpful to a greater portion of the students, but I think it would help your image in the U.S. to those who are concerned about boarding schools.

36

Growing with Single
Staff Members

Ed Danielson
Christian Heritage College

Lord Send Me, A Handbook for Single Missionaries was written with the help of two of the counselors at Faith Academy. We would do one chapter at a time and circulate it among singles who would add things and make comments, so that's what the final flavor of the book is. Our message is that there are things we as administrators and couples can do to be more sensitive to the needs of singles. Everything is designed for the couple on the mission field, even the orientation programs, but roughly twenty percent of the missionary community are singles. Out of those twenty in a hundred, four are male.

We developed a checklist for potential house partners. They are very practical statements that could be marked "Never, Seldom, Sometimes, or Frequently." Here is a sample:

• You are artistic and enjoy decorating.
• Your quarters usually look neat and tidy.

Do's and Don'ts for Those Who Want to Befriend Singles

1. Do treat singles as adults, not as teenagers, not as your daughters. It has amazed me how many times families have taken on missionary daughters. (We didn't forget the male in this book, but the situations are more commonly female.) Isn't it amazing that we have a situation on the mission field where a twenty-eight-year-old couple can have a twenty-six-year-old daughter? They might even introduce that individual as their adopted daughter. Frequently this causes feelings

that are difficult to express, because the couple has not done it out of meanness or contempt, but out of sincere love.

A lady in a remote area of the Philippines wrote, "Can I be seen as me, oh Lord, a single woman, complete in my relationship to you, not unfulfilled, a social cripple, or someone's co-worker, a solution to another's workload, but me, an individual with interests, preferences, and individual identity, not linked to any other but you?"

2. Don't tell singles they're incomplete without a spouse. I was recently at a meeting where the speaker said, "God created man as a whole being. Then he separated woman from man in order to be complete in the way God intended man and woman to be rejoined. Therefore God established the institution of marriage so that we could be complete." At this juncture, a young, attractive, single missionary spoke up firmly, yet not with antagonism, "That is the kind of false ideal that the typical women's magazine preaches page by page. We need to help teenage girls realize this is a worldly standard. Colossians 2:10 says, 'And in him you have been made complete.' Since God tells us that we are complete in him, then we don't have to have a spouse to make us a whole being. I believe that this doctrine could be used by Satan to discourage singles and make them feel they lack God's special blessings. In Christ we have everything." She got more of an amen in that meeting than the preacher.

3. Do invite singles out by themselves sometimes. The common error that couples make is that if there are two singles living together, they tend to invite them both out at the same time. That forces them to always be together. We recommend that you invite one and say, "We would like you to invite somebody else."

4. Don't joke about the issue of marriage. It's not always easy being single. There's an amazing amount of joking that goes on about this. You don't hear too many singles reacting strongly against it because they understand that the person is really doing it like a junior high boy teasing a girl. It demonstrates interest and concern, but it really isn't a good idea. I would suggest to the singles that they go to the individual in private and tell him how they feel about the jokes.

5. Do include singles in your family as a friend, not just as a baby-sitter or someone to watch the house. I think it's an insult to consider singles as the ones who ought to sit with the

kids. You are going to find that there are some singles who really thrive on that, but there are a lot of them that don't enjoy it. Just because they're single does not mean that they're going to enjoy baby-sitting. If they do baby-sit, at least give them proper remuneration.

Don't think of singles as a threat to your marriage. Obviously if a single is a threat to your marriage, some changes need to be made.

6. Don't assume singles have time on their hands. In the school I directed in Central America, the single teachers were also the dorm parents. During vacation, we have a missionary conference. Guess who were asked to take care of the kids — the same single teachers! What was worse, the single teachers would do it. They were so easy to get along with. They would do anything for anybody, but they resented it.

7. Do feel free to show affection. It isn't easy being away from family. Some singles don't want any touching, but others enjoy a hug now and then.

8. Don't expect a single to be able to do everything just because they're missionaries. Nobody is self-sufficient. Many singles felt that male administrators asked them to do things they wouldn't ask their wives to do.

9. Do recognize that singles have responded to God's leading. The level of spirituality can be just as high in any single as in any married person.

10. Don't assume singles can't be administrators. God's wisdom is available to them, too. I'd like to read something from the *Evangelical Missionary Quarterly*, "My Past Executives":

> Although women missionaries have been at the front edge of what has happened in missions for more than 150 years, they are regularly bypassed for executive opportunities and not expected to participate in the decision-making process, even though it controls their lives and ministries. Men assume exclusive leadership for a task force whose majority is feminine. The following simple suggestions could revolutionize relationships within mission groups if given a chance.
> • Acknowledge women's contribution to world missions.
> • Let mission board leaders study women's potential.
> • Include women in decision-making.

There may be a doctrinal problem here for some missions, but for most missions it has just been tradition that men must be the leaders. We need to check if we're talking about traditions or theology.

11. Do be sensitive. Sometimes singles need help and don't always know how to ask for it. That isn't true just of singles, but husbands and wives have a communication system and if functioning properly they would automatically pick up this need, whereas the single does not necessarily have someone, especially if they're living alone.

12. Don't extend pity. Singles feel as though they're pitied. One single said, "Don't extend pity in the false clothes of friendship. I have something to give you in this relationship."

Guidelines for Adopting a Family

This list was compiled by a missionary from Africa. For six years before going to Africa she had lived alone. Because of the availability of housing she chose to live with two other girls. The situation lasted about a month because she had never been a successful roommate. She sensed the need for a family and began to pray for one. "God gave me a terrific family. In fact I have several really good family friends and have formulated my own set of guidelines to follow when adopting a family."

I asked her to write these things down because I happened to be in the home and I saw this interaction. It was fabulous. These guidelines are:

1. Always choose a family whose marital relationship is very secure.
2. Choose a family whose dynamics are to your liking. I abhor bickering.
3. I always choose a family with kids.
4. Never reprimand a child in front of his parents. Never suggest how to discipline. Never tell them what is wrong with their kids, even if they ask. I'm no authority, and when it comes down to it, my kids will probably misbehave. *[There's always that idea that maybe some day the Lord will provide a husband. There's a longing there. That's why it's very important not to joke about marriage. It persists on up to later years in life.]*
5. If you can't stand their kids or their pets, eventually your feelings will surface and come between you and the family. "Love me, love my child. Love me, love my dog, too."

6. Do not develop the relationship with the husband more than with the wife. I try to spend more time with the wife than with the husband. If I pop in and find only the husband home and no kids, I usually make tracks unless I'm very comfortable. Never come between the husband and his wife. Even if you know you're right, never tell the wife what's eating you about the husband. I try to find ways to give them time for each other like taking the kids on a hike some afternoon. In this way I'm adding to the family, and I'm usually on the receiving end eventually.

7. Be considerate of family time. Don't pop in at supper time and stay past bedtime.

8. I learn a lot about marriage by just being around, and I mimic the wife in little things. If the wife powders the baby after a bath, then when I bathe it, so do I. If the family hates soup, for Pete's sake don't them serve soup when they come to your house. I've learned a lot of neat things this way.

9. If I really want to be involved with the family, I must help lighten the load—wash the car or the dog, offer to baby-sit or bake cookies, etc.

10. A very kindred spirit is developed when I take an active interest in the things the family is interested in. This is a real blessing. I need families, and yesterday my family told me they needed me.

That's a neat relationship. Those are the things we work towards in counseling.

Discussion

Regarding housing for singles, do they want to own their own, or are they content in mission housing?

I think we took two chapters on that subject because that's one of the keenest ones. We get varying attitudes. Some singles absolutely cannot live without singles. Others just absolutely cannot live with others.

I think if missions are building units for singles, they should consider units that could be changed readily. Maybe they would share some facilities such as laundry but give as much privacy as possible.

Think for a moment. You've got two singles in a home. One single wants to invite a couple in, or a fellow, or a girl. The other one has got to go along with it. They might not have that much in common. I'm for spending a little more money.

Could I make a plea about single accommodations on furlough? This is a great bone of contention. Many missions assume that singles automatically will return to the home of their parents on leave, which automatically makes your single feel dependent, childish, and immature. It is extremely harmful. I have been fighting against it for thirty-six years of missionary service.

There are some missions that actually have this policy. On furlough there is no rental allowance for singles, and for the couples there is. Singles have to go live with somebody. Talk about discrimination, you've got it.

You mentioned something about not sending singles to the hard places. We have found that singles produce a lot more in the hard places than a lot of the couples do. When we first came to the field some thirty-five years ago, we were in a province where there were nine singles. We were the only couple. We would not have seen the people movement that we have seen among the Quichuas had it not been for the faithful plowing and planting of the singles. You get a lot more mileage out of the singles if you provide good housing for them.

When mission directors assume that two singles just automatically ought to live together, I'd comment, "How long did it take you to find your living-mate?"

I was a single lady missionary, and then my husband found me. I suddenly found that the men didn't talk to me any more because I was just Derrick's wife. I wanted to be an individual in my own right as well as Derrick's wife. They assumed that then I would only want to talk about babies and cooking. But I still wanted to talk about other things.

I'd like to emphasize the two Scriptures mentioned: We are complete in him, and he will not withhold any good thing from us. If marriage is a good thing for me, he will not withhold it. If he withholds it, then it must not be a good thing at any particular time.

One thing I appreciate in my mission family is that I've always been treated like a lady. That really has meant a lot in keeping my femininity. The men in our mission are gentlemen. It's so precious to have a door opened and to be treated with respect and affection. It keeps you from feeling that you've been rejected.

One frustration is that so often the older single ladies are so used to doing their own thing, they embarrass the guy that tries to be a gentleman.

Single people joke among themselves about marriage an awful lot, but I'd like you to understand that it is kind of a family joke.

Also, the term that is used for a single female is not necessarily 'girl'. I'm thirty-four. The dorm mother in my dorm is twenty-four. She is considered a woman because she has a marriage license and a child. I'm a girl. I think that's something people need to be very sensitive about.

37

Contingency Preparation for MK School Personnel

Bob Klamser
Contingency Preparation Consultants

My purpose today is to challenge you to consider the responsibilities of missionary schools as custodians of children during emergencies and crisis, and to specifically examine your level of preparedness in face of the growing threat of terrorism and civil unrest. Although we'll focus primarily on terrorism, the solutions we'll talk about apply to almost any kind of crisis or unusual event. The planning process will work equally well in preparing for natural disasters, changes in government, or any of the other situations that the schools may face.

The Need for Planning

The most traditional targets of terrorist activity—government, diplomatic, military, and business people—are protecting themselves. They're spending millions and millions of dollars every year in personal and corporate protection and using the kinds of things that mission organizations can't afford and probably wouldn't want to use overseas anyway. We don't want to hide behind bars and drive around in bullet-proof cars; that's not why we're out there. That type of protection makes people harder to attack, and unfortunately as terrorists look at potential targets, they just move down until they find groups or individuals that are less protected. Right now, the mission community is probably the single largest, most easily identifiable community that isn't protected overseas.

Statistically we're beginning to see an increase in terrorist attacks against mission organizations and against individual missionaries. We feel that's something that is probably going to continue to increase.

The publicity impact of a terrorist action against a mission organization, a school, or an MK is just tremendous. Of course terrorists are looking for that high level of sensationalism that goes way beyond the initial act.

Many missionary schools enroll children from outside the mission community, especially children of government officials and diplomats, and in many places in the world this could add to the threat. We think there is certainly no reason at all for panic, but there is reason for concern. I think the challenge for MK school people is to ensure that there is adequate preparation for responding to the threat.

Let's imagine an MK school in an isolated third world location with very limited communications. Let's imagine that the school is governed by a board that consists of one member from each mission represented. And let's say the principal of the school is a member of the national church and is subject to it.

Here is the hypothetical situation. One school morning a group of fifteen armed terrorists come on your campus and seize one building with seven children and a teacher. The hostages represent four different mission organizations and six different churches. One is the child of a European diplomat. The terrorists present a list demands: the closing of the school; the departure from the country of all the mission organizations that are represented; the requirement that the police and the military not be notified. They give you an ultimatum that a child will be killed in twelve hours if the demands aren't met and also a warning that a child will be killed if the terrorists detect any police or military presence.

Unrealistic? I don't think so. In the past twelve years there have been two terrorists attacks on schools, one in Israel and one in Holland. It is not something to be panicked about, but I think it is an area of legitimate concern. These are the standard kinds of demands that come with almost any terrorist hostage taking.

Suppose you're in the school office. You have this list of demands. What decisions or issues are you going to be faced with? The clock's ticking away. You've got twelve hours before they kill a kid.

Who's in charge? Who's going to be able to make decisions about this? Does the principal have the authority? People from the different schools I've talked to didn't seem to be sure who would have the authority to make decisions. When that happens, you either have nobody making decisions and everybody just looking at each other as time goes by, or you have a lot of people making decisions, which is just as bad.

Who knows or who decides if any concessions can be made at all? Do you know if your organization would make concessions in a situation like that, be it a mission or a school? Would your denomination make concessions to the terrorists under any circumstances?

Do we notify the police or the military? They said they were going to kill a child if we do. But what's our decision? What about the parents? What about the rest of the students? Do we contact the other missions?

Who's going to talk to the terrorist? Who is the person to answer the letter? Who normally would go out and respond to that? The principal, right? The person normally in charge. We suggest from our experience that that's the very last person in the world we want to have talking to terrorists or negotiating in any type of hostage situation. I'll explain why.

In any type of negotiation back and forth with hostage takers, a bonding called the Stockholm syndrome develops between the hostages and the hostage takers as they are together. Take it on faith, it really happens. As they begin to relate to each other, they begin to see each other as humans. They begin to care about each other, and that's good. In hostage situations, we use that. That's how we get hostages out safely without sending in a SWAT team. But it also works between the hostage negotiator and the hostage takers. When I put a police negotiator in contact with a hostage taker, after a few hours there's going to be some relationship developed there. It's enough to cloud judgment. It happens all the time. In a good negotiation situation, we want to foster that because it builds trust, and it helps break down the barriers between people.

But what if that's the guy that's making your decisions too? It takes a lot of time negotiating. After an hour of talking with those guys in a negotiation situation, you're just drained. It's so intense. For those reasons, we wouldn't want the principal or whoever is in charge negotiating.

What about the twelve-hour deadline? What are we going to do eleven and a half hours from now? We haven't left the country, that's for sure. There hasn't been time. What are we going to do about the deadline?

I think this situation is one any school could face anywhere in the world. And I think if we try to resolve issues while a crisis is going on, we're probably not going to make good decisions. We're going to be pushed. We're going to fall under the pressure of time, and the terrorists will use that twelve-hour deadline to pressure us. They are very adept at what they're doing. They know how to negotiate for the other side. They know how to create terror. They know how to put you in the defensive position and then press that advantage against you.

Establishing planning

What can we do about it? Well, we can engage in a planning process that makes as many decisions as can be made before the crisis happens. We can give people an opportunity to think through these issues beforehand and establish policy.

I want to make sure we understand the same thing when I say *policy*. I'm talking about a corporate resolution saying, "This is the way our organization will handle whatever situation." Can you imagine telling the parents of a seven- or eight-year-old school child that you're not going to pay a thousand dollar ransom because that's *your* decision? Boy, I wouldn't ever want to have to do that. If that's the answer I have to give a parent, I need to have the backing of policy behind me. I need to have the assurance that I'm doing the right thing, that I'm not making that kind of a decision under the tension of the moment.

Before they go overseas, it is important for families to know what their organization's policies are in these areas. If the organization has a policy of no payment for ransom, everybody should know that and agree with it before they go abroad. Then, if it ever does come up in a real situation, there's not a clash over policy.

We need to know beforehand who will be in charge. That's really important. We worked with a mission organization that got involved in a crisis situation involving hostages. There was in that mission one individual who nominally should have been in charge of the incident. He began working to resolve it. For several reasons that had nothing to do with the abilities of that individual, the mission wanted someone else to handle it. So they sent out someone else who began working on it, but never told the first guy. So two guys were working on it. Of course by the time it was finally resolved, they crossed paths. They ended up having to go back and rebuild relationships with three governments. And of course, these guys had to put their own personal relationship together. It probably created a situation where some hostages were kept in captivity weeks or months longer than they needed to be just because of the confusion.

We need to know what authority the people in charge have. If the principal of the school is in charge, does he have the authority to pay ransom? If there is a demand to publish some type of manifesto, does he have the authority to do that? Does he have the authority to close the school? He needs to know what his limitations are beforehand. Trying to find out what they are during a crisis situation, especially if communications aren't good, is really going to be tough. We owe it to that person to make sure that he knows what his limitations are.

We need to make sure that the bureaucratic obstacles and processes that we deal with in everyday operation don't become stumbling blocks in an emergency. In an emergency the leadership needs to be free to respond in a timely manner to what's going on.

Advantages of planning beforehand

When we engage in planning beforehand, we basically have time to do three things that we can't do in a crisis.

We can evaluate objectively the potential impact of the crisis. Sometimes when we're handling a crisis, we may feel that on a scale of importance of one to a hundred the issue is a ninety-nine. But if we stepped back and looked at it, we might see it's really about a fifty or a twenty-five. It gives us a chance to look at those kinds of issues and see how critical they are going to be beforehand. What are the consequences of a particular emergency, be it a hostage taking, arson, or a bomb threat? What is the potential impact?

We explore alternative strategies and resolutions, and take a look at their consequences. There's not time to do this in a crisis. Usually in a crisis we make decisions because of time pressure, and we don't have the opportunity to think through the consequences. What's going to happen as the dominoes start to fall? When we do planning beforehand, we can look at the experience of others who have been in the same position. We can go through brainstorming sessions. There are lots of different ways to look at a situation and get a handle on what the consequences of different decisions might be.

Finally it gives us time to seek the advice, counsel, and guidance of other people — professionals in the field, others who have been through the experience. We have the opportunity to get a lot of input that we wouldn't have in a crisis.

Organizational policies

The first thing we think an organization needs to do is to establish their basic policies in some of the following areas:

1. A policy about negotiating with terrorist or hostage takers. We need to differentiate between negotiating and making concessions. Negotiating is just talking, discussing, communicating. Contingency Preparations Consultants would always recommend negotiation. You don't give away anything through negotiation. It gives you time, and time in a hostage situation is the biggest single factor that will add to the chances of the hostage's survival. The longer a hostage is in captivity, the greater are his or her chances of surviving unharmed. That's an interesting thing. Sometimes we have the impression that we need to resolve this thing today. A hostage negotiator or a professional in this field will come in and say, "We don't even want to start resolving it until tomorrow because we want to let the emotions go down and let people start to get to know each other inside there."

2. Payment of ransom. I would just make one point to you. The U.S. government pays ransom for hostages. Israel's government has paid money for hostages. Every large business concern in the world does pay ransom for hostages, regardless of published statements. My concern and that of my organization is that a mission organization following the recommended policy of the various governments of the world may find themselves in actuality being the only entity out there that doesn't pay ransom. That could have some implications with the terrorist group that routinely takes hostages and routinely gets ransom. It is something that an organization should consider. Regardless of what the American government says, everybody's doing it.

   Let's say you're working in an environment where kidnapping is a way of life. Most large businesses have ransom insurance. When an executive gets kidnapped, the insurance company writes a check after they have negotiated down to an agreed upon amount. My concern is that a terrorist organization or just a group of criminals that routinely gets money by kidnapping people takes someone from a mission organization. (I think we all understand that these groups don't see a difference between a missionary organization and an American business.) And they say, "Wait a minute. This is routine. Everybody pays ransom. Why don't these guys?"

They may get stuck in a place where they don't have a way out. They need a way to save face. That's dangerous. My concern is that mission organizations understand that dynamic. A lot of people say, "We don't pay ransom to terrorists," but in fact everybody is doing it.

3. What about other concessions? Would your organization not pay ransom but instead spend a thousand dollars to distribute milk to children in a needy area of the city? That could be a face-saving way out for the hostage takers. What other concessions might the organization make?

4. What about the rest of the family if you have hostages?

5. How about the media? If the media knows what's going on, they'll descend on your organization and demand lots of information and lots of time. Who's going to deal with them? It certainly shouldn't be the person in charge, for lots of reasons. How are we going to deal with the media?

6. What about when it's over? What about counseling? I think most of us now are at the point where we understand we need to provide some type of counseling for victims of sexual assault, victims of child abuse, and hostages. What about their families? What about the leaders in the organization who had to deal with that? Our strong belief is that those people all need to have counseling. If the organization does not back that policy, people will resist going. So we recommend that counseling be included in your policy.

Organizational response

Somehow your organization needs to know and have written down in your policy who's going to be in charge, who's going to make decisions, and what authority they have.

After we've got these policies, what do we do with them? Having them in a nice notebook on the shelf in the headquarters in the United States or Canada doesn't do anybody in the field any good. They need to be put down in written form as part of a contingency plan available to everybody in the field. Contingency plans should give you a step-by-step procedure for working through some of these different types of emergencies. As we brainstorm, as we go through the evaluation process, we can develop ideas and strategies. We can understand the steps that might be unique to a particular situation and put those in a step-by-step plan of how we are going respond.

Now I realize the contingency plans can't cover every possible scenario. The craziest things happen. People do strange things, but these plans provide you a framework. Put down on paper those decisions that can be made in advance. As the person in charge works through a crisis, he is able to rely on this prior planning.

We are trying to prepare a generic plan that would fit missions and have a lot of blank spaces for people to fill in. If you're interested in having a copy, just let me know.

Contingency planning tends to be done at the middle management level of any organization. There's nothing wrong with that. However, two things need to occur. We need to make sure that the top administration is involved in the planning, at least to the point where they understand these policy decisions and agree with them. You certainly don't want them to be surprised by your ransom policy during a crisis and say, "What do you mean we're not going to pay ransom?" or "What do you mean we are going to pay ransom?" Your top administration has to be involved, understand, and buy into the plan beforehand. They may well be the people that are executing it.

Also, you need to make sure that the people affected in the field buy it. If they aren't involved in the preparation of the plan, they need at least to be able to review it and give you their input and comments on it before it becomes the law.

When I did contingency planning for my organization, I did a dam failure plan. This particular plan I wrote with the help of the city emergency services worker. I was working at a desk at that point. I hadn't been out on the streets in a couple of years, so I wasn't real familiar with some of the areas. When we got it all finished, we sent it out to our patrol sergeants. We asked them to take it out at night when they had time and just drive through all the steps. They did. From the feedback we got, we found one of the things we had done was send a policeman to an intersection that within about ten minutes would become a little island. He would be standing there directing traffic in nothing but water. And it would probably be a day and a half before we could get him out. That was just a matter of us not knowing what was going on out there. We didn't understand the geography well enough because we were inside.

The same thing could happen in any type of contingency planning. What looks good to us in the office may look very different to the people on the field that are going to have to carry it out. We should make sure they have the opportunity to review it and catch our mistakes.

What does this document look like when it's all done? I suggest you have a three ring notebook. In front put all the major policies your organization decides upon. Then it should have a section for each emergency. You just have to evaluate what your priorities are. It may be that where you are the most likely emergency is an earthquake or a coup or a terrorist takeover of the school. Just prioritize them and do a section for each one.

Let's take hostage taking as an example. The first thing you do is evacuate the rest of the school. They should go to such-and-such a location. The next thing you do is call so-and-so, if that's the next thing you have decided on. It actually says step by step what to do. You actually put phone numbers in there.

Now I don't know how it is in the mission community, but I know in law enforcement sometimes we promote a guy to sergeant that in retrospect we wish we hadn't. I suspect in almost any organization we have those people in administrative or leadership roles who probably shouldn't be there. They are more suited to other tasks.

When I do a contingency plan I think of that sergeant that I wish we'd never promoted, and I remember that he may be the one that's going to be in charge if anything happens, and I write the plan for him. I think that's the way we should write contingency plans. Make them very simple. Anticipate that the person you least want to be in charge is in charge, and he can't reach anybody else, so he's got to go through this step-by-step process. I realize we can't anticipate every step. He's going to have to do some independent thinking and that's good, but that's the type of document I'm talking about.

I would even go so far as to recommend that you use only half the page. Leave the right hand of the page for whoever is using the plan to write notes on as they go through. Encourage that it be a working document, something that's actually used in a crisis.

I think that in the planning process the people that are involved need to understand that a plan does not supersede common sense. You have to have room for common sense and judgment.

Several years ago we had a dam that failed. Actually the dam was outside the incorporated city limits, but everything from the foot of the dam onto the flood plain was in the city. In a heavy winter storm, this dam began to fail. It was eight or ten hours before anybody realized the thing was leaking. The city and the county got together, and they kind of butted heads for a while. Finally after eight or ten hours, the decision was made to activate the contingency plan. What that involved was the evacuation of some 250 homes and the closing of a shopping center. They were closed for over a day and a half.

The common sense part that did not enter into it was that the most water that would have hit any of those places had the dam totally failed was eight inches. The dam did not fail. And even if it had, the risk on a scale of one to a hundred was about a ten. We did not use common sense. We had a plan in place and we implemented that plan without thinking or using common sense. Of course our constituents were angry.

I think any organization could get involved in a situation like that. We have to have common sense included in the planning process and in the execution of the plan in the crisis.

I don't use the terms *terrorists* and *guerrillas* synonymously, but in their training and their planning they do interact. We believe they are currently being trained at five major training camps in the world. These training camps are fourteen to sixteen weeks in length, which is longer than almost any law enforcement police academy in the United States. Their regimen, discipline, and curriculum is much stricter than that of any police academy in the United States. In addition to that, in any single class going through one of these training camps, you will have terrorists literally from all over the world and from many different groups. They go through as classmates, and they develop relationships, friendships, and professional associations. They share information. They study all the kinds of things that we are talking about. They study hostage negotiations and crisis management techniques in far more detail than we do. They are planning and training all the time.

Fortunately most of the time they do not have the resources to implement their plans. Terrorists are very, very few in number. They are very weak. That is why they rely on terror. That is why they have to pick actions where they get a maximum degree of publicity. Statistically, you are more likely to be the victim of a homicide in any American city than to be the victim of a terrorist act anywhere in the world. In appearance, terrorism becomes far more than it is in fact.

Prevention

I would like to mention some specific things that missionary schools can do as far as combating terrorism directed against the school or their students.

Fortunately, avoiding terrorism is not difficult. Terrorists almost always rely on surveillance and planning beforehand. They will do extensive surveillance. They will sometimes watch targets as long as six months to a year before an action. They do not have the resources to use a whole lot of people in cars for surveillance. That gives us a tremendous advantage. If we can detect their surveillance, we can probably cause them to break off their plans to attack us. When terrorist headquarters or safe houses or homes are raided, time and time again we find records. They keep good records. And we find where they have made entries recording that they felt someone detected their surveillance of a particular target, and they abandoned that target and went on to someone else.

There is no trick to detecting surveillance. It is just being aware and observant. It is just noticing that there is a car parked out there in front of the school or in front of your house, and this is the third time it has been there this week. Or, "Why has that couple been sitting there across the street in the park watching our school every lunch hour this week?" It is as simple as that.

Then you have to do something about it. Go up and just greet them, "Hi, can we help you?" or "Are you looking for something?" Something as innocuous as that. It can actually be something more aggressive than that, like going up and writing down their license plate number or taking their photograph. If the police or the military is available, notify them, and ask them to come by or at least increase their patrols.

You might ask, "Well what about danger? These are terrorists. If I go up and write down their license number or say, 'Hi,' aren't I putting myself at risk?" No. When terrorists are acting violently, they are doing it in a preplanned operation where they have all their support and logistics. But when they are out on surveillance, they are going to do anything they can to avoid a confrontation.

If you are in an area where there is an increased risk, vary the routine in your school just a little bit. Terrorists rely on routine. They want to know that at 8:05 there is going to be a whole bunch of kids out in the courtyard, or there is going to be a bus dropping off a group in front, or whatever the activity may be. They want to know that it is going to happen at a certain time. They want to know that when a bell rings, certain things are going to happen, and this bell is probably going to ring at this time. You can change those things just a little bit. Throw off the routine so they can not detect a regular pattern of activity. Send kids home at a different time or start school at a different time. I realize some of these things become a little more difficult logistically, but maybe you can ring the bell at a different time and not change your pattern at all. Anything along the lines of varying routines is going to go a long way towards discouraging terrorists from attacking your school.

If there is a substantial risk and parents are really worried about their kids being kidnapped, there would be flexibility on their part. You can be creative. You can think of all different kinds of things to do. Maybe it is just having the staff go outside. Maybe it is just saying, "Half an hour before school starts to half an hour after, we are going to have three staff people walking around the outside of the campus. Maybe we will not do it tomorrow, but the next day we will do it again." Anything like that can be used, because terrorists are really going to look for that pattern of activity. They want to be able to get in, do their activity, and get out in less than five minutes. If you are changing your routine they are not going to be able to do that.

The other key thing that we recommend is the establishment of relationships with the community around you. I probably do not need to emphasize that very much for schools. But I do want to point out that next to awareness, that's the single biggest thing that will protect you from terrorism. As you become known and understood by the people around you, you will be protected. If nothing else, I think you will get advance warning of an increased threat level, or maybe actually an attack.

We have all kinds of examples of that happening in the mission community. People in the village or town have detected a threat against a missionary family or a center and have communicated that threat. We know of cases where missionaries have been taken hostage, and villagers have actually come in and physically intervened. They told the hostage takers, "Look, this guy is ill. You need to get him medicine." "It is not right to have this family separated. At least bring them together." "Give them their Bible and let them worship, and make sure they are getting their food." There has actually been that much intervention on the part of the people with the hostage takers. And that comes as part of building relations.

The closer your personnel are to the community, the more a part of the community they are, the safer they are. The relationships with people are much more of a protection than a big facility with lights, cleared areas, and night watchmen.

I recommend strongly that your school or the mission, if possible, develop a relationship with whoever is in charge of the military or the police. Now, I know that in some situations that is risky in and of itself. But if it is not, and if you can do it, it is beneficial. We all know in dealing with any bureaucracy, if you call the government you get the government response. But if you know somebody in government and you can call them and deal with that person that you developed a relationship with beforehand, you get a thousand percent more.

A school or a mission organization needs to know what the government's policy is going to be. Some governments prohibit negotiating. Many countries prohibit the payment of ransom. Some countries have laws against it but encourage you to do it anyway. In one Latin American country where Americans were taken hostage, an outside firm came in and negotiated a hostage incident successfully with the government's knowledge, and everybody was happy. They came back down within a month to the same city for another hostage incident and were arrested for negotiating with the hostage takers. (It was resolved within a day.) We need to have at least some understanding of the government's position about what we are doing. Having a relationship beforehand with the officials and the government is, in our view, as much a part of contingency planning as writing these documents out.

Assistance

Our organization, Contingency Preparation Consultants, is a nonprofit group. We do not do anything commercially. We exist to serve mission organizations. We are available to help you with training or contingency planning, and we want you to know that should your organization get into a crisis or a hostage situation, we are available to help while it is going on. We are available to come to the scene, provide assistance and advice. We can not make decisions. But we are certainly available to come and help or to give advice over the phone. We hope you will never need us but if you do, we want you to know we are available.

We offer a two-and-a-half day training seminar. We ask that the cost be covered by whoever makes the request. If an organization needs either training or emergency services and it can not provide the costs, we will find a way to work it out.

Recommended references: *Crisis Management, Product Tampering, and Other Corporate Tragedies*, by Ian Mitroff. *Terrorism and Personal Protection*, edited by Brian Jenkins and published by the Rand Corporation, has several excellent chapters on contingency preparation and crisis management.

38

Caring for the MK in Times of Crisis

Priscilla Bartram
Principal, Lomalinda School, Colombia, Wycliffe

The crisis situations I'm going to talk about are not the common, ordinary, everyday crises. I'm going to zero in on major crises. During the twelve years I've been principal I have learned a lot, and I have a lot more to learn. I want to give you an idea of the things that have helped us make it through. When Chet Bitterman was kidnapped, we were not prepared, and we had to do some fast thinking.

At the time we knew we were in a vulnerable situation. The soldiers had moved into our area, and we had expected to be attacked at Lomalinda. We had not expected it to come in Bogota. It was about time to go home for lunch when a teacher handed me a phone message, "Chet Bitterman was kidnaped out of the group house."

You need to know your channels of authority and who is going to call the shots. As the senior administrator I needed to make some quick decisions. We stopped and prayed. That's the thing I will emphasize the most. You've got to have the relationship with the Lord. That's your source. As you go to the Lord, he will calm you. He will also give you what you need. He has never failed. We had no security plan for the children. We are a day school. We have a few children living in a children's home, but most children live with their parents.

After we prayed, I said to the teacher, "You call high school and tell the teachers I want them to meet when the bell rings. I'll get to the elementary teachers.

I thought it was better for the parents to tell their children the news, because each parent knew the temperament of their children and how they would handle that news better than we did. But somebody picking up somebody had told somebody, and the news had already gotten to our high schoolers while I met with the teachers and gave them the news.

You need to know the types of reactions children will have to this type of experience. Some won't change expression. Some will be mad, angry, fighting. Some will be dazed.

Let me tell you what had happened several years earlier that helped prepare us for this particular situation. In 1974 it was announced at conference that probably within the year we would be out of Lomalinda. We have a lot of couples there with young children whose only roots were at Lomalinda. We had to deal with children who were not functioning because the parents were not functioning. They were not ready for this news, therefore they could not meet the needs of their children. We would have children sitting in class just staring.

You need to let your parents know that they need to work on preparing their kids for change, especially if you're in a nice cozy place. You need to do contingency planning. At that time we grappled a lot more emotionally in some ways than we did when Chet was kidnapped. By that time we had begun to think, "We're not here forever. This is not our home. We're pilgrims. We don't know what God has for us."

All of us who work on foreign soil need to keep that uppermost in our minds. The security cannot be in the location. It has to be with the family unit or the people who are around. We need to work for that. We had struggled through that in 1974, so when Chet was taken in 1981, we found that the children who came from homes where the parents were prepared for this were having their needs met. However, our new people had not gone through any of this.

In the office my first need was to become calm before the Lord. The rumors and newspaper reports were coming, and I found myself getting up in the air and getting very frightened. We need to be able to admit we're frightened. The military moved in immediately because they figured the guerrillas were going to try to get our director who was living in Lomalinda. We had no guns on the hill right above the school. We were very vulnerable.

We were assured that the guerrillas did not want a bad name and so would not harm the children. We were given instructions, "Talk with your kids. Be prepared." Parents had to bring their children and pick them up if they were younger than fourth grade. We had a curfew. I was told to give the teachers instruction to have the children get down on the floor. To keep the scare element down as much as possible, we decided it would be best not to do drills, but the teachers were prepared. We felt that the children would do whatever the teachers told them to do. You may make a different decision, but that was ours.

Planning

Since that time I have been asked, "What are your contingency plans? If we had to move out of here in a day, what would you take? What would you do?"

Now, we have our records ready. I could reach into the file and pull every transcript out. We have things organized so anything that has a name on it could be burned. I have a separate file of addresses that I need, that could be pulled out, but because we've had a lot of change, I do not have my personnel to the point of knowing what jobs they would take. Mothers would go home and others would fill in. One of the most disturbing things for a high school student would be not to be able to go on and get the credit for the classes he has taken. So every time the grades come out, we make a copy and send it to our Children's Education office. Our permanent files of all the graduates are now being kept in the States. You need to think through things like that. You need to think about what might need to be destroyed.

You need to think about the instructions that need to be given to the children if you should have soldiers come in. In our group this is basically a parent responsibility. But those in a boarding school situation might have to face that type of thing. The soldiers do not have the same standards we do. Our children need to be instructed on proper behavior, being friendly but not too friendly.

Eventually all of our personnel were pulled into the center until things were calmed down. No one was left in isolation. I think that is very important. When this type of thing happens, no one should be in isolation.

One thing I insisted on was that the teachers had to be in our security meetings so they knew what was going on. I feel that your teachers cannot be isolated. They have to meet the kids' needs. I feel your high school students cannot be isolated. They're old enough to understand and be a part. It was the parents' final decision, but the majority of our high schoolers sat in on those security meetings. The security might be an adult-only meeting.

What are you going to do with your kids? What information are you going to give them? I personally feel some of our parents gave far too much information to younger children, things that they did not really need to know in detail. We need to counsel parents on that. Young children need some information so everything is not all scary, but they don't need every little jot and tittle.

We found that praying with the kids in class was a very important thing. We had prayer meetings all the time. They were necessary for teacher and students. When we got an announcement we would just stop class and pray. One of my biggest problems was the rumors that were flying. Finally I'd say, "Tell me your rumor. I will check it out on official channels to see if we will repeat it." Fear is a normal reaction in this type of situation. If someone is frightened, we need to be caring. Those who are stronger should strengthen whose who are weaker.

In a crisis situation you have to be willing to forget the mundane. There were things I should have been doing like ordering books. We didn't get our books the next year, but at that point that was not the most important issue. People—kids, staff, parents—they were the important thing. For about two months about all I did was counsel. I listened. I shared.

When Chet was killed, we all had a meeting. We wept together. We buried him at the center.

One couple had gone to Bogota to negotiate. Their daughter Virginia was left at Lomalinda. When the news came and we went into the auditorium to share what Chet had meant to us, we were asking, "Shall we leave? Shall we stay? What does the Lord want us to do?" Virginia stood and said, "If you leave now, everything my parents and Chet have done will be worthless." I think we realized then that the Lord wanted us right there in Colombia and that the was going to open the door for the work to continue. It hasn't been easy. We've had many people who can't get into the tribe, but we have one New Testament that's being printed now. There's another one ready to be printed. We are thankful for God causing us to zero in and get our job finished. Sometimes he shakes us up to do that. We begin to get the priorities in the right place.

We had a graduate come back from the United States on his motorcycle. He was known and loved by all the kids. He had been on the center less than twenty-four hours when he was "cat walking" on his motorcycle at eleven o'clock at night and hit a trench he didn't know was there. We had a funeral service the next morning.

The reaction of the students to that was very interesting. We had hoped it would calm down some of their motorcycle riding. It did not. Some of them were more wild than they had been before.

We have to remember that students react in different ways. I remember one of the teachers saying, "It's as if they don't care." But that was not really what was going on inside of them. They were trying to deal with it.

Shortly after that, we had a senior girl make the trip from Bogota to Lomalinda by motorcycle along with another senior and one of the fathers from the center. She was clipped by a car and had a very seriously damaged leg. We prayed that Catherine would not lose her leg. I was concerned because we were getting a lot of negative answers to prayer. Catherine eventually lost that leg up to the knee, but because we had prayed and asked for the Lord's will, he has enabled most of our kids to handle it. I'm not saying it's all resolved.

Joanie was our homeroom teacher for junior high and the art teacher throughout the whole school. Her life had influenced and was influencing many. We were at the lake and our former night watchman stabbed Joanie. Before anyone could get to her she was gone. Not many of us were in any shape to counsel the teenagers who where there. We again had a service the next morning. As an administrator, I could not deal with going back to school, and my teachers were not stable enough to meet the needs of the kids. We felt it was better for them to be with their parents. We delayed starting school again, and we talked it through ourselves. I think this is very important. We shared our emotions, our tears, and our frustrations. We shared that we didn't understand what God was doing. It was hard to handle. We prayed together, and I really think that helped us be able to face the kids the next day and begin to meet their needs. The parents had done some good counseling, and the kids were ready to go back into the routine.

Routine is a stabilizing influence for kids. So we went back into routine as quickly as we felt we could handle it. We did the same thing when Chet was taken. Some said, "You shouldn't have any expectations for the students. They should come when they want to. If they're having difficulty they shouldn't have to stay in school."

I said, "We will have school as usual. We will be understanding of people who have special needs." I told parents they could keep a child who had an emotional problem at home, but to please let me know so we knew why they were not in school. We gave homework. We had expectations of the kids. I would like you to know that our kids maintained their grade point average throughout that time. They didn't bury their feelings, because they were given a lot of time to talk about it. A lot of teachers gave assignments that enabled the students to write about their emotions. But we have found that it does not help the kids just to be turned loose with no objective. The sooner you can get them into some kind of routine, the better off they are.

Joanie's death was May 4, 1986. School ended around the fourteenth or fifteenth. On the nineteenth our group house in Bogota was bombed. Some of the people on their way to furlough were in the house that night. We were trying to do some care ministering ourselves, but we needed an outside counselor to work with us. You need to be aware of that. Sometimes it takes an outside person to be able to help.

We have a new English teacher this year who knew nothing about the situation. She's been having the high school students write a daily journal. It's amazing how many times Joanie's death, the kidnapping of Chet, the death of Doug, and Catherine's accident will come into those writings. She has made herself available for counseling at the level she can do. Some of the kids are confiding in her. Even though she wasn't there, she can listen and understand.

When New Tribes pilots Paul Dyer and Steve Still were kidnapped by a guerrilla group, their five children in grades three through seven were in our school.

To encourage the kids we took a familiar song like "God Will Take Care of You" and put our friends' names in it. "God will take care of Steve. God will take care of Paul." That really personalized it for the kids.

We choose Scripture verses full of promises and wrote them on big sheets of construction paper and hung them all over the classroom. Our room was just covered with promises of God's care and protection. Whenever we looked up and looked around, the Scripture was right before us.

You need to think through your situation and the types of things you would want answers to, and try to search them out now.

Know your personnel. Know your weak links in an emergency. You can't always tell that until it happens, but you can notice who seems to have trouble dealing with everyday situations. I found that as an administrator, I continually had to work with the personnel under me. My door was open.

You need to talk through some of these things ahead of time with your staff. Part of my orientation now is security—what we would be expected to do and how we would function. You don't want to scare people. That's what you have to watch. But you need to make them aware that they are in a vulnerable situation. In 1983 when soldiers moved onto the center, one teacher could not handle it. It was better that he left, because he would not have been able to meet the needs of the kids.   I caution you to realize these people need to be loved, not put down because they can't handle that kind of situation.   No one is better or greater.   It's just that we are made different.   We have different temperaments.   We have been through different things.   Some can handle it and some can't.   We're better off knowing that.

39

Building an Alumni Network

Kay Landers and Rob Quiring
Alliance Academy

Kay Landers: Many missionaries feel estranged not only from their nation and culture as a whole, but specifically and painfully from the evangelical community they've left. They feel estranged from their extended families, from their friends, and from people in their supporting churches. If we as adults are yearning for home, how much more do our young people yearn for home.

We have a week-long senior trip at the Alliance Academy. Usually we go to the ocean. A couple of years ago, a college freshman who had graduated the previous year went to his former classmates and asked, "Can I go along this year?"

They said, "No way! You've had your trip."

The first night we camped out, there was a little bonfire way down the beach. I walked down to check it out, and there was our former student. He said, "I guess they won't mind if I'm down here, and they are up there."

He was searching for home, but what was home for him?

Many people claim that school becomes home for our young people. I thought, "Well, all right, if the Alliance Academy is home, and they come back and home isn't there as they remember it, an Alumni Association especially might help our younger graduates."

One reason for an Alumni Association is to help our graduates find each other, to provide an address list for our young people.

Rob Quiring: The most important reason is just to keep our graduates in touch with one another, so that there's information flowing back and forth. Another reason is to have a way of distributing current information about the school so that they know who the superintendent is, who the principals and teachers are, what's happened to those who were there before.

*I graduated from the Academy fourteen years ago. A friend
and I worked for two years to put together a ten-year
reunion. Unfortunately this was before Kay came up with
the Alumni Association. We ended up pretty burned out
from all our efforts, although we very much wanted to do it.
That ten-year reunion was a shining example of why we need
something to pull us together. We had a whole lot of fun at
that reunion, but there was also healing. There was redirec-
tion of some lives. I just can't express to you all that happened. So we were all very thrilled when we heard that the
Academy had started an Alumni Association.*

*Most of us really feel attached to our school. We care
a lot about what's happening here, what happens to the kids.
We want to help. An Alumni Association will allow us to
help and to get together not only for our own benefit, but to
help those kids that are going through the school like we did.*

Landers: One of my ideas for the Alumni Association was that it
would provide a literary journal. I don't want it just to become a list
of who marries whom and how many babies. I have a dream of
really making it a journal for ideas and poetry, concepts and concerns.
I would like to see it be a forum for their struggles. Our graduates
are so special. They have so much to share.

I am anxious to establish a job network, but that is still just a
dream. I envision a job network all through the United States with
hundreds of people willing to have MKs work for them during the
summer and also willing to provide a place for them to stay.

Another goal is to alert alumni to fellow MKs in their area. I
also want our missionary staff to know where our kids are.

Clearing: To help our current students, we keep a record of which
colleges our alumni attend. A lot of times when kids look at a college, it seems so far away. They would love to write a letter to an
alumnus from the Alliance Academy who went to that college.

Starting an Alumni Association

How do you go about starting an Alumni Association? We
started with our present students. We made sure we had a home
country address — grandma, aunt or uncle — somebody who will stay at
one address. That's not complicated, we can all do that.

The second thing we have to do is find the graduates — they're
everywhere. The Alliance Academy is a school for missionaries' kids,

but we also have business people and embassy people, and I suspect when we're through we'll find we have kids in every country in the world. How do you find them? I advertised in a newsletter for people who have lived in Ecuador. I used mission publications. I put up notices at the post office, "What's happened to your kids?" I got in touch with people here to try to get to other people. Addresses began filtering in, and then they began flowing in, and then I began to have so many that I began to get in trouble. The school was quite supportive. Ben Schepens, our principal, said, "We'll just put it in a computer, no problem."

> *Over the years our school has had an incredible record of classes maintaining newsletters. In some cases we found our addresses just by finding who is still in charge of those newsletters. We have about 700 graduates from Morrison and I think we have accurate addresses right now on about 640 of the 700. That's after two years of scrambling.*

> *Apparently you include teachers and former teachers in your listing. Do you also include students whose parents are transferred, who leave in perhaps tenth or eleventh grade?*

Landers: Yes. One of the categories is "actual/intended graduation." Intended graduation covers all those kids that were there for a short time, but didn't graduate for one reason or other. There have been some kids that have spent kindergarten through seventh grade at the school. They still feel a part of their class. Anyone who attended the school for almost any length of time became part of the community, so we like to include them as alumni. The real purpose of the Alumni Association isn't for the school. It's for the kids and getting them together.

You can put out a newsletter or a newspaper — whatever you feel most comfortable doing. In Ecuador we have publication facilities available to us, and that's the area I work in. I decided to jump right in and do an honest-to-goodness publication.

Quiring: But actually I beat you by about six months on publication, because that was the year that I was in charge of the yearbook, and one of the things that I did was list that current graduating class' four-year projected home base address in the back of the yearbook. When some graduates who were back in the country saw this page in the yearbook, they said, "Oh, you got an Alumni Association going. Here's my address, stick it in for the next time."

Kay mentioned earlier that Ben Schepens was originally supportive of the idea and put a lot of things in the computer. He was using a database system that was too sophisticated for Kay. If you're trying to set up something like this and you don't have sophisticated computer users, you can use a filebox or something like that. The computer is useful for us in that it allows changing of information rather easily. We chose to use the Appleworks database system simply because so many people at our school knew how to use the Appleworks program. It works fairly well for us.

These are the categories that we set up:

Name:	Marital status:
First name:	Spouse:
Maiden name:	Children:
Address line 1:	Class of:
Address line 2:	Actual/intended grad:
City:	Parents' affiliation:
State:	MK/non-MK:
ZIP code:	Dorm/non-dorm:
Country:	College:
Telephone:	Major(s):
Birthday:	Profession:
Home base name:	Current date:
HB address:	Etc. 1:
HB address 2:	WP file name:
HB phone:	

Birthdays are important to us because when we need an excuse to write to someone we haven't written to in a long time, we can send them a birthday card and get something going again.

One of the most important pieces of information for us is the home base name, address, and phone number. We've got a couple of lines for that to make it easier when I'm setting up the mailing label. The home base is somebody that is going to be there and know where the graduate is and be able to forward some mail to him.

Whether they were an MK or a non-MK is not so much for the Alumni Association as it is for the administration to be able to look back over the years to see what the fluctuation of population has been for the school, to know what kinds of changes have to be made in policy if another mission comes to the country. *Dorm/non-dorm* again helps administratively at the school to anticipate what kinds of changes need to be made in the community.

College, Major(s), and *Profession* are all useful for us to know, but also I want our current students to be able to contact the graduate and say, "What are you doing? Can a good doctor come out of the Alliance Academy?"

Current date is to keep track of how current the address is. If someone writes a letter to us with information that we may be wanting to use for the alumni journal, we can type that on the word processor and save it. *WP file name* is a reference point for us to say, "Who's written in, and where do we find that elsewhere on the disk?"

When girls get married, do you list them under their maiden name or their married name?

Quiring: That's one of the nice things about the database. We can set it up any way we want to.

We list people by class, alphabetically by their married name. We figure as long as we include the maiden name in the list, everyone will be able to recognize who they were before they got married.

What to Include

Landers: Include address lists, student information, school information. What other suggestions do you have?

Case studies: "There was this family and these circumstances came up . . . How would you respond to that?"

We featured our graduates who are currently teaching in the school, with pictures of families and things like that. That really went over quite well.

We try to include some of the significant happenings during that school year that we think the grads will be interested in—new buildings that were built, changes in the campus layout, staff that have come or gone, and such things.

Current pictures of alumni.

Around Christmas time we have an alumni dinner with the people that have come back to visit their parents. We're able to take pictures and hopefully get them into the publication.

Techniques, Technicalities and Lessons Learned

Landers: How often to publish depends on how often I can get the strength to do it, but I aim for at least twice a year. October and March are low months for our college and Bible school students, so I aim to have the publication come out during those months. I have appreciated from the very beginning the support of the administration, especially because the school has given financial support.

Quiring: Theoretically if it works properly it should almost pay for itself or even help attract funds to the school. I realize that's probably not one of your stated goals, but I would expect that most graduates would have a certain amount of loyalty and would at least be willing to defray the costs of the association,

We have had some people send in checks with letters saying, "Hey, we know that printing something like this wasn't free. Here's some money to help with that." Someday I'd love to see an alumni scholarship for one of the seniors that has a genuine need.

We all have had the experience of college alumni newsletters that hit us with one or two things right up front. One of them is, "This is what you can do for the school." The second thing is, "We need your money to keep this particular project going." I think those are two dangers you want to avoid. What we're doing is trying to maintain a friendship and a contact.

About four or five years ago, one of our former graduates really took an interest in starting a newsletter. She married an MK from a school that has an Alumni Association and wondered, "Why can't we have something like that?" She started working on a mailing list and we coordinated the efforts from the school end. That has really helped us as a school to get an updated list. Then, to take the burden off the school, she has kept that.

One teacher sends news of events and special articles that come out in the school to this gal in the States, who has much better printing facilities and can put out a quality letter to the alumni. The alumni, then, are totally responsible for getting this paper out. She has mentioned special projects that "we as alumni can do," so it's coming from them, and we really appreciate that.

Quiring: If you're doing an alumni newsletter or something, we'd really love to see what you're including.

Part VI

ISSUES FOR MK TEACHERS

40

The Christian Philosophy of Education

H. Gene Garrick
Pastor, Tabernacle Church, Norfolk, Va.

A philosophy of life is a way to look at life as a whole. There are two central things I believe a philosophy must have. First is a unity. It must be able to relate everything to everything else in a sensible, unified way, in a way that makes us realize we aren't in a disparate world. Everything is not flying off in all directions. There is purpose and there is meaning to all of life. The second attribute a philosophy must have is a center point, a point to which all of that relates, which brings it all into relation with itself and each other. Dr. Mark Fakkema, who has been called the father of modern Christian school education, stated that "Christian philosophy is the romance of seeing all things as one whole with God as the ultimate."

Philosophy asks the great questions such as: "What is ultimate reality? What can I depend upon to be ultimately real in life and in the world?" Once we find out what reality is, then we have something to hold onto, and something to aim at. It gives us ultimate purpose in life. Along with that question come the questions: "Who am I? What is my real nature? What is my purpose in life? Why am I here?" Then comes: "How am I to know all of these things? What is my point of knowledge?" Out of that comes a fourth question: "What then has value?" Out of these questions we are going to frame what education is all about.

A philosophy of education is simply a philosophy of life brought down to the educational level. We're taking a Christian understanding of all of life and bringing that down to how it applies to education. Once you grasp the philosophy, it has to be a part of your everyday life as a Christian school teacher. No matter what you're doing as an educator, you've got to take the framework of basic understanding of life to which you subscribe, and apply it to the present situation.

We're talking about more than classroom teaching. We're talking about the life and character of the teacher. We're talking about the administration. We're talking about relationships. We're talking about the athletic program, the science lab, the newspaper, paying bills on time, the philosophy of how you raise money. All of that fits in as application to our philosophy of life.

View of reality (metaphysics, ontology) — "God-centered"

Romans 11:36 probably is the key verse of the entire Bible. "For of God, and through God, and to God, are all things: to whom be glory forever. Amen." God is the center of the entire universe.

This whole idea of the God-centered nature of reality is a very important one. What is real? Paul states it this way in II Corinthians 4:18: "We don't look at what we can see, because the things that we can see are temporary. Our real focus of attention is on that which we cannot see, because the things we cannot see are eternal." When we talk about reality we're talking about that which cannot be seen, that which is eternal, as compared to that which can be seen and experienced in a sensory way and is temporary. Everything that we experience in a sensory way is temporary. This world is not eternal. It had a beginning. It will have an end.

When we start thinking about reality, we've got to think about God, because God is that great unseen, eternal reality. By our very make-up we understand that the nature of reality is spiritual. And Scriptures declare that it is eternal as well.

Let's begin at the center point, seeing all things as one whole, with God as the ultimate. The ultimate means "that from which all things come and that to which all things go, and that which is the explanation of all things, and that which is behind all things." A.W. Tozer said that God is under all, sustaining; around all, enclosing and protecting; above all, presiding; outside of all, creating; and within all, filling. God is that great ultimate reality. Everything came from him. God is the creator of everything. All things ultimately are a reflection of the God who created them. Therefore we call God "the ultimate original of all things," one of Mark Fakkema's phrases.

God was before all things. He was the pattern in some way for everything he created. So Paul could say concerning the creation around us that it declared God's godhead, his power, and his glory.

The problem of evil and sin is the fly in the ointment of any philosophy. Where did it come from? If God is all-good and all-powerful, how could evil possibly exist? It is a total contradiction of his nature.

The fall brought total disintegration and misunderstanding into man's whole pattern of thinking. But the fall and evil stem from the creation of man in God's image as to his will. Man has a limited free will to make decisions that are contrary to God's best purposes for his life. He has made those decisions, and in making those decisions with God's free will, he created evil. Actually, I think Lucifer, our enemy in heaven, created evil. Evil is not God's creation, but evil is under God's control. The book of Job, if it illustrates anything, illustrates that. If the story of Joseph and the story of our Lord Jesus on the cross illustrate anything, it is this: evil is under the control of Almighty God.

The second thing about God that this verse tells us is that through God are all things. God not only created, but God sustains. God is the God of providence. He's not the deistic god who eons ago molded the world, tossed it out, created natural law, set it in motion, and then went off. Rather we have a God who is transcendent, totally above and outside of his creation. At the same time we believe that God is present in his creation and with his creation, sustaining it. We might put it this way: The laws of nature aren't independent realities apart from the power of God. Isaiah 40, for instance, says, "Because God is strong in power, not one star falls. All of it stays in place." The same thing is said about our Lord Jesus in Colossians 1:16, 17. "By him all things consist or hold together."

I would propose that the laws of nature are nothing but the way God does things. That's the way God chooses to operate. We believe in a God who is present and active in his creation, sustaining all things. Everything has a dynamic relationship to God through his creation and his constant sustenance.

The third leg of this triangle is that to God are all things. Here we have two concepts. One is the ultimate fulfillment of all things, and second is the ultimate purpose of all things. All things are to God. That is, they will find their ultimate reality in him, and they have the ultimate purpose to bring glory to him. Paul concludes by saying, "To whom be glory for ever. Amen." Here we have defined the God-centeredness of the universe in which we live. This is a real view of the universe.

My proposition is this: We ought to teach children the real view of life, and then they can understand the present condition of life in light of the real view of what life is. It's not what life ought to be. This is what life IS. We get confused sometimes and think it is an ideal we should work toward. No. This is the way life is right now. We are far short of it. We have great needs. There are problems in our society, in our world, in our universe. What should we do in light of the reality that God is and the unreality that man has created and made? It seems to me that is the sort of contrast we need to be presenting.

View of man (anthropology, psychology) — "image-centered"

Let's look at the view of man, briefly. One former leader in American education said that if you don't believe in the perfectibility of man, you should not be in public education. He meant that if you don't believe man can solve his own problems — drugs, alcoholism, poverty, war, racism, economic development — don't get in public education, because that's what it's for. It is the evolutionary view of man, that he has evolved from nothing to what he is now, and his evolution has just begun.

The other extreme is the nihilistic view which says that everything man does is bad — that the five boys on a desert island who, left to themselves, went to total corruption, is a better view of what man is really like.

But the Christian view is neither of those. Neither is it a mixture of those. Rather, the real view of man is stated in Scriptures this way: "God created man in his own image and after his own likeness." Man is best defined in his nature as an image of God.

Man is a thinking being and has an ability to communicate. He knows right from wrong and is creative and emotional. He has a will and can make decisions. He is a creature who is able to have the dominion that God gave him.

God created man in his own image after his likeness. That is the nature of man. Our view of the purpose of man grows out of his nature. The nature dictates the purpose. Now what is man's purpose? What is the purpose of any image? It's to be like the original.

Here we have defined man's nature and purpose. He is the image of God. His purpose is to glorify God, to reflect what God is like, to bring honor and glory to him, to depend upon him. Just as the world around us in not independent of God, so man should not be independent of God.

Dr. Mark Fakkema calls man an original image. He partakes of God's originality and his will. God has somehow given man the choice whether he wants to reflect and glorify God or not. Creation outside doesn't have a choice. It is dependent on God. It does glorify God by simply being what God created it to be and doing what God created it to do. It is man that has marred the landscape and made creation deficient. Man has chosen to be independent of God and to go his own way and to glorify himself, so man cannot fulfill his purpose in life.

What is man's greatest need? Man's greatest need is restoration to his original purpose. Education per se will not do that. Only redemption can do that. So the Christian view of education must always start with redemption—restoration of man to his relationship with God in this purpose of glorifying God. Once that's done, education begins to have meaning.

Education will then help him to realize his full potential as a human being created in the image of God.

View of knowledge and truth (epistemology) — "revelation-centered"

Our view of knowledge and truth is probably the crux of any philosophy. How do you know what you believe is true? Naturalism says you must find out truth by the scientific method of investigation, observation, and laboratory methods. You know it's true because you've established it in that fashion.

There are others who say, "I believe people can know things intuitively. I believe flashes of insight can come, and suddenly you'll know truth." That was certainly true when I started thinking about my wife. We had seen each other a few times, and all of a sudden I thought, "I think I love her." Flash of insight. It proved to be true. Truth can perhaps be known that way.

Truth can be known, the world would say, through the authoritarian method. That is, the authority in the community or society says, "This is true," and then everyone needs to believe that. Somehow we believe that man has that power to come to truth by himself. Rationalism says that man is a thinking being, and therefore he can think his way into truth.

All of these are true to some extent, but they leave one important thing out, and that is that we can know truth by revelation as well. When we say that, immediately some people pull back. "No, that's mystical, and that's beyond what we can experience." But it's not, really. We've been married thirty-three years, and in a normal situation I couldn't tell you what my wife is thinking. I can't even know it if I ask all the right questions, because she's cagey. I can't know it by scientific investigation. But there's one way I can know exactly what she's thinking, and that is if she reveals it to me. If she tells me, then I'll know it. It's a human experience we all go through all the time, in every area of life.

Why should it be so strange that the God who created and sustains and is the purpose of all things should reveal himself? "We cannot by searching find out God," the book of Job tells us. And that means philosophical searching, scientific searching, artistic or whatever it might be. We can't find out God through our own means, but if he reveals himself we can find him. Now one of the presuppositions of Christianity is this: there is a God. He is a personal God, and he has communicated himself to man. He has told man what he is like. We believe that God has revealed that to us in Scripture.

Ultimately, all philosophy depends on faith. Every person who says, "This is the way I look at the world and life," is making a statement of faith. He can't say, "I know it's this way." All he can say is, "I believe this is the way it is." The Christian says, "I believe;" the evolutionist says, "I believe;" the atheist says, "I believe;" He can never say, "I know for sure."

All truth is God's truth, not just the Bible. The truth that's in nature that science pulls out is God's truth. When God built the universe, he built it on geometrical principles. Therefore, we don't create geometry, we discover it. What you teach in the math class or what you teach in music class might be just as true as John 3:16. It's not nearly as important. I would much prefer my child know how to know the eternal God and to be his child and to live with him forever, than how to build bridges. There's a difference in the quality and the importance of knowledge, but it's all God's truth.

Therefore, we believe in an integration of God's truth. God's truth in Scripture and revelation, and his truth in the world around us that is learned and discovered by man are not in contradiction to one another. Rather, they supplement one another. The truth of revelation extends the truth that we see here, and helps us understand it better. In effect, it evaluates and judges all areas of truth. But the Christian views the whole area of knowledge and truth from a scriptural point of view.

View of value (axiology) — "eternity-centered"

Real value must be centered in that which is ultimately real, that which is eternal, in God himself. It must be centered in man's ultimate nature and purpose, not in man's earthly existence as such. That's the reason Paul says to Timothy, "Bodily exercise profits a little, but godliness is profitable for all things; both for the life that now is, and that which is to come."

Jesus said, "You shall know the truth, and the truth will make you free." The truth is that which we must have in order to understand the value of anything in life.

View of education (pedagogy) — "life-centered"

The direction of learning then, is first Godward, then manward. We can't fully understand this world unless we understand God. We might understand the mechanics of it, what causes the weather and all, but in leaving God out, we have no ultimate point of reference to the eternal. And therefore, we can get very confused about life.

The Christian says, "Ultimately reality is found in God, not in man. It's found in the Spirit, not in material. It's found in eternity, not in time. That's ultimate reality." Therefore we must train our children to know God first. Then they can understand the world. It's not without reason that Jesus said, "You love God," first, and then, "You love your neighbor." That's always the right direction.

Jesus said, "Seek first God's kingdom, his righteousness, that ultimate spiritual reality, then those things which you need — food, clothing, shelter — will be added to you."

The purpose of education, as we have said, is restoration to God's control and ultimate purpose for our lives. Education has that function of helping the development of the person to his ultimate potential. The power for education, from a Christian point of view, is from God. Whereas we can teach children science and history and these things, and they can learn them and memorize them; an understanding of who God is, who man is, and our relationship with God comes only as the Spirit of God works. There's got to be a power outside of ourselves.

We aren't simply academic schools. We're teaching the student about life. We're doing it through the tools of academics, sports, and many other things, but nevertheless, our whole context is that we're teaching about life. The school should be applying the truth to life. There shouldn't be simply academic learning, not the memorizing of facts alone.

Education could perhaps be summed up better from the wisdom of the Old Testament. Wisdom is the understanding of knowledge as it applies to life in a way that will produce good, rather than bad. All of our educational processes need to be thought of in terms of how they are going to affect the total life of that student.

A Christian educator always looks to God. A Christian educator prays. A Christian educator recognizes his own limitations. A Christian educator doesn't try to convince but rather tries to help a person understand the truth in a spiritual way. The power of education comes from the Holy Spirit. It comes from the Word of God, which is powerful. It comes from the whole revelation that God has made of himself. Because of that, the process of education is not methodology so much as the dynamic of the Christian persons who are involved.

This understanding of life isn't something that is taught academically in the textbook. It's taught because a person who sees the world that way begins to communicate that to his pupils. It can be the parent of the home, the teacher from the school, or the pastor in the pulpit. Education is communication. But communication has to be of life. We're communicating a view of life. We train up the child in the way that he should go.

View of authority and responsibility—"partnership"

I believe that a Christian school is a return to parent responsibility and authority in education. The Christian school says, "We believe God gave children to parents. They are responsible. They have asked us to be their partners. We will help them educate their children for the glory of God." There must be a concurrence of philosophical views between the home and the school.

The school must never look at itself as being independent of the home in what it's trying to do and how it's trying to carry on that work. We often look at ourselves as the educational experts. We know about children, we know about teaching, and we don't like parental interference. We would like to conduct our work and let the parents conduct theirs at home. I don't believe that's possible if we believe in life education. If we believe that all truth is God's truth, then we believe that the teachers at home are just as important as the teachers at school. But there must be a relationship.

> We've had experiences where we related what the child was like at school, and our parents have said quite frankly, "You've got another child in mind. That is not my child."
> Then I said, "Well, how do you view the child?"
> They told me, and I said, "Well you have another child in mind. That is not your child."

We need to begin sharing, because we're working with the same child.

I believe when we're working with a non-Christian home, we still must recognize the child belongs to those parents. We must be honest with them in working with them and working with their child, and not subvert their family by leading the child to faith in Christ without the parent's really knowing what we're doing. I think we've got to be totally honest, but I think we must work toward the salvation of that family as well.

All of us, whether we are on the field or whether we are at home, must have a philosophy of education. It must be a biblically-derived philosophy. It must be an all-encompassing philosophy with God at the very center. You need to think that through, and then you need to think through the uniqueness of that philosophy as it applies to your school in your particular framework.

Discussion

Out of eighty-five participants from forty-one countries of the world in the boarding conference, only one school had a philosophy statement regarding boarding and its relationship to the natural parents of those children.

I've been in MK schools where the teachers and the house parents never communicated. I've been in MK schools where the parents never knew much about what was happening. Even when the parent came back into the station, the teacher and parents never got together. That reflects a philosophy, the philosophy that the school is the teachers' domain. They educate the children. That philosophy needs to change to say the school is an extension of that home and a partner with that home. We need to work together.

What about turnover of personnel?

The administrator needs to take seriously the fact that when new personnel come in, there's got to be continual re-education.

How does the education philosophy become a reality in the school?

By taking it seriously. In other words it's not just written out for accreditation purposes, it's written out to actually apply. Many schools don't know why they admit the students that they do. That goes back to your philosophy. "It's because this is our philosophy and these are people with whom we want to work." You've got to define your constituency. Then you choose the people related to that overall philosophy.

As an administrator you have to systematically relate the philosophy to every part of the school program. It'll take years. It's a lot of hard work, but it has to be planned hard work.

Six times a year our parents come together to be educated. Our teachers do the same thing. The development of our handbook and all the rest was with the idea of communicating that philosophy again and again. It takes at least five years of intense hard work by the administrator for a person coming new to the Christian school to begin to think somewhat Christianly about his teaching and about the whole program of the school. So there has to be an intensified, planned, hard-work, long-range program to carry that out.

41

Values Development in
the Christian Schools

Kenneth Hall
Superintendent, Southfield Christian School

In his book *Christian Behavior*, C.S. Lewis tells the story of the little boy that he asked one day what he thought God was like. The boy thought for a few minutes, and then he said, "As near as I can figure out, God is a grumpy old man who goes around seeing if anybody is having a good time, and then tries to stop it."

Some people think the same about values and moral education. They think it is something to rob life of joy. Those of us who are followers of Christ know that joy is the result of a life that is founded on biblical values. The word *value* itself has an interesting history. It comes from the Latin *valore* and means 'to be strong, to be forceful and courageous'. We get our word *valence* from that word. In chemistry, valence is the power of elements to combine and interact with each other. We also get our English word *valor* from that same word, which means 'to be brave and strong'. A clear set of values results in the valiant person.

Values affect three areas of life. (1) Values affect relationships between people. (2) Values relate to the internal harmony within an individual. (3) Values relate to the purpose of life. Values are like ships travelling in convoy. The ships are likely to reach their destination if all of the ships stay out of each other's way so they don't collide. Secondly, they're likely to reach their destination if each ship is seaworthy and in good working order. Thirdly, they are likely to reach their destination if they're headed in the right direction. If their destination is New York and they end up in Bremerhaven, it was not a successful voyage.

In a Christian school, values instruction is a very pressing issue. For most of our schools, that's what we're mandated to do. We're there to transmit biblically-based values. It seems to me that task involves four aspects of instruction. (1) It involves how we communicate values to the young. (2) It involves the understanding of values. Do the students understand what we're talking about? (3) It involves making judgments on the basis of values. When students make a decision about a moral situation, to what extent is the decision based on biblical values? (4) It involves moral action. The actual behavior in the real world that results from moral judgment.

There are lots of values issues in the Bible. Let me call your attention to two of them as examples of other kinds of situations of a similar nature.

> Mark 2:23-28. And it came to pass, that he went through the corn fields on the Sabbath day; and his disciples began, as they went, to pluck the ears of corn. And the Pharisees said unto him, Behold, why do they on the Sabbath day that which is not lawful?
>
> And he said unto them, Have ye never read what David did, when he had a need, and was an hungered, he, and they that were with him? How he went into the house of God in the days of Abiathar the high priest, and did eat the shewbread, which is not lawful to eat but for the priests, and gave also to them which were with him?
>
> And he said unto them, The Sabbath was made for man, and not man for the Sabbath: Therefore the Son of man is Lord also of the Sabbath.

Jesus is in a values conflict between principled morality and the Pharisees' interpretation of Old Testament regulations. Jesus issues the principle that the Sabbath was made for man, not man for the Sabbath.

Luke 4:16-30 is an example of the public affirmation of a value that may get you into trouble. So far as we know this is the first public sermon of Jesus:

> And he came to Nazareth, where he had been brought up, and as his custom was, he went into the synagogue on the Sabbath day, and stood up for to read. And there was delivered unto him the book of the prophet Esaias. And when he had opened the book, he found the place where it was written, The Spirit of the Lord is upon me, because he hath anointed me to preach the gospel to the poor; he hath sent me to heal the broken-hearted, to preach deliverance to the captives, and recovering of sight to the blind, and to set at liberty them that are bruised, to preach the acceptable year of the Lord. And he

closed the book, and he gave it again to the minister, and sat down. And the eyes of all them that were in the synagogue were fastened on him. And he began to say unto them, This day is this scripture fulfilled in your ears.

And all bare him witness, and wondered at the gracious words which proceeded out of his mouth. And they said, Is not this Joseph's son?

And he said unto them, Ye will surely say unto me this proverb, Physician, heal thyself; whatsoever we have heard done in Capernaum, do also here in thy country.

And he said, Verily I say unto you, No prophet is accepted in his own country. But I tell you of a truth, many widows were in Israel in the days of Elias, when the heaven was shut up three years and six months, when great famine was throughout all the land; but unto none of them was Elias sent, save unto Sarepta, a city of Sidon, unto a woman that was a widow. And many lepers were in Israel in the time of Eliseus the prophet; and none of them was cleansed, saving Naaman the Syrian.

And all they in the synagogue, when they heard these things, were filled with wrath, And rose up, and thrust him out of the city, and led him unto the brow of the hill whereon their city was built, that they might cast him down headlong. But he passing through the midst of them went his way.

Jesus didn't have to use those examples from the Scripture that God had mercy on Gentiles as well as on Jews. He takes two Gentile examples from the Old Testament. He knew the audience to whom he was speaking, and yet publicly he affirmed the value of God's mercy on all people. The result was enormous upheaval threatening his life. But Jesus stood by the value that he proclaimed.

Difficulties in developing Christian values

As you and I work in a Christian setting to develop a set of biblical values in the lives of the students with whom we work, there are some difficulties.

- Lack of agreement among Christian leaders and Christian parents as to what values ought to be affirmed and taught.
- Cultural biases, and sometimes sorting out the difference between a principle and what a preference or cultural bias may be.
- Poor knowledge of the Word of God.
- Lack of training and preparation.

- The values dimension of our instruction is not real high in our consciousness.
- Double standard of living. Making promises and not reinforcing it with behavior.
- Pluralism. We talk about the different value systems and then say, "We'd better not be too strong about one."
- Rate of social change. Mobility, so that the sense of accountability to some group isn't there.
- Temptation to substitute a cookbook of prescribed behaviors for values and principles. There is certain amount of choice and freedom that is involved in working with values and principles that is often uncomfortable.
- Drive for personal peace and affluence.
- Unwillingness to change. Theologically we think of the old nature and the proneness to do what is contrary to righteousness and justice.
- Developmental issues.
- Progression of moral development in child.

Approach to moral education

In the light of the difficulties, there have been several approaches to values instruction. One approach would be relativism. Values seem to be so different from one locality to another or one time period to another. How can you choose what set of values to teach? So, rather than try to teach any, say, "All values are equally valid for the time or the place at which they exist."

There are a couple of problems with that. (1) There are not so many differences as some people suppose. (2) The fact that there are lots of different value systems throughout cultures does not mean that all of them are equally valid.

The second approach to the teaching of values is cultural transmission. We can't sort out which set of values to teach, so teach whatever the prevailing set of values happen to be wherever you are.

There are two problems with that. (1) Moral and ethical issues are never settled by majority vote. Majority vote may be a great way to run a democracy, but it is not the way to determine morality and values. (2) Values have to do not only with what is, but with what ought to be. Simply transmitting culture, you are transmitting what is, whereas principle and morality deal with what ought to be.

Another approach to values instruction is not to bother with it at all. Rather, concentrate on ego strength, self-esteem, and emotional stability. One of the clearest expressions of that viewpoint is by A.S. Neal in his book *Summerhill*. He says on page 4:

We set out to make a school in which we shall allow children freedom to be themselves. To do this we removed all discipline, all direction, and all moral training. We have been called brave for doing what we did. But it did not require courage, just a complete belief in the child as good, and not an evil being. A child is innately wise and realistic. If left to himself without adult suggestion of any kind, he will develop as far as he is capable of developing. I believe that it is moral instruction that makes the child bad, not good.

Later in the book Mr. Neal relates this incident:

A few years ago we had two pupils arrive at the same time, a boy of sixteen and a girl of seventeen. They fell in love with each other and were always together. I met them late one night entwined around each other and stopped them. I said to them, "I don't know what you two are doing, and morally I don't care, for it isn't a moral question at all. But economically I do care. If you, Kate, have a baby, my school will be ruined. You have just come to Summerhill. To you it means freedom to do what you like. Naturally you have no special feeling for the school. If you had been here from the age of seven, I'd never have to mention the matter. You'd have such a strong attachment to the school that you would think of the consequences to Summerhill."

So here it is. Clearly he wants to avoid moralizing about sexual behavior, but he's got to make some regulations in this area if only because of economics. This is the typical outcome of trying to duck values training in favor of mental health and personal freedom. You end up with a hidden moral curriculum.

Another approach to the values issue is the developmental approach. I suppose that got the most publicity in relation to Lawrence Kohlberg of Harvard University.

Fifth is the Christian approach to values instruction and moral development. There are at least three Christian approaches.

One was expressed first by Augustine and then later picked up by Martin Luther and is summarized in the little quip, "Love God and do what you please." Augustine and Luther said that if you love God with all your heart, soul, strength, and mind, then you will do what is right. You don't need instruction about specifics. You need only to love God and then do what is right.

At the other end of the spectrum is the cookbook of rules and regulations. In *The Brothers Karamazov* by Dostoevsky, the Grand Inquisitor comes to the Christian and says, "You and Jesus had it all wrong. You thought that what people wanted was freedom to make choices. That's not what they want at all. What they want is bread and authority. People are going to resist you and rebel against you because freedom is the worst burden to carry." In light of that, some people have said that the way to handle values instruction and moral development for kids is to tell them what is right in every situation.

The third Christian approach is to focus upon principles of justice and righteousness. I would like to carry that one a little further.

School-Based Values Education

I would like to suggest that a comprehensive values instructional program might consist of four or five parts.

Direct instruction

You might call direct instruction indoctrination or even moralizing. Moralizing usually has a negative connotation to it, but I'm using it in the best sense, and that is telling kids the principles of biblical righteousness and biblical justice. Honesty, truthfulness, and integrity are right. The full weight of God's revelation is behind them. They are good. Dishonesty, falsehood, and lack of integrity are wrong.

Precautions in relation to indoctrination or direct instruction are: (1) Sometimes this kind of instruction is carried out in a loveless, self-righteous manner. It leads to a rejection of the principles without due regard for their worth. (2) Direct instruction, if it stands alone, is insufficient. For one thing, it needs to be done in an environment that is just and righteous. Instruction in biblical values in an unjust environment sabotages the instruction. (3) It needs to be supplemented with practice opportunities.

> Hebrews 5:13-14 For every one that useth milk is unskillful in the word of righteousness: for he is a babe. But strong meat belongeth to them that are of full age, even those who by reason of use have their sense exercised to discern both good and evil.

Interesting emphasis there on the importance of practice, the importance of exercise, the importance of struggling with moral issues. So maturity and moral understanding a result not only of knowing the value but also of practicing it and struggling with its applications.

Modelling or example

This is a powerful form of learning. The Bible appeals to it again and again. For example Paul writes to Titus, "Adorn the doctrine of God our Savior in all things." That doctrine about God and about life in all of its glory and radiance, dress it up in the clothes of a captivating character. Don't just preach it and argue for it, but adorn it with life.

One of the great words in Christianity is incarnation, enfleshment of the truth. Our Lord is the supreme example of the embodiment of truth. But we, too, must embody what we teach. Paul says, "Be followers of me as I also am of Christ Jesus."

Victor Franco, a psychiatrist from Austria, told the story of a man who bought a parrot. He wanted to teach the parrot to call him Daddy, so he would say again and again to the parrot, "Call me Daddy." When the parrot didn't do it, he'd smack the bird up alongside the head. Finally in utter frustration the man took the parrot to the chicken coop for the night. The next morning he discovered that the parrot had killed all of the chickens but one, and the last one he had down on the ground strangling it and saying, "Call me Daddy." The parrot had missed the point of the lecture, but he caught the behavior.

In our values instruction, if behavior does not support instruction, you can be sure that the kids are going to follow the behavior. When there's conflict between action and instruction, it's action that will be followed.

Values clarification

I realize that values clarification has been hammered by Christian writers in the past few years largely because of its basis in relativism. I should probably find another word to call this, but I don't know another word for it. What I'm talking about is what wise parents have done for years and years, and that is to work with their children to develop a deeper understanding of values as they apply to a situation.

We teach and we model, but what are the kids really owning for themselves? We've tried to include some strategies and activities that will open up the opportunity to hear from them and to talk with them. Let me suggest two exercises that we have used at our school:

One of the activities is called a values barometer. This is a series of ten statements about which we ask the students to indicate the extent of their agreement or disagreement. If they strongly disagree, they put a -2 beside it. If they disagree, they put a -1. If they agree, they put a +1. If they strongly agree, they put a +2.

Let me give you an example of five of these statements:

1. The penalty for those guilty of first-degree murder should be death.
2. It is OK to lie if it is done to spare someone else's feelings.
3. Spanking children teaches them violence.
4. The decision to be a missionary includes the acceptance of a low standard of life.
5. Children should have the right to waste their money.

After completing the exercise, we ask if there is someone willing to volunteer their response to a statement and why they indicated their agreement or disagreement. Sometimes we've done it as an actual activity. We've labeled different locations in the room with the values and asked students to go to the place in the room where their agreement is indicated. And then we have asked them to defend why they are where they are. At the end of that time of defence, we say to all of the, "Would you like to change the place where you are?" Some of them move at that point. The point is to get them talking about values issues, and the point is to get them conscious that there are decisions to be made about values issues.

When the students give their value judgments, does the teacher finish with any kind of judgement on that?

Yes. We do not leave them openended.

We don't have a curriculum in our school that's called values development. We try to merge it with the regular curriculum. For example, one of the stories in the reader in the primary grades is a story about a child who's ostracized and ridiculed by the other children. Obviously the teacher is going to ask comprehension questions, vocabulary questions and recognition questions, but then the teacher may also ask this: "How would it feel to be rejected by your friends? What would you want somebody to do for you, if you were the one being rejected? "What do you think the Bible teaches about dealing with others in the group?"

Here's an example related to math. The math problem is this: "Bill brought a Stingray bike for $100. Three years later he sold it for $35. While he owned the bike he spent $9 on repairs. How much did it cost Bill to use his bike each year? What percent of the purchase price did he use when he sold it?" The teacher might also follow that up with some questions like these: "If you were selling your bike, and a perspective buyer came to see it, would you tell him what was wrong with it? What if she or he didn't ask? Would you lower the price for somebody that you knew was really poor?"

Moral dilemmas

One other kind of activity is the moral dilemma. The use of moral dilemmas was popularized by Lawrence Kohlberg. Kohlberg said that there are two parts to moral judgments. One is the content. The content says, for example, that shoplifting is wrong. But the other part of the moral judgement is structure. And structure is the answer to the question, "Why is shoplifting wrong?"

Kohlberg says that if someone says to you, "Shoplifting is wrong because you may get caught and have to pay a fine, that that is low-level moral reasoning or preconventional reasoning. He says that if somebody says, "Well I don't shoplift because my parents taught me that it's wrong, and it's against the law," that's popular-level moral reasoning or conventional-level reason. That's law-and-order reasoning. If somebody says, "I don't shoplift because the Bible says to do unto others as you would have others do unto you, and I don't want somebody taking my possessions," Kohlberg would say that goes above popular-level moral reasoning and appeals to a universal principle in making moral decisions.

Here's an example of a moral dilemma Kohlberg would use with primary grade children:

There's a little girl by the name of Holly who is the best tree-climber in the neighborhood. One day Holly fell from a tree and hurt her knee. After that her Daddy made her promise that she would not climb trees again.

A couple of months later Holly is walking down the street and she sees a group of her friends standing beneath a tree and looking up into it. When she gets there, she discovers that her best friend's kitten is up in that tree. And her best friend says to her, "Holly will you go up there and get my kitten?"

The question to the kids is, "Should Holly go? What should Holly do?"

Here's a moral dilemma that Kohlberg would do for high school students. "During the Civil War in the United States it was against the law to harbor runaway slaves. But there were some people who provided protection for runaway slaves. Did they do right? Or did they do wrong?" Now you can imagine if you threw that out to a class of high school students, you'd spend an interesting time as they wrestled with the values issues and the moral issues that are involved with that.

Obviously these dilemmas can be developed for our particular situation, because their only purpose is to get students struggling with the principles on which they would make their decision. Suppose you include these kind of activities in your curriculum in your school. Is there any reason to think that students who make moral decisions based on biblical values in a classroom situation are likely to make those decisions in the real world? There's some research that indicates that young people who have the experience of practice with moral decisions in a safe environment under the guidance of a teacher are more likely to act in accordance with their values in the real world when a decision is called for.

Discussion

Another variable involved in the transfer proces is the variable of self-esteem. Those with self-esteem who have had practice in wrestling with moral issues are more likely to carry it over than those who may have had the same exercise and same practice, but who have poor self-esteem.

How do you train teachers?

We have a set of staff development activities that we go through, encouraging teachers to include this kind of activities in the curriculum. Every once in a while the teacher will say, "But I don't think of that. Why don't we make it a class?" We've resisted that simply because we'd rather have it pervasive, so that it becomes almost incidental teaching rather than just formal instruction, "Now we're going to talk about values."

The issues of family structure in the book of Genesis are tremendously interesting moral dilemmas. Yet I find we don't want to touch these issues.

I'm not sure yet about the argument Jesus gives about the Sabbath. The Old Testament law was very strict. There are so many moral dilemmas created in Scripture that it should make Bible curriculum very rich, and yet I find it is often a wilderness experience.

One of the concerns I would have with trying to avoid moral dilemmas of Scripture is that they arise again later. And if the kids have not had some experience in wrestling with them at the time they arise, then when they arise later, the students will say, "They were afraid of it."

Another helpful area in terms of values clarification is to use the real life decisions that the child is wrestling with. It may be whether to go to the football game tonight or to stay home and study.

If the child is struggling with a decision the parent has made, help him to step into the role of the parent. Ask, "What values could be guiding your parents in what they're asking you to do, and what values are important to you in terms of what you would want to do in this situation?"

We have a few teachers in our school who enjoy taking the classroom discussion model of William Glasser in *Schools Without Failure* and combining it with values clarification, so that if an incident occurs in a play ground, they make that a topic of values wrestling in the classroom. They feel confident and competent about doing that. Not every the teacher does.

Could it be that young kids need the cookbook as a basis of understanding? If we get a teenager who does not have the cookbook basis, is there not a valid place for that kind of approach? And does the student not need that before he can discuss values dilemmas?

I certainly think the way in which you would do it would be different than you did with primary grade kids, but I still think that often direct teaching has to be done.

We need to consider how kids process information. With literature, kids are so involved with the characters that you do not have to add the moralizing process for the young child. The nature of moral dilemma in story form is so powerful that we are afraid of it. The difference between the story of Joseph and the story of Snow White is the issue of redemption and reconciliation. Often in trying to interpret a story, we will in fact destroy what children have gotten.

42

Keeping Up-To-Date Professionally

Grace Barnes
Azusa Pacific University, Operation Impact

Some definitions of growth and development

In our department we talk a lot about growth and development, and we base our perspective on what we call a developmental view of mankind. People are individually different and unique, and we need to celebrate differences as well as the many things we have in common. We also believe that not only do children go through stages in life, but so do adults.

Generally we are not prepared for moving from one stage of adult life to another. Growth is something that is more of the same. It's the natural process of life. Development is a change in structure. It requires new assumptions and new ways of looking at things. It generally occurs as a result of some sort of a crisis or time of transition in life. A lot of times it can be very uncomfortable and very difficult, but it's what spurs us on to be better. Development in our lives is absolutely imperative for us to move in any kind of direction. But what is sad is that when people are going through transition, we think of it as negative. We don't provide the necessary kind of support for people in those transition times.

When missionaries have outgrown their mission or what they're doing, they feel like they've got to do something different or new. At the same time, they feel guilty because they have committed their lives to this area, and they think it's not spiritual and not right to think about doing something else.

John Nesbitt, author of *Megatrends*, says that from now on, a person will have five and six careers in his lifetime. In order to do that, there's going to have to be continual educating and training going on.

I would like to suggest, too, that growth and development relates very much to our philosophy of what we think vocation is. James Fowler talks about vocation being a partnership with God in this world. Our job is really to orchestrate all of our time, talents, relationships, and values in the kingdom work of God. That might take on various expressions, so the job or career is not so much the issue, but rather how we look at our vocation. If we're in transition we need to ask, "What is our purpose?" Then we can develop some new goals to help us grow and develop further. I know in my own personal life, I've had at least five distinct careers, but they all seem to flow out of a general purpose. My vocation is still intact, but I have had different ways to express it.

The nature of transition

We find people in their thirties and forties and then later in their sixties and seventies going through some major transition times. Sometimes we call it mid-life crisis. But there comes a time when we evaluate. The kids are grown or almost grown, and we're looking at our past life and wondering what we're going to do for the next big segment. Sometimes we need new input and professional updating and a new sense of direction. It can be very uncomfortable. That transition involves endings and new beginnings and a neutral zone, which is where we feel this discomfort. The neutral zone is that period where the focus tends to be on ourselves rather than other people.

That transition is a necessary part of evaluating where we are and where we might want to go in the future. It's a time to reflect on our current interests, likes, talents, gifts, abilities, and experiences, and to re-evaluate where we are going. The tendency in our Western culture is to be so task-oriented that we feel like we've got to keep going and be busy to be productive. It's hard to sit back and reflect. Development really takes place in process, not in one minute, or one month. A lot of us in the Western culture are very results-oriented. We want things to hurry up and happen. We burn out in terms of our own emotional involvement in life. When you go though some process of reflection, you find yourself revitalized.

Becoming an effective activities manager

Becoming an effective activities manager is one of the things that helped me a lot in the last two or three years. There really is no such thing as controlling time. Time has been the same since the Year One as it is now. There are still twenty-four hours in a day. In this generation, we realize there's so much to do out there, that we must become project managers and activities manager. Time is not the issue. It's activities that are the issue.

How do you select what you'll do, and how do you set your priorities? They have to come out of your purpose and your goals. If we just live according to what we've got to do today, and what we've got tomorrow, we end up being crisis managers. If you work out your purpose and your goals, then you can decide whether your activities fit those or not. If they don't, you don't do them.

Professional Development

Most growth plans are based on growth and not on development. Growth plans are "I want to do this. I want to do better in this." Development plans focus on the development of areas of our lives that we really have not given ourselves permission to work on or that we've had difficulty with, or that are real risky areas. We need support people to help us with those. When we focus on professional development, we need to deal with four areas.

As the first step in professional development, you need to asses where you are. Assess your current strengths and likes, your current weaknesses and dislikes, your current preferences. Then ask yourself, "What are my goals? What are my choices?"

Next ask yourself, "What knowledge and skills do I have at this point? What skills have I developed through my experience? What are the things that I have to contribute?" Consider not just academic areas or learning areas, but attitudes as well.

Now ask yourself, "What are the resources available to me to reach my goals?" We need to take time out to research the resources that are available. We're in such a hurry to get going on something that we don't even think about all that we're going to be going through in that experience. When you're exposed to new information, you're going to be going through a tremendous amount of growth and development and change. You gain some new knowledge and skills, but it's the personal growth and development that takes place that changes lives and is appreciated the most.

Evaluation needs to be done on an on-going basis. Continue to evaluate where you are, what you're doing, and how it really affects your life. Ask yourself, "Is this really what I want to be doing?"

Discussion

How do we know when it's time to make a change?

I think it's an inner thing. It's feeling restless in what you're doing. It's the sense that you need something new in your life. It's the desire to do something very different or to take a risk. Maybe it's some observation by family members or people you work with, "Hey, maybe you should think about something new in your life."

The tendency is to feel guilty. But I think as we develop, we are going to feel this way at different times in our life, and that's OK. I think when you're ready, you feel ready, and it's right. It's almost like a new calling.

Is there any indication as to the best way to approach professional updating? Is correspondence on the field, while you're involved in the work as effective as taking time out when you're back home to go to school and take courses?

There are so many ways to look at that. People have found that furloughs can be good times for studying. Others have found them terrible times for study. Correspondence is limited because there's not much interaction with anybody else. In our program there is a year-long project you work on. You have mentors and people on the field to help. We find this is a good balance. I would see that kind of arrangement as better than just the correspondence or trying to fit something in hit or miss on a furlough situation. Some people take an extended furlough, so they can concentrate entirely on studying, and that seems to work fairly well.

Bear's Guide to Non-Traditional College Degrees includes a wealth of information on programs that can be done overseas and in the States. Many are not accredited. They may be authorized or approved or licensed, but not accredited. Most accredited programs require some kind of residence, which may be as short as one week per year. There's one in doctoral program at the Fielding Institute in Santa Barbara, California, which requires a very intense time of seminar only one week per year.

The California University for Advanced Studies has a School of Professional Management. They have B.A., Masters and Doctoral programs which can be done entirely overseas. It only costs a couple thousand dollars for the whole degree. It is not accredited, but it is approved by the State of California. They're hoping to turn it into an accredited program soon.

Regents College Degrees of the University of the State of New York could be helpful to anybody who has not finished their B.A. degree. This school will put together a program for you, especially if you've had a lot of courses through the years. They may say you need to take one or two more courses in a certain area. They have been very helpful to many of the Operation Impact students.

Tennessee Temple and Pensacola Christian College offer short two and three week segments for furthering studies. Westmont is trying to put together ways that people can get credit for their life experience and get a B.A.

Three Boxes of Life, put out by Ten Speed Press, is a fun and an excellent resource book for anybody who's considering more of a transition or a change in career.

43

Programs for Non-Academically-Inclined Students

Dennis Vogan
Superintendent, Faith Academy

[Those in attendance at this session began by filling out a question-naire on programs for non-academically-inclined students. Participants included nine teachers, four boarding home parents, and nine school administrators representing sixteen different schools. They reported their schools had no vocational/technical programs. One high school had a work program. Only four reported that it was possible for MKs to work in the community.]

Summary of Questionnaire and Responses

Does the need for non-academic programs exist at your school? *Has never existed (3), Has always existed (17), Has recently developed (last 5 years) (2), Will increase in the future (8).*

MK schools should provide non-academic programs for MKs who are not able to succeed in the academic programs. *Strongly agree (12), Agree (9), and Neutral (4).*

MK schools should provide non-academic programs for MKs who desire these programs. *Strongly agree (8), Agree (12), Neutral (4), and Disagree (1).*

Discussion

Deciding about special programs

Do you think we should consider what students desire in pro-viding programs that are not for academically inclined students? Do you think we should only provide these programs for students who need them?

We should provide possibilities for the kids that have those desires. Depending on the field where you might be, there may be many resources that have not yet been tapped.

We should really consider the desires of the kids, because that may turn them on academically later.

I have one kid who is working in the mechanic shop half day, and he is the one that wants to go to school.

If one of your goals is to meet the needs of the kids and bring them to their fullest potential, then certainly consider their desires, but be careful because they may change next year.

I think that they should have such programs because there are kids who are not able to do the standard school curriculum. Because of that, their parents may have to leave the mission field so that their kids can have an opportunity to proceed on their level.

In a good strong vocational tech type of program in the United States, we would love to see academic students. We never get them.

I am the mother of three girls with learning problems. We left the field for three years because of the academic problems that we had with our kids. Coming back, it has been very difficult for my three girls to fit in. No one knows the stress level that these kids are under, until they are home and they explode. They are worth a program.

We at MK schools have a responsibility to all the MKs. We may be limited by our size and our abilities, but we should stretch as far as we can and know the alternatives we can offer those MKs.

Are we pushing the average students too hard?

Some research has indicated that MKs score significantly higher on some standardized tests than their counterparts in the homeland. If that is true, and we're striving to maximize our students' capabilities, are some of the students who would actually do well in the homeland struggling in our schools?

Based on the comparison with American schools, it is my opinion that most of you people work with a skewed curve. I think you need be aware of what skewed curves do to self images.

I went down to Amazon Valley Academy one time and was visiting in a home. I asked the girl, "Have you considered Wheaton?"

She said, "No, I'm at the bottom of the class, and I couldn't get into Wheaton."

I found out later she had a 1200 SAT score. That was the worst at Amazon Valley that year. She was at the bottom of the class and wouldn't even apply to Wheaton. We've got an image problem here.

In our school, kids we would probably have directed into a vocational tech program, had we had one, are pulling much higher grades and showing a capability far beyond what we had expected by the time they're juniors and seniors, simply because the other students in the classroom have a tendency to bring them along. When they hit the United States they're average or above-average students.

What are other limiting factors?

Peer pressure and pressure from parents in the mission field. We have great difficulties in convincing some parents that their children need a program like this. They don't believe that their children have learning disabilities. Therefore their children must go into the normal system.

Resistance from teachers who are so academically oriented. I've had one say, "If a child has any kind of academic problems, those parents should not be allowed to come to the field."

We have enough trouble getting ordinary teachers, let alone special class teachers.

Availability of materials. What is available in terms of textbooks and materials at different reading levels, different achievement levels? This year, we are getting some correspondence material from the University of North Dakota that is geared toward some of the non-academic areas. We have been amazed at the success of some of these kids in this area. It has been very helpful for their self image too. It blew some of our teachers' minds that these kids would sit down and actually write something, but they are turning in good work.

We are limited by the amount of faculty that you can put into a small school. We offer vocational tech courses, and we try to put these students into as many classes as we can. Obviously they are not going to be able to handle chemistry and physics and other advanced classes, but we try to provide general math or even remedial math if a student needs that. We just don't call that a special track because each year we handle the situation as we need it. It's hard for us to have a special learning disability teacher come in when we only have those students occasionally.

We also have different tracks as and when needed. We've just changed our graduation requirements. Instead of having one diploma, we've now got three diplomas. For a normal academic diploma, you need twenty-four credits. We've now instituted a general diploma with nineteen credits. At the same time we thought, "Let's go the other way, too, and do an honors diploma with twenty-seven." Guess what everybody wants now. They all want to get the higher one.

Within a classroom and in special groupings we can meet the needs of these kids in math, English, languages, sciences, and such. We can do that just as elementary teachers have been doing for a long time.

Sometimes because we do not have enough expertise or enough resources available locally, we throw LD kids into some type of vocational program rather than properly diagnosing their problem and working on resolving it. One of the frustrations of the voc teacher is that he gets those kind of students rather than the students that really want to be there.

Are finances a significant factor?

For financial reasons, MK schools should not be expected to establish non-academic programs in their curricula. *Agree (2), Neutral (5), Disagree (10), Strongly disagree (7).*

That's the main objection that we receive. "It's too small a program. We can't justify it financially."

*We have a school of ninety-three students, and we're just
beginning an LD program. As the principal of the elementary, I am amazed at the change that it has made in our
school in just one year of implementation. Now we think
back, and we see all the kids that have gotten away that we
thought were undermotivated. Several years ago we felt that
perhaps we couldn't afford the program, but I've been impressed by how little it has cost us, because we already had
faculty members who were very anxious to get involved.
What it entails is allowing them to commit a significant portion of time.*

*Another thing that impressed me is how many students
we have. At one time I might have said, "Well, we have two
or three students who could use this program at any given
time." But we have a lot more. I'm amazed at how many
we have.*

What do you do when there is no program?

Parents anticipating missionary service overseas where non-academic programs are not available and whose children require non-academic programs, should stay in their homeland until their children
are beyond school age or the field is able to provide the necessary
programs. *Strongly agree (4), Agree (4), Neutral (6), Disagree (7), Strongly
disagree (3).*

*Just because you stay in the United States does not mean
that you will get what your child needs. We went back to the
States and our kids were tested. Oh, they needed the program. They had room for them, but they weren't allowed in
because the test scores weren't what they were supposed to
be.*

*There are a lot of people that come to the field when their
children are very young, or their children are born on the
field. I really don't feel people should have to leave the field
if the Lord has called them to that area. The school's goals
are to meet the needs of the children that are there.*

*I think the parent has to contact the schools that are available and explore with them. Our MK schools are better
caring communities for those kids who are hurting than
schools in the States. We have worked with the parents of a
child in Haiti to develop a special program. It's about half
academic. He is developing as a person, and the community*

is so much better for him.   The school has to be willing to reach out, and the parents have to be willing to see the limitations of the school.

Who relates best to non-academically inclined children?

I found that the Christian teacher that is coming out of a public school is much better equipped and much more willing to work with the non-academic student than those that have come out of the Christian school.   In the United States, the Christian schools tend to take only top level kids, so these teachers don't know how to deal with the non-academic student.   Public school teachers tend to have had a very wide range of kids in their classroom and have learned how to work with them all.

Re-entry for the non-academically inclined

Is there something that we should do to help the non-academic kid in his adjustment back at home?   To help him investigate areas that most kids won't be investigating because they are off into the mainstream of higher education?

We're already beginning to do that as parents.   Right now, we're contacting families about different careers that maybe don't take all the academics.

I think families need to utilize their furloughs to explore the resources that are available to them near their home base, through a guidance counselor in the local school system, through state employment offices, or through a voc tech school.   Just as those with children who are college-bound should utilize the high school years whenever they are on furlough to explore colleges.   Those with non-academically inclined children need to do the same.

44

Gifted Children in the Classroom

Joy Limburg
Teacher, Faith Academy

According to the U.S. Office of Education, gifted children are defined as those who consistently excel or show the potential to consistently excel above the average in one or more of the following areas: general intellectual ability, specific academic aptitudes, creative thinking, leadership ability, visual and performing arts ability, and psycho-motor ability. Probably in our classrooms we'll spend most of our time dealing with the first two.

There are many things about gifted children that are very demanding and difficult for us as classroom teachers, but they are clues that help us to understand who these people are. Margo Long, of Whitworth College, has compiled a list of characteristics of the gifted child that tend to screen him out of programs: bored with routine tasks, refuses to do rote homework; difficult to get him to move into another topic; self-critical, impatient with failures; often disagrees vocally with others and the teacher; makes jokes or puns at inappropriate times; emotionally sensitive—may over-react, get angry easily or readily cry when things go wrong; uninterested in details; their desks and their work are often messy; refuses to accept authority, nonconforming, stubborn; tends to dominate others.

When these characteristics show up in a child that is in your classroom, you have a challenge to help that child know how to fit in with others and to keep the flow of your classroom going.

There are three areas that we need to consider. The first is the personal philosophy of teaching and education of the leader of the classroom. Then we will consider the students, who they are, and what their needs are. Lastly we'll talk about developing some appropriate curriculum to meet the needs of these students.

The classroom teacher or administrator

The things that I am going to suggest today really boil down to just one thing. Do you really believe that your responsibility is to take every student where he is right now and move him forward? It's a big responsibility. Yet it has to be the underlying philosophy if we're going to meet the needs of different children in our classroom.

Very often when teachers move into a new culture, especially if it's their first experience in an overseas school, they are only functioning on the survival level during those early years. All they can handle is taking the whole class as a unit and starting to move it forward, because they are going through so much adjustment in getting used to a new school, a new culture, and new companions. That's normal, but if they stay on that level year after year, they are not meeting the needs of the students.

If you're on that level, see if you can start moving from that level by doing something different. It's so much easier to stay on the survival level. It's so much easier to do what the professor did who said, "I'm afraid I thoroughly messed up the seating chart, so you must take care to remember your new names." If that's where we are, we're forcing our students into a mold that the majority do not fit into.

We have to look at our teaching and ask, "What is the focus of my teaching in my classroom? Am I really teaching my students how to learn? Am I giving them the tools that they need to move forward and to really learn, or am I one of those who says, 'I have the content of this book that I must cover, and no matter what happens, we've got to get to the end of this book'"? If that's your goal, you would be like the teacher that said, "I don't care how well you can read. You have to pick a book from the fourth grade shelf."

Because the gifted child has a special God-given ability, there are certain demands that are put on him. The behavior that results from those demands leads the child to have a strong need for curriculum that is geared his needs.

When we have in our classroom a child that has a learning difficulty, our sympathy, empathy, and concern flow out to that child. It seems to be a natural part of whatever it is that makes us teachers. That same flow needs to be going towards these characters in our classroom that drive us nuts sometimes, these very special individuals that are called gifted children.

It comes back again to your philosophy. Do you really believe that the gifted and talented in your classroom need special attention?

Or are you one of those who says, "He's got all that going for him. Can't he make it on his own?" Can he? Let me tell you why I started the program at Faith Academy for gifted elementary children.

Ten years ago as a regular classroom teacher, I had a student teacher come to my classroom. She worked with the students, taking over more and more of the classroom responsibilities, but she couldn't handle all thirty-three of them in math class. There was one group of about six children who really bugged her. These six kept putting such pressure on her that finally I took them out of the class for the math period every day. I taught them math, but in ten minutes they were done. The student teacher would still be explaining the lesson for the fourteenth time to the rest of the class. I had a lot of extra time with these children.

In this group were two boys who all year long had kept asking their mother, "Mom, why doesn't Miss Limburg like me?" As I spent more time with this group of children, we started talking about interpersonal relationships and extra things. Those boys' story began to change. They found out that Miss Limburg really did like them after all. The only thing that was different was that I spent time with them. I had always put my capable students to work on a worthwhile project and had gone off and helped a child that was having a problem. These boys were suffering because they thought I ignored them. I wasn't giving them the time and attention they needed.

That was my motivation for starting a special pull-out program for gifted children at our school. At that time our classes were large. The teachers just could not do the things that they would have gladly done if they had just had the time. That was my frustration, too.

The students

Gifted students tend to be bored very, very easily with routine tasks. Routine tasks, until they have a purpose, have no value to a gifted child. They will turn them off. I think of a second grade girl, a highly capable child, who just refused to read as a first grader. Nothing turned that child on until she was in second grade and her older friends were reading a book that she wanted to read. In two weeks she had taught herself to read. She was not motivated until she had a reason to read that seemed important to her. When that motivation came, the skill came with it.

We must consider the student when we start thinking, "What are we going to do with these kids in our classroom?" We need to get acquainted with the student as an individual to know who he is, what it is that makes him tick. You need to look at your students and diagnose them as individuals. Pull out every skill you have ever learned to diagnose your students and find out who they are. Find out what their strengths are as individuals and as students, not only in the classroom, but outside the classroom. What is it that makes that child a strong individual, personality-wise, skill-wise, academics-wise? Know the areas where that child is strong. You need to know what their learning styles are and have appropriate materials and activities for the child who learns through his eyes, the child who learns through his ears, and the child who learns only if he can stand up and wiggle and experience it? Many of your gifted children will be the doer learners, the kinesthetic learners. They are difficult to have in your classroom.

We need to know what their interests are, inside and outside the classroom. And we need to know where they are in their self-concepts. How do they view themselves? Is it OK to be a gifted person? As you get to know that child then you can begin to see a picture that will lead you to something that might help him.

Madeline Hunter's ITIP techniques for diagnosis are great, because they are quick and not time-consuming. It would be ideal to do this kind of diagnosing for every child in our classroom, but if you have a child that's giving you trouble, start with him and see if you can build a profile. Once you determine who he is, his needs will begin to form a pattern for you also. His characteristics will begin to reveal the key to motivation.

When we have a child with a learning disability in our classroom, we try to diagnose that disability and work with that disability to bring it up to an "average" level so that child can function in the classroom. When you're working with a gifted child, the opposite approach seems to be the one that works best with him. You don't take the weak areas, even though your gifted child may have some very weak areas because they tuned out in the lower grades. You find where the gifted child's strengths are and teach to those strengths. The motivation from working with his strengths turns him on and enables him to pick up the skill he missed and move on from there. He sees there is a need to learn how to spell or to punctuate or to read more carefully.

Gifted students do get bored with routine tasks, and they will turn them off, no matter what you do to try to teach to that weakness they have. They are unique individuals. And that makes it super demanding on us in a classroom, because we're also teaching children that are struggling, we're trying to keep the flow of our "normal" children going, and at the same time we're working on the special interests of gifted children. Of course we get frustrated because we can't do all of these things. But we need to turn on the "I can" for gifted children.

If you can find those strengths where your kids are challenged, start with those. Gifted children have such strong positive needs. An impulsive reader has got to read. Capitalize on it. Somehow find a way to use that reading to lead him into the things that will pick up his skills. The humorous has to have a release. Find a positive way to help that child release that humor. The problem solver has to have problems to solve.

Curriculum

Once you discover who he is, then you can begin to do something about it in your curriculum. When a child comes into our classroom, it's our responsibility to teach that child to learn how to learn. You may get a high school senior in your classroom that doesn't know how to read a history book, doesn't know how to approach the idea of history, or the flow of history. It's your responsibility to teach him those skills. If he doesn't know how to research history, you're the one that's supposed to teach him that. We need to teach him the skills of how to learn.

Then we need to teach the child concepts and generalization. What are we going to do with a set of facts when we get them together? What's the value of them?

If kids have gotten to high school and don't know how to think, then that is the time to teach them. Teach them how to think through history or geometry or whatever it is. We must teach all students the basic skills they need—how to study, how to read, how to handle information in our own subject matter.

Then we have those students who already know the material. Are they a threat to you? You have a student in your high school history class who could come up to the front and teach the Civil War as well as you could. What do you do with that child in your classroom? You need to have an appropriate curriculum planned for that student also. We have three alternatives:

1. We could give them more material. "OK, you did that beautifully. Do this one now. You've got that page finished, try this page." But you know what your gifted child is going to do, don't you? Turn it off.

2. We can enrich their program horizontally, which many of us as classroom teachers attempt to do. We can give them an alternative. "You are fully aware of what has gone on in the

Civil War. Would you then begin (if this is where the interest of that child lies) analyzing the conflict that is taking place
in Lebanon and relate what you learn from the Civil War to
what is happening today in this situation?" They spend their
full time working on this while you are building the background on the Civil War with your other students.

3. Or, the gifted children can be accelerated, moved on into a
totally new program. Maybe that student doesn't belong in
your classroom but belongs in an Advanced Placement class.

This is a quickie little example of what could be done to enrich
your program horizontally. Let's go back to kindergarten when you're
teaching each child the color green. We give the child a trunk, five
limbs and forty-two leaves. "If you put them together just like this
you can have a beautiful tree." Then we put all the trees on the wall.

What if you said to that same group of children, "If you wish to
arrange your limbs in a different manner, that's OK. You go ahead
and do that. And if you have an idea that's totally different, talk to
me or the aide, and we'll see that you have the materials you need to
make your tree." We put them all up on the wall and give them all
the same attention and value to show that it's OK to be a creative
person, and yet every child has learned green at the same time. We
take a simple lesson and restructure it in order to meet the needs of
our gifted student at the very same time that we are meeting the
needs of the regular classroom.

In first grade maybe we are learning the short sound of e. Your
example picture is an elephant. The children are going to color their
elephant. Before you give them their elephant, have one picture of
the elephant that you have cut into little pieces. You hold up one
piece, put another piece with it, and keep adding one piece at a time
until the children discover what that picture is. They say, "Oh, it's an
elephant." They've had a chance to predict, to put together ideas.
Then they can go ahead and color their elephant. Thirty seconds of
your time and the child has had a chance to think as well as to practice the short sound of e and to color his elephant.

This next idea comes from the magazine *Super Think*. Ordinary
questions that might be asked in your classroom can be turned into
thinking questions. For example, instead of saying, "Who was it that
discovered America?" you ask, "Why is it that Columbus is credited
with discovering America?" You have the child put into words what
it is that this man did that causes his name to be so famous today.
Just switching the question around so the student must use higher levels of thinking is one of the most important things we can do to help

the gifted children that are in our classroom. If you can encourage your high school teachers, especially those structured teachers who find it very difficult to move out of their ordinary frame, to begin using the higher level, open-ended questions in their classroom discussions and on their tests, that alone will begin helping these children to relate to what is going on in their classroom.

If you watch for ways that you can expand the ordinary things that you do in your classroom, no matter what level you're working on, and start building a file, then you have some activities that will help you meet the needs of your special students.

I know that by now you are saying, "I believe everything you're telling me, but I'm thinking about leaving teaching and getting myself a nice, easy twelve-hour-a-day six day a week job." That's where we are as teachers. It is a big responsibility. We just get to the place where we say, "I can't do all that." Don't. Start with one thing that you can make work in your classroom and move on from there. Check out your own philosophy. See where you're really going with this idea of seeking to understand the special needs of your children and meeting the need of every child in your classroom.

Be very careful of labels, of calling any child gifted. My program is called "The Far End." It's at the far end of the hall. We can say it's at the far end of the curriculum. But the children say, "We're going to the Far End." They don't say, "I'm going to the gifted room."

Let me also remind you that not all high achievers are gifted students. We have many very capable children in our classroom, and these ideas are going to help them. Not all gifted students are high achievers, either. We can't set a little box up there and say, "OK, gifted kid, you're going to fit right in here." They won't. They will never fit in any pattern that you give them.

This is a story that Frank Lloyd Wright, the architect, told long ago. He said that at the age of nine he had an experience that helped set his philosophy of life. He had a solid, no-nonsense type of uncle who had taken him for a long walk across a beautiful snow-covered field. At the far side of the field his uncle stopped him and turned him back and said, "Look at the tracks across the field. See how your footprints go aimlessly back and forth from the trees over there to the cattle over there, back to the fence, and then over there where you hurled sticks, and finally you ended up over here? And now look, see how my path comes straight and strong right across the field? I want you to learn that lesson, my boy."

Frank Lloyd Wright said, "I learned a lesson from my uncle that day. I determined right then not to miss most things in life as my uncle did."

Resources

Books

Clark, Barbara. *Growing Up Gifted*. Columbus, OH: Charles Merrill, 1983. (Best general textbook on gifted)

Rimm, Sylvia B. *Underachievement Syndrome, Causes And Cures*. Apple Publ. Co., W. 6050 Apple Road, Watertown, WI 53094. 1986

Roedell, Wendy Conklin, Nancy E. Jackson, and Halbert B. Robinson. *Gifted Young Children*. Ithaca, New York: Teachers College Press, 1980. $8.25 (Pre-school gifted children)

Saunders, Jacqulyn, with Pamela Espeland. *Bring Out The Best: A Resource Guide for Parents of Young Gifted Children*. Free Spirit Publ., 123 N. Third St., Suite 716, Minneapolis, MN 55401 (612-338-2068) 1986. $12.95.

Magazines

G/C/T. P.O. Box 66654, Mobile, AL 36660. Monthly, $24 per year

Challenge. Good Apple Inc., Box 299, Carthage, IL 62321-0299. Five issues per year for $20.

Gifted Children Monthly. P.O. Box 115, Sewell, NJ 08080. Monthly, $24 per year

Gifted Children Quarterly. National Association for Gifted Children, 5100 N. Edgewood Dr., St. Paul, Minnesota 55112. (Requires joining; magazine comes with membership.)

Catalog Addresses

Midwest Publication, P.O. Box 448. Pacific Grove, CA 93950

A.W. Peller and Associates, Inc., Educational Materials, P.O. Box 106, Hawthorne, NJ 07507

Good Apple, P.O. Box 299, 1204 Buchanan St., Carthage, IL 62321-0299

Dandy Lion Publications, P.O. Box 10888, Palo Alto, CA 94303

Opportunities For Learning, 20417 Nordhoff St., Dept A, Chatsworth, CA 91311. (Have several catalogs—specify "for gifted")

Creative Publications, 5005 W. 110th St., Oak Lawn, IL 60453, 1-800-624-0822

Zephyr Press, 430 South Essex Lane, Tucson, AZ 85711. (Ask for: *Reaching Their Highest Potential* catalog.)

45

Curriculum Development: Science

Sherry Long
Ben Lippen School

When it's all said and done, my students will not remember all of the details and facts that I try to get across in science, but I can guarantee you that they will remember me. For good or for bad, your students will remember you.

Role of the Teacher

The teacher who most affected my becoming a teacher was an English Literature professor. I can hardly remember anything about her classes, but her life has affected mine even to this day. Likewise, as a Christian model of the Lord Jesus and as a person who is enthusiastic about the material, you affect your students lives.

One of the things that has helped me most of all in my life, was meeting a person who had a deep, deep commitment to knowing truth. No matter how many questions I came up with, this lady's commitment was to knowing truth. That commitment was the fork in the road for me. As a model, I want to have that commitment to truth, and finding truth. That has a tremendous effect on a life every once in a while.

We're all trying to motivate students. I've spent fifteen years of my life trying to motivate students. Some came highly motivated. When others walked in my door their first words were, "I hate science." I was discouraged, and I thought "Oh, they hate me." No, that's not what they said. They said, "I hate science." For one reason or another their experience had taught them that this was not their forte. I started responding "Well, I hope something this year might be of interest to you." or "Just stay around a while and let's

337

see what happens." It was not a reflection on me, but on something that had happened in their past.

As a motivator I consider two areas important. One is communication. Communicate clearly. Let them understand your terminology. That's a principle in any course.

Secondly, develop their curiosity by doing some things in the classroom that are fun and different. Make them ask, "How did that work?" Arouse their curiosity.

I want my students to learn to ask good questions. Even little fellows in grade school can begin to be taught how to ask good questions. When they say, "Tell me how that worked," respond, "Well how do you think it worked?" They may not come out with the right answers, but they learn how to ask the questions. In doing so, they begin to learn how to think. They start saying, "Well, if this happens then that must be true." They begin to arrive at answers by themselves. That's probably one of the biggest issues that I hear teachers dealing with, "How do I teach people to think?" (And in a few of these simple little demonstrations I hope to approach that issue.)

Presentation of the Material

There are two basic ways that I go about presenting science material. One is with words. But if science is just left in the book, most students respond, "Oh no, here comes another chapter." So, I've really worked hard at putting lab material into the courses. Lab work can take hours of preparation for a fifteen to thirty minute demonstration, but there are things to be seen, and we acquire a great deal of knowledge if we learn to ask questions about what we see.

I aim for demonstrations that are profoundly simple, requiring materials found at home, in your office, in your desk drawer, or in your kitchen drawer. One of my desires for children is that after they leave a science class they can go home and say, "Mom, look what the teacher did today!" They can run in, get two pop bottles and a dollar bill and show Mom what was in science:

> Balance one pop bottle on top of another in hourglass fashion with a dollar bill between them. The object is to get that dollar bill out from those two pop bottles without them falling over. If people start to pull the bill slowly, the friction is too much. (You can move into all kinds of friction ideas.)

You grasp the bill at one end and very quickly hit it. That's Newton's law that one object is moving and it wants to keep moving, but the bottles don't want to move yet.

So you can approach that on all kinds of levels. If I were to have my physic students explain that, I would certainly have them deal with Newton's laws of motion.

An airplane works because air pressure is greater on the bottom and lifts it up. That principle can be taught by inverting a little funnel over a ping pong ball and blowing to make greater pressure underneath so it lifts the ball up.

Sometimes in a science class you have to look a bit ridiculous or sound a bit ridiculous, but you'll be loved for it. Here's a very simple way to illustrate the principle of molecules sticking together because they like each other; they have an attraction. Stick a spoon on the end of your nose. You have to get some water vapor on it and that's provided by a little breath. You need to get your nose a little bit damp. I have to have a mirror to do this. If you're real good at it, you can put two on your eyes, and lay one across your forehead.

The entire Bible. Genesis through Revelation, King James Version, almost 1300 pages, is printed on a small piece of plastic. I use these micro-Bibles when I start teaching the microscope. They can be purchased for $2 from Christian Projects Services Inc., 530 El Camino, La Habra, CA 90631. It does take a microscope to read them. I don't tell the kids that things are upside down and backwards; they begin to realize that themselves. The more I let them discover on their own, the better I find that to be.

Lab equipment is extremely expensive. But I've worked hard at taking complex labs and improvising and writing up how to do something simply with material I can buy or materials that I can find in the shop. The best places for getting microscopes are colleges that are throwing out their old ones and hospitals that are getting rid of old microscopes or that have old ones sitting around that they don't use anymore. Go in and try to buy those.

Resources

Here's a list of several books that give simple experiments or present simple concepts.

Chen, S. Phillip. *Entertaining and Educational Chemical Demonstrations.* Chemical Elements Publishing, 529 Mission Drive, Camarillo, California 93010

Hechtlinger, Adelaide. *Biochemistry Units for High School Biology Teachers.* Parker Publishing Co., West Nyack, New York

Mullin, L. Virginia. *Chemistry Experiments for Children.* Dover Publication Inc., 180 Varick St. N.Y., N.Y., 10014

Sund, Robert, Bill Tillery, and Leslie Trowbridge. *Elementary Science Discovery Lessons.* Allyn and Bacon Publishing Co., 470 Atlantic Ave. Boston, Mass 02210

These three are sold through major book stores in America on a special order.

Dresner, Simon. *The Science World Book of Brain Teasers.* Scholastic Book Services, Scholastic Magazines, New York, N.Y.

Epstein, Lewis and Paul Hewett. *Thinking physics.* Insight Press, 614 Vermont St. San Francisco, Ca. 94107

Walker, Jearl. *The Flying Circus of Physics.* John Wiley and Sons, Inc., Physics Dept, Cleveland State University, Cleveland, Ohio 44115

I would also like to get a communication network going. I could send you the labs that I've written. You can go down to any hardware store and buy the equipment for $400-500. I built it for $10, and it works just as well. That's the kind of thing we need to be sharing.

46

Developing Thinking Skills
in Young Children

Lucretia A. Pelton
Elementary Principal, Southfield Christian School

Someone once said there are two ways to slide easily through life—to believe everything or to doubt everything. Both ways save us from thinking. I don't know if believing everything or doubting everything makes you slide easily through life, but I do think it limits thinking.

One of the dangers that we face in teaching in a Christian school is that we have a strong desire to help children learn academic things and we have a strong desire to teach them God's truth. We tend to do that in a manner that says to children, "I've got the answers. I will tell you what you need to know. Believe me and accept it." We indoctrinate the children in God's truth as well as in knowledge.

I'm not saying that all indoctrination is bad, but we need to think about not staying at that level and teaching children just content. All of a sudden we expect children to make decisions. We scratch our heads and say, "What is wrong? Don't they ever think anything through? Didn't they see what was going to happen?"

It is dangerous to be so concerned about young people that we present the truth in a way that doesn't give them opportunities to think. We need to make sure that they have the ability to evaluate that and make wise decisions and judgments. One way to prepare children to live in a society that is going to challenge them is to help them develop thinking skills.

People in the educational circles are telling us we aren't doing a very good job of teaching children to think. Research done by the National Assessment of Educational Progress reported in 1979-80 that

341

nearly 40 percent of the seventeen-year-olds could not draw inferences from written materials; only one fifth could write a persuasive essay; only one third could solve a mathematics problem requiring more than one step. That's not very good.

The hue and cry has been, "You're not doing the job." I truly believe that teachers really have a desire to be the best they can be in their classroom. They're anxious for any new ideas and techniques that come their way. I think that most teachers not only want to improve personally but are concerned about the educational profession in general.

Because of our strong desire to do a better job, I think teachers are vulnerable to new ideas, new approaches, new technology, new materials. Through the years, we've tried new technologies and techniques. Unfortunately we often find the solutions they promised were not there.

Thinking skills is not just another educational fad. God was concerned about our thought life. Philippians 4:8 says, "Finally brothers, whatever is true, whatever is noble, whatever is right, whatever is pure, whatever is lovely, whatever is admirable, if anything is excellent or praiseworthy, think about such things." God was concerned about the kind of thoughts we have. We should be concerned about the kind of thoughts students have.

God wasn't concerned just about the kind of thoughts. He was also concerned about how we used our thinking. He created us with a mind, and he expects us to use it. We need to seek his will and his guidance, but he does expect us to use those abilities that he has given us.

I John 4:1 says, "Dear friends, do not believe every spirit, but test the spirits to see whether they are from God, because many false prophets have gone out into the world." Young people can get caught up in a lot that is being passed off as truth. God says we need to test those. If we're going to test them, it seems to me that we're going to have to collect the evidence, weigh it, sort through it, and make a wise decision with God's help. We can begin helping children to do that in the classroom.

Thinking skills are particularly important for missionary children. Missionary children move from one educational setting to another. If we can help them know how to think through and apply the knowledge they are given to new situations, we will move them further ahead. I believe you can start teaching these skills in kindergarten.

Thinking necessitates a sound knowledge base. It would be very difficult to reason or to think wisely if we didn't have any knowledge base or any standard against which to measure it. As Christians, our standard of measure is God's truth. We do need to teach knowledge. But it's important that we not stay at that level with children. Teaching thinking does not rule out teaching content. But just because we're teaching content does not necessarily mean we're teaching children to think.

I'm afraid too many times as teachers we put students into situations where we simply expect them to think. We expect them to do it the best they can. That's not teaching thinking skills.

We falsely assume that students will automatically learn how to engage in higher levels of thinking. They need to understand the process through which they are going. Just because they are sitting in our classrooms and we're sharing knowledge with them that doesn't mean that they're somehow going to learn this thinking process. Research tells us that 80 to 85 percent of all the questions asked by teachers in the classroom require students to recall only facts while only 20 percent require students to think. Most teachers wait only one second for a response before repeating the question, calling on another student, or making a comment. We don't give children time to think. Even increasing that to three or five seconds allows for more contribution from students in the classroom. We're not talking about taking a whole lot of class time.

Research says that 75 percent of our class time is spent on instruction; 70 percent of that instruction is classroom talk; only 1 percent is inviting open responses, the kind of questions that ask children to express their opinions or require some reasoning. I don't think it's going to cause chaos in our classrooms if we change our questioning methods. I do think it is important that children understand that when they're expressing their opinions we're not debating absolute truth, and that those opinions have to be supported by evidence. It's important to ask children why they believe what they believe and how they got their answer. They must express those opinions in a respectful manner.

I think we're going to have to make a conscious effort to teach thinking skills and not just assume that it's going to be happening. How are we going to fit it into our schedules? I'm convinced the only way it'll get done is if we integrate it into what we're already doing. Use the content that we already have, but develop activities and questions that will stretch their thinking processes.

We need to look at our classroom. Is it the kind of classroom that encourages boys and girls to think?

Developing Minds: A Resource Book for Teaching Thinking, edited by Arthur Costa, is a good resource book that costs around $20. In the back it tells about a lot of the different thinking programs, gives a little evaluation, what ages the programs are for, what they're trying to do. These ideas on learning environments to promote thinking are adapted from that book:

- Create a classroom climate that is safe for what I call risk taking—a classroom that has trust, rapport, and warmth so that the children will feel comfortable about expressing an opinion that might be different from the other students' or even different from yours.

- Ask broad and open questions. Work on becoming a skilled questioner. Make sure that your questions are not only factual questions but also questions that ask for an understanding of the material or for application to a new situation. "Put it in your own words." Or "What do you think would happen if we changed the ending of the story?" Everybody's answer does not have to be the same, but lets make sure they tell us why it's going to end that way.

- Have students ask questions of their own. Create a climate of inquiry. Let them know it's OK for them to create their own questions.

- Follow up student responses by asking for clarification, elaboration, evidence, and thinking process. Ask, "Why do you think that?" or "How did you get that answer?" "What evidence was there for you to think that?"

- Wait before calling on students. Students need time to think. As teachers, we get a little bit frightened if we have quiet time in the room, because we think they didn't understand, or we didn't communicate clearly. But they need time to think.

- Have a clear purpose and plan a sequence of activities to accomplish it. Plan to teach thinking skills in all subject areas. It can be done in every single subject area. I wouldn't start in all the subject areas at the same time. Pick one and begin work in that. If we spend two to three hours a week trying to help develop thinking skills and do it for two years, we will probably see some results. You might take just one subject area and work on it for a week. Then maybe try it in another subject area. Some start is better than no start at all, so I would encourage you to begin.

Bloom says there's a hierarchy of thinking skills. He says we move from one to the other. We spend a lot of time in elementary school at the knowledge level, and rightly so, because that's the data input base. They do need some knowledge to make judgments.

Most elementary school activities are probably dealing with the bottom four—knowledge, comprehension, application, and analysis— although I do think it's possible to do the synthesis and evaluation with young children. I think it is possible, for example, to ask them an evaluation question after you've read the story of Goldilocks. "Do you think Goldilocks was good or bad?" A young child might say Goldilocks was bad because she went into the bears' house and ate their stuff and slept in their bed, and she shouldn't have done that. Maybe the reasons aren't going to be very sophisticated.

I think junior high and high school students should probably be spending most of their time at the synthesis and evaluation levels, but we all begin with knowledge.

I think it would be important to have more than one kind of question on a test. I think it's OK to test for knowledge, but I think it would be nice to have some questions on there that ask them to apply that knowledge to a new situation. Then grade more on how well they support their reasoning, not whether the answer is right.

With young children begin with knowledge of the concrete and work toward a goal of more abstract evaluations.

47

Predeparture Re-entry Preparation

Ron and Rita Young
Fortaleza Academy, Brazil

Ron Young: I remember well looking forward to my first furlough with a great deal of anticipation. I also remember noticing that some of my colleagues who had been on the field for quite some time were not quite so enthusiastic about going on furlough. I thought that was strange, but I attributed it to their being more attached to the Brazilian culture. I realize now that another factor was fear of returning home and being "out of it." Clothing styles, syntax, economics, vocations, and avocations all change. The list could go on and on. The longer I live in Brazil, the more acute those differences have become. When I went home on my last furlough several years ago, I remember having a gnawing uneasiness about returning to the United States, in spite of the fact that I had lived my first twenty-nine years there. This experience helps me identify a little better what that missionary kid going back to the United States feels.

Predeparture Orientation for the MK

What is the goal of our missionary schools? Two things stand out:

1. We want young adults who can comfortably function in both the home and the host cultures. We want them to feel comfortable in the host culture. We want them to go back to their home country and be able to adapt and fit in also.

2. We want them to be functioning members of the body of Christ.

There are holes that need to be filled somehow, and we need to try to examine ways that we can do that. That could come through predeparture preparation.

Rita Young: If you're going to work on a predeparture re-entry curriculum, you need to establish your needs. To make an assessment, I used my own experience, questions from Ron's survey of our students, and the booklet, *Especially for MKs Going to College*, by Robert Wright. (Western Bible College, 5000 Deer Park Drive, SE, Salem, OR 97302.) From these sources I determined our needs to be in three basic areas:

A Sense of God's Will

The MK needs to be committed to a sense of God's will in his life. Robert Wright lists how MKs handled adjustment: through prayer, recognizing the situation as God's will, and confiding in the security of God's leading. Suggestions for MKs by MKs: accept the situation as God's will; put Christ first in your life; maintain a proper devotional life; get involved in a church; make friends with older students who are solid Christians.

Personal Development

The MK needs to have an interdependence with his family so that he accepts responsibility for his own actions after he has counseled with his family and significant others in his life. He needs the ability and desire to reach out to others. This comes from teaching him personal development skills and allowing him to practice them while he's on the mission field in his mission school where he is comfortable. He needs to be secure in his personal standards of belief and conduct. He needs to define what his personal standards are.

Culture Adjustment

The next step is to choose what materials you're going to use to present this information to your students. What I chose for the study of God's will was a Sunday School quarterly, *Found: God's Will* by John MacArthur. (Victor Books, Scripture Press, PO Box 1825 Wheaton, IL 60187.)

Some resource materials that I felt very helpful in the preparation of a retreat plan were: *Understanding Love*, (Lester A. Kirkendall and Ruth Farnham Osborne, Science Research Association, 259 East Erie St, Chicago, IL 60611) and two books by Walter Trobisch, *I Married You*, and *Love is a Feeling to be Learned*.

When we did our graduate studies our professor talked about KISSMIF, Keep it simple, stupid; make it fun. I think you can't beat that for selling ideas to young people. So I incorporated that philosophy into a retreat idea.

We've held a three-day retreat for seventh through twelfth graders. We have mini-sessions for everyone. This last time tenth graders had "How to Break a Stubborn Habit" and seventh graders talked about relationship problems. We saw a considerable decline in how many times they poked each other per day after they had studied that.

Then we initiate the culture study, and I continue it by working it into my Family Living class, into devotional periods and into my English classes.

Everyone has stress. I introduce our study of culture shock by giving a stress test. I ask the kids to picture their situation over the next year. Which of these things are going to be stressful to you? How do you envision your situation? Add up the points. Do you have stress? Yes, obviously they all have. On the stress test that I use, if you had over 300 points within one calendar year, you were subject to a major physical ailment. Most MKs hit somewhere between 350 and 400.

Culture shock is not going to last long, and there are ways of overcoming it. As you teach the MK ways of overcoming it, you go over into personal development. You want to teach him self-acceptance. First of all improve relationships with his family. Help him to see himself in his family so that he can help his family and they can help him. If he has a helping attitude toward his family, he's already developing a skill that he needs to reorientate himself. He's taking his eyes off himself and putting them on another person. That's one of the biggest things he needs to do to become oriented into the new society—think about others and stop thinking about himself. You want to make him self-confident in Christ, so that he can take his eyes off himself; so he can become involved; so he can interact with the new college environment. Make him more secure in his family situation. Help him to understand that what he is, is what he is going to become.

Then teach him to have confidence in God's love and to commit himself to God's plans. Teach him the importance of being secure in the fact that God placed him there. When the going gets rough, God is there with him. If he's committed to God's will in that cultural adjustment situation, he will stay where God placed him. I've heard over and over, "It's rough in the beginning, and then it passes." What we want to do is keep him in a good environment while it passes. If he is in a Christian college and he leaves, he will have another whole set of adjustments.

I give the true example of a kid who came to us one noon and said, "I just withdrew from school this morning." I say to the kids, "Let's analyze how wise that was. In the morning when he got up and wanted breakfast he had a meal ticket. Can he go there for supper? He had a place to sleep last night. Does he have a right to that place tonight?" They start to get this overwhelming feeling that maybe there is security, even though it's rough. Maybe it's worse in a different situation.

What is the attitude of students when dealing with a section on re-entry?

Rita: This re-entry seminar is given as "We're going on a retreat to meet our own particular needs." One of the things we notice is that as our seniors continue through their senior year, they start to draw apart and together. They start to become much more united than they were before, and they start to see themselves as having particular interests.

One time we went to the ocean and sat under the stars and talked about our place in God's universe. Use the kinds of things that you have. Young people can absorb so much when you give it to them with fun in an exclusive situation that's totally theirs.

Ron: Dave Brooks mentioned that at Morrison Academy they introduced re-entry as a course of study in the school. It flopped. I can believe that. Kids love the idea of a retreat. They look forward to it all year long. The senior classes are specifically re-entry oriented. All of these courses are re-entry oriented, even when we start with the juniors. We give them the PSAT and the interest surveys. That's career orientation. It can start way back in the earlier grades. Some of the things aren't meaningful at the time. But when they hit that senior year, they're starting to think "United States." They're going to be leaving. It's more a matter of timing than just hitting everybody at the same time.

Seniors are very conscious that they're going to be leaving in a few months. Therefore they are very receptive to this.

Rita: We present a great deal of our re-entry material in a class called Family Living. It's more a personal development type of class.

This class works through "Where are you right now?" If you don't like what you are now, or you see weaknesses, let's work to change that, so that as you work through a dating relationship and into a commitment to marriage and eventually into marriage, you will be a quality person. You will make that marriage successful because you yourself will be that kind of a person.

I have each student write a paper on "What can I do to help my parents at the stage of adjustment they're in?" Their parents and their families are in a definite state of adjustment simply because that high school senior is going to leave home. Each student writes a paper and then tries to work on those things during the semester.

I'm not sure what will work best in your situation, but they need some help and some time to analyze themselves and to learn to see themselves in their whole family situation.

The Jay Adams books, *Christ and Your Problems* and *Godliness through Discipline*, (Baker Book House, Grand Rapids, MI 49506) are excellent. I use them as devotional books at the beginning of my English classes. We read two pages each day at the beginning of class. That way it's not overwhelming. I've found that some books are more effective when studied in that slow way.

Perhaps the secret of predeparture re-entry curriculum is to give it according to the students' particular needs. I don't care if you do it in your history classes or your English classes or your Family Living classes or a special class or a retreat, but you need to be very conscious of doing something, and that something needs to meet the needs of your students.

Wright in his book talks about the fact that everyone has frustrations. We want to teach the biblical response where the MK accepts his frustration, becomes involved, and is obedient to God, and does not stay in any of the more negative areas of response such as anger, fear, self-pity, and bitterness, or eventually even depression. We want him to pass through these stages quickly. Perhaps there's discomfort, not an actual anger and fear. We don't have to determine that in our predeparture preparation, but we do need to be conscious of trying to help meet his needs.

The MK is going to have stress. What can we do to defuse his stress? The only thing you can do to defuse stress is to know what's coming. If you think you're going to fail a test, project yourself as having failed that test. Think of the worst things that can happen if you do fail the test. Then you have defused the failure, and probably because you have removed some of that tension you will do better.

We can help the MK to project himself. Early application and acceptance to a college helps him in this. He thinks, "We're going back to our country on such and such a date, and at this time I'm going to do this, and this. And I'm supposed to be at college for orientation on such and such a date." And so in March his family is already making their preparations for that orientation date. When he goes home for his spring break, he knows that is going to be his last time in his father's church. He knows that he must say good-bye to his Brazilian friends at home then, because he'll be leaving from the city of Fortaleza immediately after graduation. Or is he going back to spend the summer? Is he going to have a summer job in his home country? He starts to mentally prepare himself for that. You can put this into every class.

When I have a Home Ec class, one of the options of study I offer the girls is wardrobe planning. Let's assess your wardrobe. What's good enough to take along with you, and what are you going to leave here? Now what do you need to add to your wardrobe? Plan your wardrobe for what kind of climate you're going to be in and what you can afford. All of these things help her to project herself into the situation that she's going to be in. I think they actually begin to see themselves walking around that college campus, either from actually having been there or the pictures. They think about what it's going to be like that first cold day when a sweater or jacket isn't enough. They need to think about those things to defuse the stress.

Do anything you can, in any class or in any school activity, to help prepare them socially. Responsibility for planning class parties or all-school parties prepares them for other responsibilities, discipline, and leadership. Perhaps one person is only responsible for putting the announcement on the bulletin board. Perhaps he's not even used to that much responsibility. When the announcement isn't up, peer pressure will come to play. Just constantly be thinking, "I want to prepare these students." You have kids going in and out all the time because of furloughs and home visits and that sort of thing. You're helping all of them all of the time, and then hitting an extra concentration with your seniors.

48

Computers in the Classroom

Neal Peterson
Lomalinda School, Colombia, Wycliffe Bible Translators

Introduction

I'm so excited about the possibilities that computers offer educators. I find it challenging to be involved with introducing and fostering the use of this technology in the classroom. Yet as educators we must be aware of some of the pitfalls that lie in front of us as we begin using computers in the classroom. I'd like to briefly discuss the use of the computer as both a tool and tutor for instructional purposes and present some trends that I see developing in the computer education field.

Computers as an Educational Tool

Computers can offer us powerful assistance with our tasks as educators. Word processing, electronic filing, and electronic spread sheeting can all be utilized by teachers to facilitate student and class record keeping and lesson writing. While a commitment to learning these programs will take time, the rewards include increased efficiency in the long run and a more professional appearance to any written document you create.

Students benefit in similar ways. What student's writing assignment doesn't improve if he or she has access to a word processor? While data filing and electronic spread sheeting are normally not utilized by students, some familiarity with these types of programs is certainly desirable from an employer's point of view.

Much is being made of "student level" word processors and data filers. While many of these are good products, I'd recommend using the commercially available software programs whenever possible. The advantages of using these programs over the educational versions are as follows: (1) They are more powerful, with more advanced features. (2) They are more readily available. (3) Documentation is just as good if not better than the student software. (4) A student is more likely to encounter the commercially available software in the business world.

At Lomalinda High School we offer the students in the upper grades the electives of word processing with Superscript, data file management with PFS File and Report, and electronic spreadsheeting with Visicalc. If students elect to take all three, we are finding that it will take them, working one hour a day, approximately one school year to learn these programs well.

Using the computer as a tool implies that you are giving students both a reason and an opportunity to use it. It is fundamental to their understanding that they comprehend the basic concepts underlying such programs and experience the practical application of the computer in meeting their specific needs. For example, teaching about a word processing program should not be the major focus of such a course. Learning how to really use a word processor will require that students prepare their own documents such as term papers on a computer. Allowing them to experience the quirks ultimately proves more valuable than drilling them on particular control keys and terminology.

The computer as a tool offers exciting possibilities both to teachers and students, as an organizer of information and a resource for information. Care must be taken that we don't so entangle this type of learning experience with our own educational strictures that we actually hinder student usage and make the computer less of a tool and more of an obstacle to learning.

Computers as a Tutor for Education

Computer assisted instruction (CAI) is the most obvious use of computers in the classroom. The variety of software available for classroom computers is tremendous. Unfortunately, a high percentage of the software available is not very useful to the average student or educator. While drills and practice certainly have a place in education, flash cards may be just as effective and certainly more affordable! Tutorial materials, a presentation of a series of concepts or facts, or simulations may make better use of computers and better justify their cost.

Benefits of CAI for students

The benefits of quality CAI for students are well documented. An IMPAC study presented the following conclusions:

- CAI saved significant amounts of time over conventional instruction (20 to 40 percent).

- Fewer students involved with CAI are retained in a grade in comparison with students involved in conventional instruction.

- Students using computers generally have more positive attitudes toward continuing to use the computer as a learning tool.

- Student gains of two to three months in mathematics, reading and language arts were typical when instruction was supplemented with basic skills CAI.

Benefits of CAI for teachers

- Teachers are freed from merely being dispensers of information and have more time to manage and coordinate instruction activities.

- Students who use computers generally have better attitudes toward learning and are more positive toward education in general and the school environment in particular.

- Computers allow for greater individualization within the classroom.

- Microcomputers can transmit information, teach certain skills, and help students solve problems.

Factors which adversely affect educational programs

The field evidence definitely validates well-designed CAI. However these are factors that adversely affect any educational program:

- Ill-prepared teachers unfamiliar with either the hardware or software that they are trying to use.

- Inflexible teachers either unwilling to learn and apply new technology or intimidated by the computer.

- Inappropriate software-software designed and produced by programmers for a general audience but purchased and utilized by schools with more specialized needs.

- Lack of software to run on the computers.

- Lack of adequate number of computers so that all students are able to spend significant amounts of time (ideally at least twenty minutes every other day in grades 4-6) on the computer.

Suggestions to counteract negative factors

To help counteract these negative factors that can severely cripple a computer education program, I'd suggest the following:

- School administrators must require that school personnel learn about computers. Summer vacations and furloughs need to be times of professional development and exposure to this new technology. Teachers need to learn about computers as much as students do and that takes time.

- Consider the purchase of authoring software. This software is designed to allow a non-programmer to write customized courseware using normal English. While authoring software is not inexpensive, if utilized sufficiently it will be considerably less expensive than attempting to purchase all the various software packages you'll eventually need.

- Consider having your older students write software for your younger ones. The motivational factors of giving programming students a task that makes sense and contributes toward the education of others is sound pedagogically, a wise use of resources, and can also be a time saver for you.

- Try more flexible scheduling so that students can take turns using the computer. While this will take some creative planning, more students will benefit with fewer machines. Shorter time periods of twenty minutes several times a week appear to be more beneficial than longer periods one or two times a week. Avoid having more than two students on the computer at a time. The addition of the third child severely detracts from serious work.

At Lomalinda School we are using our computers to supplement the teaching or provide remedial instruction in mathematics, grammar, spelling, and reading comprehension.

For the first time we can give opportunity for our students to learn about computer assisted drawing, programming in Basic and Logo, and computer terminology and processes.

I also see the potential in using the computer to supplement the teaching of such varied topics as geography, history, and Latin culture. As much as possible, we must integrate computers into the regular curriculum. I feel as if we are just beginning to scratch the surface of incorporating the computer into our educational system.

As a by-product of these activities, our students are becoming more computer literate and are beginning to use the computer to help them tackle the types of problems they will be facing in an increasingly complex world. We do not teach any classes on computer literacy as such, but that computer literacy is a secondary benefit of using the computer to enrich our basic educational program. This approach makes the computer an aid to education not simply an objective in itself.

Trends in Educational Computing

Speculating on the direction educational computing is moving is similar to forecasting the weather. While certain developments may seem quite obvious, whether they catch on in the classroom may be a different story. I'm sticking my neck out by mentioning certain trends that appear to be major developments in educational computing.

Networking

Networking of computers is becoming more popular in schools. The advantages of a system by which student stations can access a host computer as needed saves on resources and avoids the floppy shuffle. It also permits the teacher a greater degree of control and organization through the host computer and controller. Computer managed instruction becomes much more feasible as organization is centralized, and downloading and saving of student files is more directly monitored. Our particular network at Lomalinda connects a host computer with six non-disk-drive units and two disk-drive units.

Disadvantages

- Much of the available educational software cannot be used on a network. This is changing as networks become more popular.
- The increased complexity of the network does reduce reliability somewhat compared to units that stand alone.
- A computer lab becomes essential and computer education more departmentalized.

IBM-Compatible Computers

A second trend that appears to be gaining momentum is the push to purchase computers that are IBM compatible. Competitive pricing has placed the IBM compatible within the budget of many more school systems.

Advantages

- A faster, more powerful computer with more memory
- A wealth of available software for business applications, including large integrated programs.
- Wide availability.
- More powerful graphic capabilities.

Disadvantages

- Less specialized software for educational needs. This is rapidly changing as the major publishers promote software that runs on the IBM computer.
- Competition from adults in using the computer for personal needs. The increased power and versatility of these computers make them specially attractive for adult use. Care must be taken that the computer remain within the students' realm.

Electronic Communication

A third trend involves computer modems and electronic communications. While communicating using computers is not a new development in the business world, it has experienced explosive growth in recent months in home and school use. This particular aspect of computer usage may be the most potentially powerful application to our lives today. Classrooms around the country are now able to communicate with one another. Experts in various fields can be interviewed over the computer from the classroom. Local and national libraries are making their reference materials available to computer networks. Airlines, hotels, and car rentals are only a few of the many data bases accessible by the computer in the home. This allows an individual to make reservations, as well as purchase or inquire about a multitude of goods and services.

Where is all this leading us? We cannot afford the luxury of complacency about this new technology. Our students will need exposure to computers and computer skills sooner or later. We must do what we can to foster computer knowledge in the classroom now! As our students return to their home countries, they will be confronted with an array of new technology and an accompanying explosion of information centered around the computer. While we most likely cannot provide the most up-to-date hardware and software, we must help them develop the conceptual understanding they will need to cope in our modern society. We need to foster the skills and attitudes necessary so that they approach the computer as an aid to learning, not as an adversary.

Comments in Response to Questions

It is possible to get a card for some IBM-compatible computers such as the Tandy 1000, which makes it possible to run Apple software.

Apple will have to go a step above the IBM or will have to become IBM-compatible.

If I were strictly focused on elementary grades, I could be happy with Apples. But for high school, I would want IBM-compatibles.

The price is quite comparable between Apples and IBM-compatibles.

I expect that in the near future word processing will be taught rather than typing.

If you want to get the latest and best advice, I'd suggest you subscribe to a user's group magazine, a magazine written especially for the computer you own. There is a wealth of information, not only about the machine, but about programs available for your machine.

My focus is not the computer but on using the computer to do something else. We are trying to use the computer as a cross-cultural tutor. Because of that, we were given a grant from Tandy which gives grants based on the creative use of computers in education. Application forms are available from the Wycliffe's Children's Education Department in Dallas.

Regarding a course for computer literacy, we teach BASIC language at fourth grade. What can you learn in computer literacy that you wouldn't learn programming in BASIC? It's easier to learn in bits and pieces. For the older children who haven't had this experience, a computer literacy class is a viable option, but I would center it around learning a programming language.

Teacher preparation is essential. Some schools offer on-the-field training with college credit.

49

Itinerant Teachers in Remote Settings

Sharon Haag
FES Coordinator, Christian Academy of Guatemala

What I'm going to share with you are some things that I have been feeling from my experience as an itinerant teacher. I have asked mothers that I have been working with, "What kind of a person would you like or need as an itinerant teacher?" I'm going to focus on the characteristics and attitudes of a successful itinerant teacher from my perspective and experience.

First we need to define terms a little bit. I'm thinking of itinerant meaning a traveling teacher, a person who goes to families' homes, and lives with them for different periods of time. In FES program, itinerant teachers go for two one-week visits three times a year, so they're in each family's home about six weeks out of the whole year. In other programs, like the one I was in in Mexico, we itinerated for more time than that, a month up to six months.

I think this could apply to tutors as well. Some missions are sending tutors to specific families to spend the whole school year with just that family and tutor those children, but I think a lot of the same qualities are necessary in that kind of a situation as in itinerant teaching.

In the Bible we have an example of an itinerant teacher, Paul. He went around traveling to different places, staying in people's homes for differing periods of time, teaching the people in different areas. I have considered how his characteristics and attitudes helped him be a successful person. I want to take his example as a model for myself too.

A Servant Heart

One of the things that I think is very important, maybe the most important, is that an itinerant teacher have a servant heart, a commitment to service. And in that service their life needs to be a living demonstration of the love of Christ for the families that they're going to serve. Also it's a commitment to serving that family so that the family can get on with their ministry of sharing God's Word with the people God has called them to.

One of my co-teachers in Guatemala said that one of the most important attitudes was to go into a situation expecting to fit into the family's lifestyle and to their ministry. I need to adapt to their way of life and help out in any way that I can. Before I go out to a village, one of my prayers is that I be a real joy to that family, that they look forward to my coming. I think one of my biggest roles in the village is to be an encourager, especially to the mom in the educational situation, and also to the children.

You find that you can have a real role as a listener. You're someone who's coming in from the outside, who's not involved in all that's going on in that village situation. And it really helps that person out there to have someone come in that they can talk to and who really can talk to them on their level, because it's different when they're relating even to the national Christians that they've been working with. And then through that too, you have a real opportunity to be a prayer partner with the people in the village. You get to know their lives in detail, and their concerns, and what it's really like to live out there, and so I think your prayers can really be much more effective and in that way be an encouragement to that family.

And then in practical ways lighten the load wherever you can. Often it's really hard for a family working in a remote setting to have much time as a family to do things together, because there are people coming to the door all the time asking for this, and that, needing them to go here and there, especially if they're involved in medical work or other service capacities. And so, for one family I decided to do the evening dishes so that after supper the whole family could go down to the sleeping house and have a couple of hours together to play games, read to each other, have their devotions, and that sort of thing. It was a real encouragement to that family.

You have to be sensitive to each different situation too. Maybe some mothers really don't like a stranger in their kitchen. Pushing to take over doing the dishes or the cooking could be an imposition in that setting. Maybe what would really help them is if you took the kids off in the afternoon to take a hike or play something to give the mom some free time to catch up on correspondence and those kind of things that she needs to concentrate on. So look to lighten the load wherever possible.

Another attitude within the servant heart category is to pay our own way. One way is helping with the household work, not acting like a guest. I feel if you stay over a week with someone, you're not a guest anymore. Just do what you can in the family life. In our situation we pay for food costs, and if they have provided any transportation to get out to that area, we pay for that too. The tuition that they paid to the school covers transportation costs, and wherever we are, we'd be paying for food anyway. Now, some families don't want to accept that, and that's fine. You need to let them give to you, too. Several of the families I've worked with have said, "No, we don't want you to give us anything." They want to do that. Other families really need it, and it's a help to them. It helps you not be a drain on them.

Contentment

The second attitude that I feel is important is that an itinerant teacher be content whatever the circumstances. You recognize that from Paul's writings. Whether you have much or whether you have little, you need to be a person who's content with whatever situation there is. Now, this could mean physical things. The places you may go as a itinerant are very, very different. One place that I went to in Mexico was in a large city. There was running water, electricity, a washing machine, a dryer, and all of that. I had my own room kind of separate from the house.

Other places where I go it's a dirt floor and a tin roof. Sometimes I share a bedroom with one of the kids and have to be careful about not taking a long hot shower, because all you get is what's in the bucket.

Also there may be much or little as far as social contacts or fellowship is concerned. And that can be a really hard thing for an itinerant teacher, because in a remote setting, the family you live with may be the only ones you can understand and talk to. There's a real temptation to rely on them for all your social contact and good feelings as a person but they're so busy that they don't have time to give you all of that.

A single itinerant teacher really needs to deal with the question of singleness. If that hasn't been resolved that can be a real hard thing if they're out in remote areas. I mean there are no prospects around, and there may not be a whole lot of fellowship. I was in one village in Mexico that was in an Indian area. I speak Spanish, but I don't speak the Indian dialects, and so in that area I couldn't talk to anybody. The only people I had to talk to were the family that I was with. The wife of the family was one of my closest friends. That relationship had developed back in the center where we were in the center school. In that setting she had a lot more time to spend with me, and a lot less drain and stress on her, so that we had some good conversations and fellowship together. It was really hard for me in the village, because there was so much demand on her that we didn't have the same kind of relationship out there. But I realized that the Lord is sufficient for those situations too. He's the one that needs to be my best friend and supply my deepest needs for a relationship.

There are some practical things that you can do to help in those kinds of situations, though. An itinerant teacher needs to look at those times of isolation as times for personal growth. Some of the things that have helped me have been to take with me some special Bible studies that I've always been wanting to get to, or do some Scripture memorization, or take some special books that I've always wanted to read and never had time to do back in the busy center when there were so many people around for social contact.

I've also been able to learn special skills. One year while I was home for the summer I got scraps of material and I cut all the pieces that I would need to make a quilt. When I went out to the village I had my little packs of pieces. I hand sewed an entire quilt for a double bed. That was really fun and rewarding to me. I also bought a recorder, the kind you play like a flute, and a book that teaches you how, so I was able to learn that too, while I was out in the village. It's a good time to catch up with letter writing, or develop special interests or hobbies like wild flower collection. You get to go to a lot of different places in a single country, and it's really fun to look at the variety. I bought binoculars and bird books this year.

I am looking forward to possibly going to another country where French is spoken. I bought a set of tapes that teach you how to speak French, so I've been working on that while I'm in the village.

Another thing that's important to me is to get regular exercise. In a city I can do it by jogging; that's very acceptable for women to do. But out in a village you have to wear a skirt all the time, for one thing, and also to village people it's weird to see someone running when they don't have to. So I got an aerobics tape and book of exercises I can do that in a small space on a dirt floor or whatever, and I found that the kids in the family just love to do it with me. That makes it a lot more fun for me.

There are a lot of things that you can plan for your own personal growth during a time of reduced social contact and fellowship.

A Teachable Spirit

The third thing that I feel is important is that an itinerant teacher have a genuine willingness to learn, a teachable spirit. It can't be a person who is stuck into just one way of doing things. There are a lot of excellent teachers who feel there's one right way to do things. It comes from their background, their teaching experience, and their education and it probably is a great way to do things, but when you go to a remote setting, you're in a very different situation.

Actually it can be a really freeing thing. You have freedom from all the restraints that apply in the four walls of a classroom. It's exciting because the whole environment can become the classroom. We can do like Christ did, using what's at hand to teach different things. In fact, you have to do that because often you don't have a lot of materials.

One day in Mexico I was teaching two boys, and they heard some commotion outside. It was too distracting to keep on with their desk work, so we went to see what it was. The neighbor's pig had been in labor for six or seven hours, and the pigs just weren't coming. They had decided to go ahead and kill the pig and open her up and butcher her. Boy, what a learning experience! It was a great anatomy lesson, and a good opportunity to talk about values and attitudes. That was a real blow to that family. They'd been really counting on having all those piglets to raise. That was the main source of their income for that year. What do you do when at one fell swoop you lose everything? There were so many things to talk about in that.

In one of the villages in Guatemala the kids went out for break in the morning, and when they came back, they said, "Miss Haag, come on over here, they're shearing the sheep next door." The schedule said break was over, but you can't pass up things like that. We went out and watched the shearing of the sheep, and asked the men questions about what they were going to do with the wool, and how they processed it. They were going to take this up to the market in town and sell it.

We had math lessons. "How much do you get per pound?" "Well, how many pounds do you think you have there?" And then the kids could figure out about how much they were going to earn from that. There were social studies lessons about trade and economics, and science lessons about the use of natural resources.

Why do sheep do well in this place? Well, it's almost eight thousand feet altitude. They ought to be able to grow a nice thick coat of wool.

What kinds of tools were they using there to shear the sheep? It was quite an operation. They had the head tied up to the fence. A little boy was grabbing the hind legs, and the dad had shears which I'm sure hadn't been sharpened in ten years and was clip, clip, clipping. It was a ragged mess.

After they were finished we went back to the classroom and had our discussion. Is that the way it's done in other places? How is this different in, say, your home country, or other places in this country even? It was a great descriptive writing assignment and practice in writing how to do something. For the little first grader it was good for sequencing: what were the steps that they went through in shearing the sheep?

We can be real models to the parents in those kinds of situations by being teachers who take advantage of what there is around us and making every situation a learning experience. It's a real encouragement to the moms to realize that teaching is not just lecturing and doing work sheets, but the reading aloud in the evenings, discussion, development of thinking skills through the questions they asked, having their kids help them with kitchen duties, cooking — that sort of thing. They're learning measuring concepts and reading, following directions and all these kinds of things.

Sphere of Responsibility

Another important thing for an itinerant teacher is to know their sphere of responsibility. I've run into this time after time. It's hard because you're used to being in charge of the kids in a classroom. They are your responsibility, so it's up to you to discipline them, to tell them what they're going to do, and all of that. However, when you live with a family, in many situations it's not your responsibility to discipline those kids because the parents are there. When it's school time and I'm in charge of them, it *is* my responsibility, and the parents have to learn that too.

In one place in Mexico, the walls weren't very high, and the mom was out in the kitchen typing the New Testament. I was in the next room working with her son, and evidently he said something to me that she felt was not respectful. She said over the wall, "You show some respect to Miss Haag."

I knew that he was really frustrated about his school work, so I talked with her later, and said, "When we're in school time, I don't want you to worry about what your kids are doing. Just let me handle that and take that burden off of you. I'll take care of it there, and I'll let you take care of it during the other times of the day."

That's a real release for parents too. In the FES program, the teacher is really in charge of seeing that things are going OK for each child. When we leave, we leave lesson plans so that when a child tells his mom, "Oh I don't want to do this. Why do I have to do this? Miss Haag doesn't make me do this in school," she can say, "Well it's right here on the list. Miss Haag said for you to do this today." That helps that relationship and takes a load off Mom.

Tact

The last characteristic I'll mention is tactfulness. There's a real example of tactfulness in Paul's letter to Philemon when he writes him about a problem regarding his attitude towards the servant who had run off with some of his money. He starts out his letter to Philemon commending him for all his good qualities: "It gives me joy to see your love for the Lord, and your love for other people." After commending him for so many good things that he had done, he gets into the problem. After he talks with him about that, he says in one of the latter verses, "And I know that you're going to even do more than I expect of you." He also adds, "And prepare a room for me because I'm coming to visit you a little bit later so we can talk and see how well you've done in this matter."

It's a neat thing to study tactfulness and speaking in love and in an encouraging way. Often there are things that you need to talk to the parents about that are in your sphere of responsibility related to the education of the children. But it's not good to jump into it whenever it hits you. It's really important to think and pray about it, and to go to them at the time that the Lord puts on your heart to speak to them about it.

About two years ago in Guatemala one of the moms was having a hard time getting the kids to do the work they needed to do. The relationship of being teacher as well as mom was a real frustration for her. I knew that the biggest problem was that when she told them to do something, she didn't follow through on it. She's a real soft-spoken, kind-hearted person. She would ask them to do something and if they didn't do it, it went by the wayside. When they got in school that problem was accentuated, and they were really resisting.

I really felt burdened about that, but I didn't say anything the first couple of times I went out to visit them. I tried to build a good relationship with her, and confidence and trust in each other. I'd go back home and pray, "Lord, do you want me to say anything? Show me the right time, show me the right way to do it."

Finally, the time came, and I said, "You know, there is something that I feel is a key to making this a much more pleasant time for you working with your kids. And if you want to continue with this program next year, there's something that I think that would really help you." I was able to share that with her, and she received it pretty well, but I could tell it was hard on her.

Just a couple of months ago we were at church and two of her kids and two others were putting their noses against the church window. She motioned through the window, "Don't do that." And her kids stopped instantly.

I said, "Boy your kids are really obeying."

Then she told me how our conversation had made a whole difference in her relationship with her kids, and that she was really grateful.

Addresses of Speakers

Mrs. Grace Barnes
MK Advisor, Operation Impact
Azusa Pacific University
Azusa, CA 91702

Miss Priscilla Bartram
Lomalinda School
ILV, Apdo. Aereo 100602
Bogota, Colombia

Dr. Peter Blackwell
RR2 Box 112B
West Kingston, RI 02892

Mr. Bob Blaschke
SIM USA
P.O. Box 7900
Charlotte, NC 28217

Mr. Don D. Boesel
Overseas Crusades
25 Corning Ave.
Milpitas, CA 95035

Dr. Henry Brandt
1101 S. Olive
W. Palm Beach, FL 33401

Mrs. Alice Brawand
607 W. Ridge Rd.
Dallas, TX 75236

Mr. David Brooks
Morrison Academy
PO Box 27-24
Taichung 40098
Taiwan ROC

Dr. Ed Danielson
336 Lilac Dr.
El Chacon, CA 92021

Mrs. Lillian Davis
135 W. Crooked Hill Rd.
Pearl River, NY 10965

Dr. Nancy Duvall
3406 Casco Ct.
Hacienda Heights, CA 91745

Mr. Roger Dyer
PO Box 205
Kingswood,
South Australia 5062
Australia

Dr. Don Fonseca
Stony Brook School
Stony Brook, NY 11790

Mrs. Rosemary Foster
Faith Academy
P.O. Box 820
1299 Makati
Philippines

Rev. Gene Garrick
Tabernacle Church of Norfolk
7120 Granby
Norfolk, VA 23505

Mr. Rich Gathro
2221 N. Vernon St.
Arlington, VA 22207

Mr. David Greenhalgh
330 South Rd.
E. Greenwich, RI 02818

Sharon Haag
Christian Academy of Guatemala
Apdo. 25-B
Guatemala City
Guatemala

Dr. Ken Hall
Southfield Christian School
28650 Lahser Rd.
Southfield, MI 48034

Mr. Bob Klamser
Contingency Preparation
Consultants
P.O. Box 4792
Ventura, CA 93004

Dr. Dean Kliewer
464 S. Kings Dr.
Readley, CA 93654

Mrs. Kay Landers
Casilla 691
Quito, Ecuador

Dr. Bill Lewter
326 Acacia Rd.
West Palm Beach, FL 33401

Rhoda Lindman
HCJB
Casilla 691
Quito, Ecuador

Joy Limburg
Faith Academy
P.O. Box 820
1299 Makati
Philippines

Rev. Lareau Lindquist
2824 Soland Dr.
Rockford, IL 61111

Miss Sherry Long
1527 Noble Ave
Columbia, S.C. 29203

Mr. David Lotz
New Tribes
Box 1200
Camdenton, MO 65020

Dr. Tom Moore
855 Molalla Ave.
Oregon City, OR 97405

Diane Morris
4822 Aurora Dr.
Ventura, CA 93003

Miss Pat Mortenson
Missionary Internship
PO Box 457
Farmington, MI 48332

Mr. Paul Nelson
Children's Education Department
7500 W. Camp Wisdom Rd.
Dallas, TX 75236

Mrs. Lucretia Pelton
Southfield Christian School
28650 Lahser Rd.
Southfield, MI 48034

Neal Peterson
ILV
Apdo. Aereo 10062
Bogota, Colombia

Mr. David Pollock
RR 1 Box 23,
Centerville Rd.
Houghton NY 14744

Dr. John Powell
1714 Linden St.
East Lansing, MI 48823

Mr. Rob Quiring
Casilla 691
Quito, Ecuador

Dr. Phil Renicks
P.O. Box 960
Northport, AL 35476

Dr. William Rice
10523 N. Rice Rd.
Fresno, CA 93710

Dr. Bill Rich
9904 Duncan St.
Fairfax, VA 22031

Mrs. Ruth Rowen
Missionary Internship
PO Box 457
Farmington, MI 48332

Ms. Frederica Schlorff
126 So. Woodlawn Ave.
Aldan, PA 19018

Dr. Lyle Siverson
523 Madera Dr.
San Mateo, CA 94403

Mr. Jim Smotherman
WBT/CHED
Box 2727
Huntington Beach, CA 92647

Dr. Glen Taylor
270 Gerrard St. East
Toronto, Ontario
Canada M5A 2G4

Dr. Bill Viser
Caixa Postal 24060
20.001 Rio de Janeiro
Rio de Janeiro, BRAZIL

Dr. Dennis Vogan
Faith Academy
P.O. Box 820
1299 Makati
PHILIPPINES

Dr. Ted Ward
1209 Courier Court
Deerfield, IL 60015

Mr. David Wells
Wesleyan Academy
Call Box 7890
Guayanabo, PR 00657

Mr. Ron Whippe
Annapolis Area Christian School
Ridgely Ave. and Wilson Rd.
Annapolis, MD 21401

Mr. and Mrs. Ron Young
C.P. 1655
60.000 Fortaleza
Ceara, Brazil

Index

266
INloK
V. 2

LINCOLN CHRISTIAN COLLEGE AND SEMINARY

T

V

W

3 4711 00092 6305